RADIO COMEDY 1938–1968

RADIO COMEDY 1938–1968

A Guide to 30 Years of Wonderful Wireless

by
Andy Foster and Steve Furst

First published in 1996 by
Virgin Publishing Ltd
332 Ladbroke Grove
London W10 5AH

Every effort has been made by the authors to list full transmission details but in a few cases the information was not available.

ISBN 0 86369 960 X

Typeset by TW Typesetting, Plymouth, Devon

Printed and bound by Cox & Wyman Ltd, Reading, Berkshire

Contents

Acknowledgements

Thanks to: Daphne Bailey, Larry Cheadle, Simon Keeping, David Gould, Ian, John and Tony Pickard. To Chris Mobbs and Tony Cadogan of the National Sound Archive, Kerri Sharp at Virgin Publishing for bringing the book together and Lew Lane for the kind permission to reproduce his photographs.

Introduction

Way back in 1993, upstairs at *The Double Six* (Steve Furst's board-gaming club), the authors and I originated the idea for this book over a couple of pints of beer. If we had known then how many hours we would be spending on this labour of love, the project might have looked too daunting to contemplate. Two years and a bit later, we're very happy we took up the challenge. Once it was commissioned by Virgin Publishing, there was no going back.

Having grown up in a household where my parents tuned into the wireless for their evening entertainment, a lot of the shows are familiar, not least for their nostalgic quality. At last I know where catchphrases like 'Right Monkey' and 'You'll be lucky' come from, and who Enoch and Ramsbottom were.

Some readers will be unfamiliar with terms such as the Light Programme or the Home Service, knowing only their modern-day incarnations, Radio 2 and Radio 4. What follows is a potted history of British radio broadcast history since Marconi made his first public radio broadcast in 1920. We hope this serves to illuminate the data you will find in the side columns of this book.

The research needed to provide the transmissions details has been exhaustive and at times mind boggling. Andy Foster and Steve Furst have worked exceptionally hard to provide comprehensive listings; a feat undertaken by two enthusiasts whose knowledge of the subject and unflagging energy has contributed to what is the most informative and entertaining guide to radio comedy I have ever seen.

Kerri Sharp October 1995

Chronology of Radio History

1920 Marconi makes Britain's first public radio broadcast

1921 The Post Office issues 4000 licences to private individuals to receive wireless broadcasts

1922 The British Broadcasting Company is formed and begins broadcasting daily from November. 2LO becomes the London station of the BBC. (In the early days the company had eight stations all transmitting different programmes. This was known as The Regional System. It was not possible to transmit the same programme from more than one station at a time until 1924.)

1923 2LO moves from the Strand to Savoy Hill

First issue of *The Radio Times* is published on 28 September

1924 The 'pips' – the Greenwich Mean Time signal is heard for the first time

1925 Radio Radiance, the first regular radio revue/concert party, ran weekly from July for over a year.

1926 *That Child* – the first domestic sitcom – is broadcast in six, five-minute episodes, beginning 12 April

1927 The British Broadcasting Company becomes the British Broadcasting Corporation

1929 Radio Paris begins

1930 The National Programme and the Regional Programme begin 9 March, replacing 2LO

1931 Radio receiving licences in Great Britain exceed 4 million

Radio Normandy – first commercial station to broadcast daily sponsored programmes for British listeners starts 11 October – silenced by WW2

1932 The BBC's Empire Service (the forerunner to the World Service) begins

The BBC moves into Broadcasting House

1933 Fixed Point programming (regular series at regular times) extended to variety programmes

Radio Luxembourg begins test transmissions 15 March and becomes regular Sunday service in Britain from 29 October. Broadcasts were in a different European language each day. Sunday was English language day.

1939 The Home Service begins. BBC Variety department evacuated to Bristol

1940 Forces Programme begins

1941 A cryptic news item, that a camel had fallen ill at London zoo, was the coded signal for the Variety department to move to Bangor, North Wales

1944 Forces Programme becomes the General Forces Programme 22 February

1945 Forces Programme renamed the Light Programme 28 July.

Regional broadcasting resumes

1946 The Third Programme starts up

1948 The transistor is invented

1958 BBC Radiophonic Workshop is formed

1967 Radio 1 begins 30 September. On this day the Light Programme becomes Radio 2, the Third Programme Radio 3 and the Home Service Radio 4

THE 1930s

The Beginnings of Radio Comedy and the 1930s

Prior to the development of radio technology, comedy entertainment was provided by variety and music hall 'turns' whose popular – and at times earthy – humour appealed to the mainly working-class audience. Times were hard for the majority of the population, and a Saturday night spent in the opulent surroundings of a large music hall could provide temporary respite from the drudgery and hardship of most working people's day-to-day lives.

A seat in the gallery of the Hackney Empire, for instance, would cost you only sixpence. Music hall stars were recorded on 78 rpm records but the gramophone and the records to play on it were luxury items, out of the reach of most working-class pockets.

Since the turn of the century, the cinema had been the major rival to music hall's popularity. By the end of the First World War, the appeal of 'old-time' music hall entertainment had faded in favour of new variety acts and increasingly sophisticated products of the film industry. People wanted something new. There were crossovers between the media, though – most notably Charlie Chaplin, who had established himself as a knockabout comedian but went on to find international fame as a star of the cinema screen. He was indisputably the most successful music hall performer of all time.

By 1918, technology was advancing significantly. The age of modernism was firmly underway and new ideas and more efficient means of production began to imprint themselves on all aspects of life. The development of radio technology in the early years of the century was stifled during the Great War by a British government concerned with its possible military applications. At the end of the war, restrictions were gradually lifted but the government was determined to maintain control, mindful of the proliferation of private stations sweeping the USA and Europe.

In 1922 a broadcasting monopoly was granted to a commercial company formed by a group of wireless manufacturers keen to stimulate sales of their sets. They had the imposing name of the British Broadcasting Company Limited. Within weeks a general manager was appointed, whose strict moral views would play an important role in the shaping of this new institution: a 34-year-old ex-engineer called John Reith.

Under his stern control, early broadcasts were restricted mainly to a grim diet of improving talks and light classical music, leavened by dance music in the evenings from the Savoy Hotel, conveniently situated next door to the new company's headquarters at 2 Savoy Hill. Despite this small concession, the more popular form of entertainment, variety, was anathema to the humourless Reith and many established performers – and their agents – were wary of exposing their material to a mass audience. Ted Ray, an established name by the early 1930s, was unable to broadcast until 1939.

Despite these obstacles, variety began to gain a foothold on the airwaves. Famous comedy and variety stars who did broadcast in the early years included Will Hay, Robb Wilton, Norman Long, Leonard Henry, Vivian Foster and Stainless Stephen. The BBC also began to develop its own stars, among them Helena Millais as 'Our Lizzie', the first comedy character to be created for radio. She featured in her own 'comedy fragments from life', first broadcast in 1922 and her catchphrase was ' 'Ullo, me old ducks! 'Ere I am again with me old string bag.'

'Wireless' Willie (Willie Rouse) was more reminiscent of the original style of music hall, delivering comic songs and patter from 1924. However, by far the most popular radio comedian of the day was John Henry, who made his debut in 1923. His lugubrious style was ideally suited to the intimacy of the new medium. Such was his popularity that his cartoon adventures were serialised in the *Daily Sketch*. He even had a rose named after him. In the exchanges with his radio wife, Blossom (beginning in 1925), the first glimmers of the domestic sitcom can be discerned.

From the mid 1920s, there were many broadcasts by established concert parties such as the Roosters. By 1925 the BBC had produced its own concert party show called *Radio Radiance*, which introduced listeners to Tommy Handley. The following year, Mabel Constanduros starred in *That Child*, generally considered to be the earliest example of the domestic sitcom.

Granted a Royal Charter in 1927, the new BBC began to increase its light entertainment output and by the early 1930s it was broadcasting more than 150 variety programmes a year; in the main, these were live relays from theatres and music halls. The corporation, now in the brand-new Broadcasting House premises, was facing competition from foreign broadcasters transmitting English-language programmes. Stations such as Radio Normandy and, from 1933, Radio Luxembourg were transmitting popular record programmes and variety shows (see early comedy programmes in this section such as *Myrtle and Bertie* and *A Question of Taste*).

Radio comedy now began to flourish in this more enlightened atmosphere. In 1938 Reith left the corporation and on his departure the BBC mounted its most concerted effort to date to rival the transatlantic and commercial influences. Its weapon – a show that really put radio comedy on the map – was to be known as *Band Waggon*.

Myrtle And Bertie

(the 'Monkey Brand Programme')
June–December 1935

Transmission Details

Myrtle and Bertie

29 Weeks

The Cast
Claude Hulbert, Enid Trevor, Lawrence Barclay, Wylie Watson, Fanny Wright, Sonny Wright, Wal Sidney, Dorothy Vernon, Jerry Verno, Henry Thomas

Episode List includes
The Wedding Reception; Honeymoon Cruise; First Day in the New House; Bertie the House Decorator; Bertie the Gardener; Bertie Goes on the Stage; At the Football Match; The Village Concert; Bertie and the Burglar; Bertie the Boxing Champion; Bertie at the Whist Drive

Sunday 9 June 1935–Sunday 22 December 1935
Broadcast 1915–1930
Broadcast on Radio Luxembourg

To those brought up on a radio diet mainly provided by the BBC, something billed as '. . . a laugh-a-minute programme presented by the makers of Monkey Brand' may seem like the sort of announcement we associate with American TV and radio. But this fifteen-minute Sunday-evening slot was on Radio Luxembourg – and Monkey Brand was a soap. It was an early domestic 'situation comedy'.

It starred Claude Hulbert, who was supported by his real-life wife, Enid Trevor. The first episode was called *The Wedding Reception* and the last was *Bertie at the Whist Drive.*

The Hulberts were a very popular radio act. They'd first broadcast their crosstalk-and-song routines during the late 1920s, with Claude very much the silly-ass character while Enid remained the sensible one. They were the stars of *At Home with the Hulberts* on Radio Normandy in 1937, and Claude also broadcast with his brother Jack, when they were billed as the Hulbert Brothers.

Mr Muddlecombe JP

1937–1953

One of the great names of both radio and variety, Robert Wilton Smith (1881–1957), began his theatrical career in 1903 playing villains in melodrama – 'Nurtured on villainy and cradled in crime, that's me.'

Later he played character parts and, finding he was unintentionally getting laughs, he gravitated towards comedy. By 1909 he was touring the variety theatres, billed as Robb Wilton, 'the confidential comedian'. He found fame during the 1920s as a sketch comedian, portraying a series of bewildered parochial officials, including the Fire Chief, the Police Sergeant, the Prison Governor and the Magistrate – this last being the inspiration for Mr Muddlecombe JP.

Wilton wrote all his stage material, and the Magistrate sketch was included in the 1926 Royal Variety Performance.

Wilton first broadcast in the early days of the BBC, and also worked for Radio Luxembourg in the 30s. He appeared on film and television and made several gramophone records. His radio work greatly increased his fame. Apart from Tommy Handley, Robb Wilton was the most popular radio comedian of the war period.

The Principal Magistrate of Nether Backwash, Mr Muddlecombe JP – an endearing, much-put-upon combination of bluster and fallibility – was first heard in 1937 and then in several series, some bearing his name, some not. In *Office Hours*, for instance, which came in 1941, he was a solicitor trying to run a ramshackle office.

Transmission Details

Mr Muddlecombe JP

Series 1 – (5 episodes)

Written by
Adrian Turner (Episodes 4 and 5 written with Robb Wilton)

9 January 1937–5 March 1937 (episodes broadcast 9 and 28 January, 12 and 26 February, 5 March)
Broadcast Saturday 2045–2100 (Episode 1), Thursday 2120–2135 (Episode 2), Friday 1930–1945 (Episode 3), Friday 1930–1945 (Episode 4), Tuesday 2140–2200 (Episode 5)
Episodes 1, 2 and 5 broadcast on National
Episodes 3 and 4 broadcast on Regional

Mr Muddlecombe JP (in the Court of Not-so Common Please!)

Series 2 – (2 episodes)

Written by
Robb Wilton on an original idea by Barry Bernard

Produced by
Max Kester

10 January 1938 and 17 January 1938
Broadcast Mondays 1945–2000
Broadcast on National

One-off special
Written by
Robb Wilton on an original idea by Barry Bernard
Produced by
Max Kester

Monday 1 March 1938
Broadcast 1945–2000
Broadcast on National

Public Futilities
14 Weeks
Written by
Max Kester and Anthony Hall

26 January 1939–27 April 1939
Broadcast Thursdays 2015–2030 (except Programme 2, at 2120–2135, Programme 11, at 2115–2130, and Programmes 12–14, at 2045–2100)
Broadcast on National, except Programme 11, Regional

The Return of Mr Muddlecombe JP
One-off special called *My Bird, I Think*
Written by
Max Kester
Music by
The Revue Orchestra conducted by Hyam Greenbaum
Produced by
Max Kester

Wednesday 13

As a magistrate, Mr Muddlecombe JP didn't command the respect of the local inhabitants, who invariably ignored his expert advice and cared nothing for his opinions.

Much of the humour in the shows lay in Muddlecombe's reaction to others, his ineffectual blethering contrasting sharply with the hysteria of his anguished 'clients'.

Most of the scripts, many of which were based on actual cases, were written by Max Kester and then fine-tuned by Wilton himself. There was no studio audience.

As well as being a magistrate and later a solicitor, Mr Muddlecombe was to be found presiding over the proceedings of the Rural District Council of Nether Backwash in 1939, in a series called *Public Futilities*. Here's a sample from *By-pass*, one of the *Public Futilities* episodes:

MR MUDDLECOMBE: **But we must keep up with the times, be up to date. Bless my life, every decent town these days has its by-pass.**

MR BATTERSBURN: **My argument is that we don't have enough passers-by to want a by-pass!**

MR MUDDLECOMBE: **No, but the passers-by who do pass by, if they had a by-pass to pass by, would be able to pass by the by-pass.**

Mr Muddlecombe was a solicitor during *Office Hours* in 1941. The contents of his run-down office included an impressive mountain of outdated legal documents and a dart board. He was assisted by Adolphus, an extremely rude and disrespectful boy, who considered that *he* ran the business and that his boss – whom he usually called 'Muddlecombe' – was merely there to help *him*.

He would often rebuke his employer, saying, 'You shouldn't have done that!' This was practically a catchphrase. Others were, 'You've really done it this time'; 'I wouldn't like to be in your shoes'; 'You're in for it now!'

Mr Muddlecombe's confidence became undermined to such an extent that he was incapable of giving the most straightforward legal advice without first consulting this appalling boy. The situation was considerably aggravated when, on joining the Home Guard, Mr Muddlecombe was made a private and Adolphus a sergeant . . .

GUARD: **The footsteps got nearer and nearer. What should I do?**

MR M: **Shoot him and say, 'Who went there?'**

In 1942 came *Mr Muddlecombe At Home*:

MR M: **You got rid of that other suit of mine just before war broke out and I could very well do with it now.**

MRS M: **Which suit?**

MR M: **That brown one with the blue waistcoat and the grey trousers.**

Mrs Muddlecombe was practically a female version of her husband, just as single-minded and slow on the uptake. Forever at cross-purposes, communication between the two was almost impossible.

December 1939
Broadcast 1920–2005
Broadcast on the Home Service

Mr Muddlecombe JP – ARP

5 weeks

Produced by
Max Kester

Episode List includes:
Evacuees; AFS; Sandbags; Careless Talk

6 March 1940–5 April 1940
Broadcast 2135–2150 (Programme 1); 2200–2215 (Programme 2); 1815–1830 (Programme 3); 2230–2245 (Programme 4); 2230–2245 (Programme 5); 2135–2150

Mr Muddlecombe JP

8 Weeks

Cast included
Ernest Sefton as Mr ('Eee-what-a-to-do') Battersburn

Produced by
Max Kester

20 January 1941–10 March 1941
Broadcast Mondays 2000–2015
Broadcast on the Home and Forces networks

Office Hours

Series 1 – (3 Weeks)

Written by
Robb Wilton and Max Kester

Cast included
Laurie Lupino Lane as Adolphus
Produced by
Max Kester

4 September 1941–18 September 1941
Broadcast Thursdays 1830–1845
Broadcast on Forces Programme

Robb Wilton made a brief appearance as Mr Muddlecombe JP in the 1954 Arthur Askey film, *The Love Match.* (See also *Hoop-la!*)

Series 2 – (15 Weeks)
Personnel as Series 1

18 September 1941–21 December 1941
Broadcast Wednesdays 1830–1845 (Weeks 1–3), and Thursdays 1830–1845 (rest of series, except Week 15, which was broadcast 2120–2135)

Mr Muddlecombe At Home
4 Weeks
Devised by
Max Kester
The Cast
Robb Wilton, Marion Dawson, Doreen Season, John Rorke
Produced by
Max Kester

Broadcast Saturdays 2045–2100
Broadcast on Home and Forces Services

Take a Note (or Leaves From a Loose Agent's Ledger)
4 Weeks
Written by
Loftus Wigram
The Cast
Robb Wilton, C. Dernier Warren, Bettie Bucknelle, Gwen Lewis, Sydney Keith
Music by
The Novachord Hornswogglers, directed by Charles Shadwell
Produced by
Henry Reed
Episode List
Weeks 1 *Entrance of the Dwarfs*; 2 *Loose Slates*; 3 *Abracadabra!*; 4 *The Close of the Ledger* (with Vera Lennox and Horace Percival)

3 December 1942–31 December 1942
Broadcast Thursdays 2210–2230
Broadcast on the Forces Programme
Programme 4 broadcast on Home Service 2225–2245
(From 11 January 1943 Wilton had a regular spot in *A Matter of Form* in the 'Monday Night at Eight' slot, written by Dick Pepper)

Mr Muddle – Private Detective
8 Weeks
Written by
Robb Wilton
The Cast
Robb Wilton, Phoebe Hodgson, Reginald Purdell
Produced by
Michael North

22 April 1946–10 June 1946
Broadcast Mondays 2115–2130
Broadcast on the Light Programme

Mr Muddlecombe JP
9 Weeks
Written by
Max Kester
Produced by
Michael North

11 October 1948–18 November 1948
Broadcast Mondays 2215–2235 (except Week 9, broadcast Saturday 1500–1515)
Broadcast on the Light Programme

Councillor Muddlecombe JP
6 Weeks
This was a segment of *Leisure Hour*, broadcast from 29 July 1953 to 30 September 1953 on the Light Programme

Leisure Hour was broadcast on Thursdays, 2000–2100

A Question Of Taste/ Cad's College

(The Western Brothers)
May–September 1937/May–July 1938

This and *Cads' College*, which followed in 1938, featured the Western Brothers, who were actually cousins. Kenneth and George had never met until they worked together as songwriters. George was the 'senior wrangler who plays the piano', while Kenneth was 'the plump prefect who reclines against it'. Kenneth wrote the words, George the music.

George had previously been a civil servant and a member of the Roosters concert party, and had been broadcasting for some time. Kenneth had worked for an insurance broker.

The duo became successful songwriters in revue, and had no intention of performing, but drifted into cabaret during the 1920s. The act made little impact until they began to greet their 'boiled-shirt' audience with a languid 'Hello, cads', and to treat them with disdain – 'The more we turned our noses up at them, the more they seemed to like it.'

They had broadcast together as the Perfectly Polite Pair in the mid 1920s and, after a long gap, as the Western Brothers in 1931. The BBC was at first unhappy about the use of the word 'cad', considering it insulting. However, their satires on snobbery were a great success and 'Hello, cads' became a popular catchphrase.

A 'Cads' Club' (motto: *ad sum ard labour*) was formed, raising funds for children's hospitals. Member-

Transmission Details

A Question of Taste

Written by
S. B. Gravenall

Music by
The Quaker Orchestra and Singers

14 May 1937–17 September 1937
Broadcast Sundays 2230–2245
Broadcast on Radio Luxembourg (also on Radio Normandy at 1715)

Cad's College

Devised and Presented by
The Western Brothers with Archie Glen as Dunce, Dave Burnaby as the Headmaster, Paddy Browne as the Botany Mistress, Fred Morris as Boots, Tom Kinniburgh as the Scotch Master, Cecil Johnson as the Commentator

Music by
The Cad's Choir, Charles Shadwell and the BBC Variety Orchestra

Produced by
George Barker

6 May 1938–14 July 1938
6 Editions
Guests included: Stainless Stephen, Harry Hemsley and Rownell and West

The Western Brothers also broadcast as 'The News Narks' in Roundabout (1939), a weekly programme to which all the regions contributed.

ship was five shillings. Kenneth and George were the Chief Cads and benefits included a club tie and blazer badge (which depicted a crossed pick and shovel and a foaming tankard with a school tie rampant). There was a secret club sign and a strict code of conduct: offences included driving an open touring car while wearing a bowler hat. Crooning and wearing button boots were also forbidden.

On stage they wore full evening dress, each with a monocle, slicked-back hair and a slightly pained expression. Sending up the public-school image, they affected a languid upper-class drawl, and appeared 'too bored to live'. Their material was always topical and occasionally satirical. Their most famous songs were 'The Old School Tie' and 'Play the Game, You Cads'.

A retired colonel once wrote to a newspaper complaining about their broadcasts, seriously concerned about the impression of Britain that they would convey to 'foreigners'.

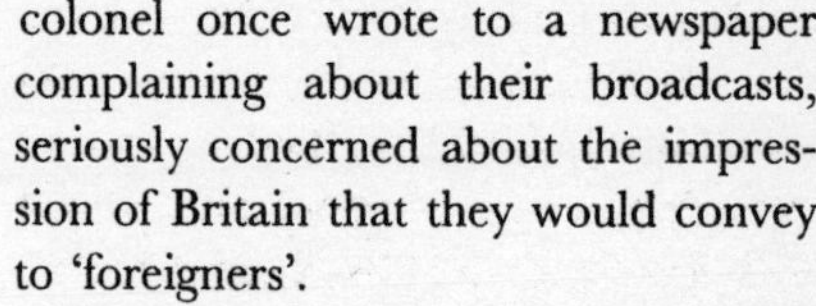

Their long and successful career embraced the variety stage, the cinema and the recording studio, and lasted well into the television era: *Cads' Club*, a 15-minute glimpse into their not-so-private lives, was screened in 1950. The act continued until George's death in 1963.

Their Luxembourg radio show was called ***A Question of Taste*** and was sponsored by the makers of Quaker Flakes. It was billed as a request show with a difference – the public were not only invited to send in requests for pieces of music, but also to take part in the broadcast itself.

The programme took the form of a musical debate in which two listeners, who were given a crash course in microphone technique beforehand, attempted to prove that one type of music was superior to another. The parameters were fairly wide, taking in everything from jazz rhythms to romantic melodies. An orchestra, complete with vocalists and a harmony trio, were on hand in the studio.

Listeners were invited to take part by sending in *their* verdict on a postcard.

The Western Brothers sang an opening and closing topical verse to the signature tune, 'A Question of Taste', and interrupted the debate with a topical sketch.

An act calling itself 'The Eastern Sisters' were heard on various shows around 1940. Their billing was 'Sorry, Cads' or 'Bad luck, Cads.' They were revealed as Mary Pollock and Dorothy Paul. Their publicity photographs showed them complete with monocles.

Band Waggon

1938–1939

This was the first of the great BBC comedy series and the first to feature a resident comedian, 'Big Hearted' Arthur Askey. It was also one of the first shows to be broadcast at the same time and on the same station every week, an idea that had at one time been considered slightly vulgar.

Askey, an up-and-coming concert party comedian,

Transmission Details

Band Waggon

Series 1 – (18 Weeks)

Taking part (variously throughout the run)

Arthur Askey, Richard Murdoch, Diana Ward, the Two Charlies, Niela Goodelle, George Formby, Gypsy Nina, Phyllis Stanley, Elisabeth Welch, Harry Richman, the Band Waggoners, conducted by Phil Cardew, Charles Smart or Reginald Foort at the BBC Theatre Organ, New Voices with Carlo, the Jackdauz

Produced by
Gordon Crier, Harry S. Pepper

Wednesday 5 January 1938–Wednesday 4 May 1938
Broadcast 1955–2040 (Week 1), 1915–2000 (Weeks 2, 7, 8), 2015–2100 (Weeks 3, 4, 6), 2055–2140 (Week 5), 1930–2015 (Week 9), 1900–2000 (Weeks 10, 12), 1915–2015 (Week 11), 2100–2200 (Week 13), 2000–2100 (Weeks 14, 16, 18), 1840–1930 (Week 15), 1930–2030 (Week 17)
Broadcast variously on National and Regional networks
(Selections were broadcast 2015–2100, 11 July 1938, on regional network in a programme featuring the Band Waggoners and Phil Cardew with Betty Bucknelle, Miff Ferrie's Jackdauz, Dudley Beaven at the

had previously been heard in *Music Hall* and *Eight Bells*. The straight man was the dashing Richard ('Stinker') Murdoch, of whom Askey said, '. . . this chap was everything I wasn't: the complete contrast. Tall, handsome, Charterhouse and Cambridge educated . . .'

Together they formed one of radio's most successful double acts:

STINKER: **Well, ladies and gentlemen, here we are with another *Band Waggon*. Arthur's here but as usual he's going to be late.**
BIG: **What for?**
STINKER: **Well we always start that way.**
BIG: **Oh yes, of course. Shall I go out again?**
STINKER: **Well it might improve the show.**

The early editions of ***Band Waggon*** were mediocre, owing to poor scripts. By the third show, the BBC had decided to cancel the series after only six editions. Askey and Murdoch were then allowed to do whatever they liked with the scripts.

They worked hard on the next show, inventing a fictitious flat above Broadcasting House (directly above the announcers' bathroom), where they both lived. They had a cleaner, Mrs Bagwash, who had a daughter called Nausea (Arthur's fiancee), and an adenoidal son, Ernie, who was the only Bagwash who actually spoke (he was played by Murdoch). They kept two pigeons, Basil and Lucy, and a goat called Lewis. ('What about the smell?' 'Oh, he'll get used to it.')

In a dramatic turnaround, the show became a great success. The first run was extended and they were offered a second series. Askcy said, 'By the time we had finished twelve ***Band Waggon***s we were very popular; at the end of eighteen we were national favourites.'

The comedy content of the show ran to 20 minutes in each hour, remaining constant when the show was occasionally shortened to 40 minutes. The pair had three regular spots and Arthur also sang a comic song such as 'The Bee', 'The Moth' or 'The Seagull'. Another regular feature, 'Chestnut Corner', was a recycling centre for appalling old jokes:

BIG: **Excuse me, sir, but can you spare me a shilling for a cup of coffee?**
STINKER: **A shilling? That's a lot for a cup of coffee, isn't it?**
BIG: **Listen, are you trying to tell me how to run my business?**

Or . . .

STINKER: **How are you getting on in your new house?**
BIG: **Oh, fine. I've furnished one room by collecting coupons out of soap packets.**
STINKER: **That's a grand idea – why not furnish all the other rooms in the same way?**
BIG: **I can't.**
STINKER: **Why not?**
BIG: **They're full of soap.**

The jokes were punctuated by funny noises: ***Band Waggon*** was pioneering in its use of sound effects. A mountain of tin cans was kept in the studio to be knocked over when required.

organ; the compere was Vernon Harris. It was re-broadcast 1945–2030, 6 September 1938, on national network)

Series 2 – (24 Weeks)

Taking part (variously throughout the run)
Arthur Askey, Richard Murdoch, the Band Waggoners and Phil Cardew with Betty Bucknelle, Miff Ferrie's Jackdauz, Charles Smart at the organ, compere Vernon Harris, Syd Walker, New Voices, Cary Grant (guest on 16 November 1938), Peter Vokes (replacing Richard Murdoch after Murdoch had an appendicitis operation)

Produced by
Gordon Crier and Harry S. Pepper

Wednesday 5 October 1938–Wednesday 15 March 1939
Broadcast 2000–2100 (Weeks 1, 8, 16, 24), 2025–2125 (Week 2), 2015–2115 (Weeks 4, 9, 10, 11, 12, 13, 14, 15, 17, 18, 20, 22, 23), 2020–2120 (Weeks 3, 5, 6, 7, 21), 2005–2100 (Week 19)
Broadcast variously on National and Regional networks

Sunday Night Excursion

18 Weeks

Featuring
Arthur Askey, Richard Murdoch, Al Bowlly, Marjorie Stedeford, Frank Trafford, Dent Stevenson, The Southern Airs/Aka The Rhythm Brothers, The Club Royal Orchestra
Arrangements by
Jack Penn
Produced by
Pat Dixon

21 May 1939–17 September 1939
Broadcast Sundays 2115–2145
Broadcast on Luxembourg

Series 3 – (10 Weeks)
Taking part (variously throughout the run)
Arthur Askey, Richard Murdoch, Diana Clare, the Three Chimes, the New Waggoners conducted by Billy Ternent, Syd Walker, compere Vernon Harris
Produced by
Gordon Crier and Harry S. Pepper

Saturday 16 September 1939–Saturday 25 November 1939
Broadcast 2015–2100 (Weeks 1, 4), 2000–2100 (Weeks 2, 5, 6, 7, 8, 9, 10), 1945–2030 (Week 3)
(Owing to the outbreak of World War Two, the old National and Regional

The show contained many catchphrases, some of which can still be heard today:

'Aythangyow' – a phrase Askey heard used by London bus-conductors.

'Hello, playmates!' – Askey was not allowed to say 'Hello, folks!', as Tommy Handley had objected, considering it to be his property.

'Don't be filthy!'

'Doesn't it make you want to spit!'

'Light the blue touchpaper and retire immediately.'

'You silly little man.'

'Proper 'oom droom.'

'Ah, happy days!'

'It isn't the people who make the most noise who do the most work.'

Apart from Askey's and Murdoch's contributions, there were features such as 'New Voices' (a talent spot) and 'What Do You Think?', a radio problem to be solved by the listener. There were also guest stars, dance music from Phil Cardew and the Band Waggoners, with a vocal group, the Jackdaws (which later came to be spelled 'Jackdauz'), and Charles Smart at the BBC Theatre Organ.

The second series introduced a regular feature, 'Mr Walker Wants to Know', starring Syd Walker as a rag-and-bone man with a weekly problem to solve. At the end of each episode the listeners were asked, 'What would you do, chums?'

Between the second and third series Askey and Murdoch did a ***Band Waggon***-style show for Radio Luxembourg, taking over a series called *Sunday Night Excursion*. The setting was a bungalow in Kennington called Seaview. The show was sponsored by Symington's Table Creams.

In September 1939 there was a third and final series for the BBC. After only 52 editions, ***Band Waggon*** finished its run, having altered the nature of radio comedy irrevocably.

There was a touring stage version of the show in 1939, and an excellent film version was made in 1940. In 1958 the format was unsuccessfully revived for television in ITV's *Living It Up*. At this time, Askey and Murdoch were supposedly running a pirate TV station while living in a flat above the head office of Associated Rediffusion.

networks ceased to exist)
One-off Reunion Show, broadcast 14 November 1947 with Fred Yule in *Mr Walker wants To Know*

A Lancashire Lad In London

January–February 1938

This short series depicted the adventures of an unsophisticated north-country couple from the fictional town of Posselthwaite, on their honeymoon in London.

It starred George Formby, along with Beryl Formby, and the show was written by Howard Thomas and produced by Max Kester.

A Formby Do
3 Weeks
19 May 1938 and 2 June 1938, broadcast 1930 and 2000 respectively, on National network; 27 May 1938 broadcast 2115 on Regional network

A Right Good Do
1 Week
(Billed as a 'Northern Christmas party')
Guests included
Beryl Reid
Friday 23 December 1938 2040–2130
Broadcast on Regional network

7 January 1938–11 February 1938
Broadcast Fridays 1825–1840 on National

Transmission Details

A Lancashire Lad in London
6 Weeks
Written by
Howard Thomas
Starring
George and Beryl Formby
Produced by
Max Kester
Episode List
The Honeymooners Arrive; *On A Thames Pleasure Steamer*; *The Night Club*; *The Tower of London*; *In Hyde Park*; *At the Wax Works*

Although this was Formby's only situation series for the BBC, he broadcast regularly throughout his career and hosted a variety of series of his own, also in 1938.

Feen-A-Mint Fanfare

1938–1939

Transmission Details

Feen-A-Mint Fanfare

Series 1 – (39 Weeks)

Starring
George Formby, Beryl Formby, Jack Train

Music by
John Firman's Orchestra, the Four Lancashire Hot Pots

Produced by
Charles Maxwell

Sunday 3 April 1938–Sunday 25 December 1938
Broadcast Sundays 0830–0845
Broadcast on Radio Luxembourg (also Radio Normandy)
(The show was previously broadcast from Radio Toulouse – but without Formby. George also took part in Radio Luxembourg's Christmas Party between 1000 and 1200 on 25 December 1938)

This was a series of laughter-and-song programmes featuring once again the irrepressible George and Beryl Formby, and was sponsored by White's Laboratories, makers of Feen-A-Mint – 'the delicious mint-flavoured laxative that keeps you fit'.

There was 'a strong supporting cast' – but this was mainly Jack Train, who provided all the male voices other than George's.

A great deal was packed into these popular fifteen-minute shows, which boasted 'a brand-new adventure each week', including 'The Formbys at Home', 'George in the Army' (and the Navy, the Fire Brigade and the Police Force).

For several consecutive weeks, George told listeners about 'Third Lamp-post Tuesday', his local football team, which consisted of himself, his best friend Syd and 'Young Alfie'.

A mystery serial began on 19 June – with George and Beryl hot on the trail of secret plans. An arch enemy, a haunted house and the Invisible Man were also involved.

Billed as 'public interrupter number one' or 'the world's fastest tap-dancer', Beryl began the series as a 'persistent lady reporter from the *Daily Gazette*', who was after George's life story. She later became a nurse, a schoolteacher and the owner of a milk bar.

Although the scripts were slightly below the usual Formby standard, there was much for his many fans to enjoy: each show contained at least three songs, with occasional band numbers or contributions from an instrumental quartet called the Four Lancashire Hot Pots. George's songs included: Levi's Monkey Mike, She's Never Been Seen Since Then, Sitting on the Ice, My Sweetie Went Away, Fanlight Fanny, Daredevil Dick, My Little Boat and Me, Biceps, Muscle And Brawn, Leaning on a Lamp-post and Believe it or Not.

Series 2 – (37 Weeks)
Personnel as above
First five programmes sponsored by Aspergum
1 January 1939–10 September 1939
Broadcast Sundays 1045–1100
Broadcast on Radio Normandy and Radio Paris

The Pig And Whistle

1938–1944

This was a half-hour of songs and sketches in a village pub setting written by the music hall comedian Charles Penrose, famous as the Laughing Policeman. The idea behind the show came from a series of gramophone records of jolly rustic scenes that he'd made many years earlier.

An authentic atmosphere was created in the studio by seating the cast around a large oak table, complete with pewter pots and other appropriate details, and a single microphone in its centre.

A small orchestra of piano, violin and piano accordion was also on hand. There was no studio audience. This arrangement was so effective that to begin with many listeners believed the Pig and Whistle was genuine.

The landlord was Jeremiah Jones (Ernest Butcher, later George Ellis). The landlady was Rosie Jones (Muriel George), and the regulars included William

Transmission Details

The Pig and Whistle

The Cast
Charles Penrose, Ernest Butcher, Muriel George, Fred Yule, Charles Wreford

Music by
The Rae Jenkins Buskers

Produced by
Ernest Longstaffe

Episode List includes
After the Cricket Match; Bob Evergreen Wins the Cup; Granfer Shines at Darts; The Rehearsal for the Village Concert; The Pig and Whistle Goes Crackers

17 January 1938–19 October 1944
Broadcast intermittently on BBC

Potter the postman (Fred Yule) and PC Bob Evergreen, played by Penrose himself. He also played several other minor characters, including Farmer Scroggins and Jolly Old George. The most popular character was Old Granfer (Charles Wreford).

The patrons took up ARP work from 28 August 1939.

Occasionally a guest would drop in and contribute to the entertainment. Over the years these included Bobbie Comber, Mabel Constanduros, Dennis Noble and *Band Waggon*'s Syd Walker.

Billy Caryll And Hilda Mundy/The Neemos

June–October 1938

Transmission Details

Billy Caryll and Hilda Mundy

3 Weeks

Written by
Vernon Harris

The Cast
Billy Caryll, Hilda Mundy

Music by
Jay Wilbur and his Band, the Cavendish Three

Produced by
Gordon Crier and Ronald Waldman

Wednesday 22 June 1938–Monday 4 July 1938

The husband-and-wife cross-talk act of Caryll and Mundy were well known to variety audiences for their domestic sketches. Inspired by a genuine row they had once had, they made an art-form of the marital spat: Billy Caryll usually portraying the classic music hall drunk. They first worked together in the early 1920s and in 1931 were part of the original edition of the Crazy Gang at the London Palladium.

Owing to a managerial contract they were unable to broadcast until 1936, but from then on were guests on many variety and magazine programmes. In 1938 they introduced two characters that were new to the radio, Mr and Mrs Neemo.

MRS NEEMO: **Let me tell you, I'm an excellent cook. My pastry is**

	famous among the neighbours. They're always asking for the recipe.
MR NEEMO:	**I suppose it's another coincidence that all the gardens round here are being laid with crazy paving?**
MRS NEEMO:	**You would bring that up, you –**
MR NEEMO:	**Only because I can't get it down.**

The Neemos argued and fought their way through two series: the first, ***Billy Caryll And Hilda Mundy***, was a mixture of Neemo sketches and dance music provided by Jay Wilbur and his band, with vocals by the Cavendish Three. In the second, retitled *Mr and Mrs Neemo*, the sketch format was replaced by complete domestic episodes, and two other members of the Neemo household were introduced: George the tortoise and, most notably, Little Reggie (His Nibbs), played by Maurice Denham. The crooner Sam Costa also joined the show.

A novel feature was 'From the London Streets'. A few days before the first show, Maurice Gaye had been spotted singing 'Gypsy Moon' in Hallam Street, near Broadcasting House. He sang it again on the air and thereafter became 'the presiding genius of the buskers', bringing a different street entertainer to the microphone each week.

(First Week on National, second and third on Regional)

Mr and Mrs Neamo

5 Weeks

Details as for Billy Caryll and Hilda Mundy but with the addition of Maurice Denham and Sam Costa in the cast

12 September–10 October 1938

Broadcast Mondays 1900–1945 on National

Almost An Academy

January–March 1939

Transmission Details

Almost An Academy

6 Weeks

Starring
Billy Bennett

Music by
Sandy MacPherson at the BBC Organ

20 January 1939–30 March 1939
Broadcast 1930–2000 (Week 1), 2130–2200 (Week 2), 2100–2130 (Week 3), 2030–2100 (Week 4), 1900–1930 (Week 5), 2125–2200 (Week 6)
Broadcast on Regional Network (first four programmes) and National Network (Weeks 5, 6)

'Somebody said that every time a man drinks a glass of beer it shortens his life by one day. Well if that's true, I've been dead exactly 136 years.' – Billy Bennett, from *No Power on Earth*

This was the only series to star the undisputed king of the surreal comic monologue. Listed as 'a musical spelling bee' this antediluvian *Name That Tune* was hosted by Billy Bennett with musical accompaniment by Sandy MacPherson at the BBC Organ.

Six members of the audience at St George's Hall were invited up to the microphone to assist in identifying pieces of music, thereby scoring points or getting gonged. A vehicle for Bennett's bizarre patter, each edition of the programme featured one of his celebrated parodies, as well as two numbers from Sandy MacPherson. ***Almost an Academy*** soon became the most popular quiz-show on the air.

'These weren't rehearsed. We gagged as we went along, and before the shows we hadn't the slightest idea what we were going to say. The result was that a real party spirit always prevailed.' (Radio Pictorial interview 1939)

A link between the eras of music hall and variety, Billy Bennett began his professional career at the end of the First World War. Inheriting something of the wild surrealism of the great Dan Leno, he achieved fame during the 1920s and in turn became a significant influence on a later generation of comedians.

Bennett wrote most of his material and often lampooned the dramatic recitations of the Edwardian era. He created classics such as 'A Sailor's Farewell to his Horse', 'The Charge of the Tight Brigade', 'The Road to Mandalay' and 'The Green Tie on the Little Yellow Dog'. He also invented the 'boom-boom' using the double-beat of a bass drum to drive home a punch line.

In appearance, Billy Bennett was the 'low' comedian supreme. Sporting a large soup-strainer moustache, usually dressed in an ill-fitting evening suit and army boots, he was billed 'Almost a Gentleman'. His act, an earthy mixture of songs and recitations, delivered in a magnificent beer-sodden bellow, was particularly effective on the radio.

There's a cockeyed yellow poodle to the north of
  Gongapooch*;
There's a little hot-crossed bun that's turning
  green;
There's a double-jointed woman doing tricks in
  Chu-chin-chow –
And you're a better man than I am Gunga din.
(From 'The Green Tie on the Little Yellow Dog')

Billy Bennett was a guest on many variety shows including *Music Hall*, *Palace of Varieties* (on which he was once master of ceremonies), *Garrison Theatre* and *The Happidrome.*

From 1930, when he was unable to broadcast under his own name owing to a managerial contract, he formed a spoof 'black-face' cross-talk act, Alexander and Mose, with James Carew (later Albert Whelan).

In 1935 he was involved in 'A boisterous, uncon-

*Informal Hindustani for 'arseholes'.

ventional gathering of famous stars' for Radio Luxembourg in a variety series sponsored by Symington's Table Creams and Jelly Crystals. It ran for four editions in May and June on Sundays at 2130–2200 (also on Radio Paris and Radio Normandy). It featured Alexander and Mose, Elsie Carlisle, Billy Bennett, the Two Leslies, Stanelli assisted by Mrs Stanelli, the Symington Twins. It was produced by the Mather and Crowther Radio Department.

Bennett died in 1942.

Danger! – Men At Work

1939–1947

Transmission Details

Danger! – Men At Work

Series 1 – (8 Weeks)

Written by
Max Kester and Anthony Hall

The Cast
Doris Nichols, Van and Allen ('the music hall boys'), Jacques Brown

Produced by
Max Kester and Anthony Hall

Episode List
Spring Cleaning; Gardening; Car Repairs; Hairdressing; Too Many Cooks; Tinker Taylor; Plumbing the Depths; Writing a Radio Script

'If you are a devotee of the type of humour typified by the Kentucky Minstrels you must go elsewhere for your entertainment.' – Max Kester

A pioneer crazy series created by Max Kester, ***Danger! – Men At Work*** brought the style of the early Marx Brothers films to British radio.

Events centred around the Hotel Mimoar and its formidable landlady, Mrs Anaesthesia Ponsonby – a rich widow with no sense of humour, played by Doris Nichols, an ex-*Children's Hour* 'auntie' who specialised in 'battle-axe' characterisations.

'I've always had the kind of face that should belong to a lion-tamer – I've seen strong men wilt in front of it.'

When anything needed doing at the hotel, the

'men at work' of the title, a violent and unscrupulous duo, were called in from the employment agency – and then Mrs Ponsonby's troubles would really start.

'Blandly unaware of what is in store for her, she faces each weekly martyrdom with the dignity of a battleship,' said *The Radio Times*.

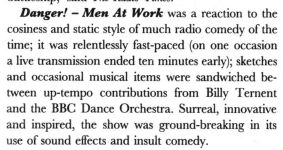

Danger! – Men At Work was a reaction to the cosiness and static style of much radio comedy of the time; it was relentlessly fast-paced (on one occasion a live transmission ended ten minutes early); sketches and occasional musical items were sandwiched between up-tempo contributions from Billy Ternent and the BBC Dance Orchestra. Surreal, innovative and inspired, the show was ground-breaking in its use of sound effects and insult comedy.

MRS PONSONBY:	**Let me tell you – I walk four miles every day for my complexion.**
EGGBLOW:	**You should live nearer the chemist.**

The first men at work were the Americans Van and Allen (the 'music hall boys'); in the second series they were Jack Train and George Moon; for the next three, Haver and Lee (aka Clay Keyes and Frank

11 May 1939–29 June 1939
Broadcast Thursdays, 2045–2145
Broadcast on National

Series 2 – (3 Weeks)

Written by
Max Kester and Anthony Hall

The Cast
As first series, except Jack Train and George Moon as the men at work

Produced by
Max Kester and Anthony Hall

Episode List
Blacking Out Mrs Ponsonby; Rationing; On Thin Ice

1 December 1939–5 January 1940
Broadcast Fridays 1845–1900 (except Week 2, at 1345–1400)
Broadcast on National Network

Series 3 – (6 Weeks)

Written by
Max Kester

The Cast
As usual, except Harry Haver and Frank Lee as the men at work, Virginia Dawn as the switchboard girl

Music by
Billy Ternent Orchestra

Produced by
Max Kester

Episode List
Plain Cooking by Plainer Cooks; Meals A La Carte

or Cul De Sac; Large Parties Taken In and Done For; Early Breakfasts, Late Dinner, Strip Teas; Fish and Chips Off The Old Block

2 April 1940–7 May 1940
Broadcast Tuesdays 2000–2030 (first 3 programmes), 2030–2100 (rest of series)

Series 4 – (6 Weeks) (renamed Danger! – Men Still At Work)

Written by
Max Kester

The Cast
As usual, but Hugh Shirreff featured as the Voice of the BBC from Week 3

Music by
Billy Ternent Orchestra (except Week 3 – Maurice Winnick Band)

Produced by
Max Kester

5 June 1940–10 July 1940
Broadcast Wednesdays 1930–2000 (except Week 6, at 1915–1945)
Broadcast on Home and Forces (Weeks 1, 2, 3), Forces only (Weeks 4, 6), Home only (Week 5)

Series 5 – (6 Weeks)

Written by
Max Kester

The Cast
As usual

Tully) played the characters most associated with the show, Duckweed and Eggblow.

The fractured English of Nikolas Ridikoulas (Jacques Brown) a helpful passer-by (and Greek surrogate Chico Marx) featured in every edition; his catchphrase was 'Ri-diculous!'

NIKOLAS: **I'm a going to a party with a boil on my neck.**
DUCKWEED: **Was it a painful gathering?**
NIKOLAS: **No – just a few friends.**

From the third series, the show was extended from fifteen to 30 minutes. For the fourth, the Hotel Mimoar and its contents were removed to the seaside.

DUCKWEED: **I'm going to give the old girl a blow on the front!**

For the fifth series, the cast were joined by Hugh Shirreff, as the voice of the BBC.

The show was revived for two series after the war; Frank Tully (Eggblow) was replaced by Charlie Irwin, who played Colonel Swivelhead, a worried character with a high-pitched voice. Susan Scott was introduced as Mrs Ponsonby's companion.

'What does this programme set out to do? A psychiatrist would say that it is the releasing of all the repressions that civilisation has imposed upon the individual, but don't let that bother you. Think of all the things you have ever wanted to do, and dared not because of "what the neighbours would think." Do them – say them – and you have ***Danger! – Men At Work***!' – Max Kester 1946

MRS P: **I've never been so insulted in my life!**
EGGBLOW: **You should get about more.**

Produced by
Max Kester

4 October 1940–8 November 1940
Broadcast Fridays 2030–2100 (Weeks 1, 3, 4), 2135–2205 (Week 2), 1930–2000 (Week 5), 2000–2030 (Week 6)
25 March 1947–13 May 1947
Broadcast Tuesdays 1915–1945 (except Week 8, broadcast 2100–2130)
Broadcast on Home and Forces (Weeks 2, 3, 4, 6), Home only (Week 1), Forces only (Week 5)

Series 6 – (11 Weeks)

Written by
Max Kester

The Cast
Clay Keyes, Doris Nichols, Jacques Brown, Charlie Irwin, Susan Scott

Music by
Stanley Black and the BBC Dance Orchestra (Billy Ternent Orchestra Weeks 8–10)

2 July 1946–17 September 1946
Broadcast 2015–2045 (Weeks 1–6, 8–10), 2010–2045 (Week 7), 1915–1945 (Week 11)
Broadcast on Light Programme

Series 7 – (8 Weeks)

Written by
Max Kester

The Cast
Doris Nichols, Jacques Brown, Charlie Irwin, Clay Keyes

Music by
Stanley Black and the Dance Orchestra

Produced by
Cleland Fin

ITMA (It's That Man Again)

1939–1949

'It should be written somewhere for all to read that Tommy Handley, in the Fiendish Forties of our century, made more folk laugh than any other native comedian. And by laugh I do not mean smile' – Ted Kavanagh

With a domestic audience of 20 million, and listeners worldwide numbering over 30 million, ***ITMA*** remains the most popular radio comedy series ever produced. Its significance, and the affection in which its star, Tommy Handley, was held, cannot be overemphasised. In recent years the show has often been unfairly criticised, accused of being incomprehensible to modern audiences, or for simply not being funny. ***ITMA*** carried its audience through 310 editions, building up characters and catchphrases over

Transmission Details

ITMA (It's That Man Again)

Series 1 – (4 Weeks)

The Cast
Tommy Handley, Celia Eddy, Eric Egan, Sam Hepper and Lionel Gamlin

Music by
Jack Harris and his Band, with Pat Taylor (singer)

12 July 1939–30 August 1939
Broadcast Wednesdays 2015–2100
Broadcast on National

(except Week 4, broadcast 2030 on Regional Network)

Series 2 – (20 Weeks)

The Cast
Tommy Handley, Vera Lennox, Maurice Denham, Sam Costa, Jack Train

Music by
Jack Hylton's Band conducted by Billy Ternent, supported by the Rhythm Octet (Billy Cotton and his Band on Week 5)

19 September 1939–6 February 1940
Broadcast Tuesdays, varying times between 1830 and 2100
Broadcast on the Home Service
(A special Boxing Day edition was called *Funf and Games for Everyone*)

Star Variety edition from the Palace Theatre, Manchester

The Cast
Tommy Handley, Jack Train, Maurice Denham, June Malo, Johnny Lockwood, Syd Crossley, Fela Sowande and Funf

Saturday 18 May 1940
Broadcast 2015–2100
Broadcast on the Home Service

Series 3 – (6 Weeks)

The Cast
Tommy Handley, Jack Train, Sydney Keith,

a ten-year period; some series ran as long as 39 weeks. A topical show (the scripts were written two days before the broadcast), it was not designed to be listened to half a century on.

'I myself cannot now understand some of the jokes. They were skits on a nine-days wonder – a headline of that day's paper, and dead the following week. Every programme is an accurate reflection of the war situation at the time,' the writer Ted Kavanagh said in 1949.

'. . . Old ***ITMA*** scripts do not read too well nowadays, and old recordings seem curiously dusty and faded, like an album of old photographs,' said the producer, Francis Worsley, in 1948.

When ***ITMA*** was first transmitted, the concept of the regular (British) comedy series was barely seven months old, only *Band Waggon* and *Danger! Men at Work* had gone before. ***ITMA*** was something entirely new, breaking away from the existing conventions of both radio and music hall comedy. Anarchic and irreverent, it was the first total radio comedy show, using the medium of sound to the full. The sheer speed of ***ITMA*** was impressive (it still is); into less than 20 minutes of dialogue the writer Ted Kavanagh attempted to squeeze at least 100 laughs, or one every eleven seconds.

No other comedy series has ever matched ***ITMA*** for consistent pace. This was due in the main to Tommy Handley's near miraculous technique. Almost impossibly quick-fire, but never incoherent, he achieved the difficult task of functioning as straight man and comedian almost at one and the same time. Although the show was built around his personality, Handley was a generous performer who always let the rest of the cast shine.

Born in Liverpool in 1894, Handley entered show business via the local amateur dramatic company, becoming a concert party comedian around the time of World War One. On joining the forces (as airman, second class) he found himself involved in a concert party again, giving over 1,000 performances in less than 12 months. After the war he formed a short-lived double-act with the future bandleader and impresario Jack Hylton. Around this time he began to specialise in improvising material based on the news of the day.

From 1921 he toured the music-halls with 'The Disorderly Room', a sketch written by Eric Blore. A burlesque on official army procedures, with Handley as the Officer in Charge, it featured dialogue set to popular melodies. It became the basis of his live appearances over the next 20 years. Handley performed it on stage, film, on record and even on television. By 1940 there can't have been many variety fans who hadn't seen it.

His first broadcast was a relay of 'The Disorderly Room' from the 1923 Royal Variety Performance. The following year he auditioned successfully for the BBC – broadcasting as a solo comedian and also taking part in *Radio Radiance* (1925), the first original wireless concert party. Later he starred in radio revues of his own including *Handley's Manoeuvres*, *Tommy's Tours*, and *Hot Pot.* By the end of the 20s, Tommy Handley was a household name.

In 1930 he formed a double act, North and South, with the risqué cabaret comedian Ronald Frankau. Later they became Mr Murgatroyd and

Paula Green, Kay Cavendish, Fred Yule, Dorothy Summers, Horace Percival

Music by
BBC Variety Orchestra conducted by Charles Shadwell (Handley was also starring in *Handley's Half Hour*, broadcast from the Criterion Theatre, London)

20 June 1941–25 July 1941
Broadcast Fridays 2030–2100
Broadcast on Home and Forces (except Week 6, Forces only)

Everyman Jack
An occasional series

Written by
Ted Kavanagh

Featuring
Jack Train, Vera Lennox, Horace Percival, Foster Carlin

Produced by
Michael North

First broadcast Friday 30 October 1940
Broadcast 2015–2030

Series 4 – (32 Weeks)

The Cast
Tommy Handley, Jack Train, Horace Percival, Sydney Keith, Clarence Wright, Dino Galvani, Fred Yule, Dorothy Summers, Kay Cavendish, Paula Green and, in Week 8 only, Maurice Denham

Music by
Charles Shadwell and

the BBC Variety Orchestra (with Billy Ternent and the Dance Orchestra appearing in Weeks 14, 15)

26 September 1941–1 May 1942
Broadcast Fridays 2030–2100 (except Week 14, 2000–2030)
Broadcast Home and Forces (except Week 15, Forces only)

A Grand ITMA Concert
Selections from the music specially composed and arranged for the fourth series
Featuring
Tommy Handley, BBC Variety Orchestra conducted by Charles Shadwell, singers Kay Cavendish and Paula Green
Introduced by
Tommy Handley
Produced by
Francis Worsley

Series 5 – (20 Weeks)
The Cast
Tommy Handley, Jack Train, Dino Galvani, Sydney Keith, Horace Percival, Clarence Wright, Fred Yule, Dorothy Summers, Kay Cavendish, Paula Green, Pat Rignold, Vera Lennox (from Week 13)
Music by
BBC Variety Orchestra conducted by Charles Shadwell

Mr Winterbottom. From 1934 they took part in many variety programmes. Their routines took cross-talk into another dimension, with shocking puns and one-liners piling up at break-neck speed. They made over 30 gramophone records between 1929 and 1940.

In 1936 Handley starred in his own series for Radio Luxembourg, an edition of the Kraft Concert Party show, *Tommy Handley's Watt Nots*. There were eight editions in all.

By the late 1930s most of the early wireless comedians were considered old hat, but Handley was one of the few exceptions. BBC's head of variety, John Watt, wanted another major 'fixed points' comedy series to follow the extraordinary success of *Band Waggon*. He also wanted it to star Tommy Handley.

Ted Kavanagh began his comedy career writing a joke column in a religious weekly. A fast and prolific writer, he scripted more than 30 shows in the first two months of the war. He wrote his first script for Handley in 1926 – this featured a dream where Tommy's deranged wireless set gave a commentary on the Grand National, the Boat Race and the Cup Final all at once.

Handley, Kavanagh and the producer Francis Worsley first worked together in *Evening in Cheddar* (1937), a successful outside broadcast. It drew criticism in some quarters over the letting loose of a 'red-nosed comic' in the famous caves.

From the beginning, the writer, producer and comedian worked together in almost perfect harmony. ***ITMA*** could not have existed without the contributions of all three.

First Series – It's That Man Again

This comparatively unsuccessful first run was broadcast from St George's Hall. Very different from the later shows in style and format, it was based on *Band Waggon*'s magazine style, with features linked by a comedy thread. These fortnightly shows were also fifteen minutes longer than in any other series.

The setting was a radio broadcasting ship. On board were Tommy Handley and his dizzy secretary, Cilly (Canadian Celia Eddy). The original plan was to base the show on the comedy of the American act, Burns and Allen; this idea was soon abandoned – Handley would have been wasted as merely a comic feed.

Also on board was Vladivostooge, a maniac Russian inventor (Eric Egan).

This floating studio, unlike the BBC, was unfettered by red tape and restrictions, and Handley as 'proprietor' was free to transmit whatever he liked. The show had two features: 'Guess Or No', a charade based on play titles, conducted by Lionel Gamlin; and 'Man Bites Dog' by Sam Hepper, where an everyday situation was turned topsy-turvy, one example being a chorus girl giving a job interview to a theatrical impresario.

ITMA's first words were spoken by Tommy Handley on the telephone . . .

'Hello! Is that Turner, Turner, and Turtle? It is? Then good morning, good morning, good morning, good morning. It's that man again. That's right, Tommy Handley!'

18 September 1942–29 January 1943
Broadcast Fridays 2030–2100 (Week 15, 2000–2035; Week 18, 2000–2030)
(The 1942 Christmas edition was extended five minutes for Christmas party music, but also to explain to curious listeners who was playing whom, and how so many parts could be played by so few people – particularly in the case of Jack Train)
Broadcast on Home and Forces Networks (Week 11 Forces only)

Occasional series *Tommy Handley's Half Hour*

First broadcast 28 November 1942 1830–1900
Broadcast Saturdays on the Forces Network
(Also this year, Handley regularly contributed to *The £250 Red Cross Radio Contest* – a monthly Forces show in aid of the Red Cross Penny-a-Week Fund)

A Grand ITMA Concert

Handley presented selections from the music heard in the fifth series, assisted by Clarence Wright, Charles Shadwell and the Variety Orchestra

Produced by
Francis Worsley

7 February 1943
Broadcast 1830–1900
Broadcast on Forces Network

It's That Man Again (film version)

Written by
Howard Irving Young and Ted Kavanagh

The Cast
Tommy Handley, Jack Train, Greta Gynt, Sydney Keith, Horace Percival, Dorothy Summers, Dino Galvani, Clarence Wright, Leonard Sharp, Claude Bailey, Vera Frances, Jean Kent

Produced by
Edward Black

Directed by
Walter Forde

Series 6 – (16 Weeks)

The Cast
Tommy Handley, Sydney Keith, Fred Yule, Dino Galvani, Horace Percival, Dorothy Summers, Vera Lennox, Paula Green, Bill Stephens (from Week 4)

Music by
BBC Variety Orchestra conducted by Charles Shadwell (Peter Akister and the Jazz Ticulators took over from Week 4)

15 April 1943–29 July 1943
Broadcast Thursdays 2030–2100
Broadcast on Home Service (except Week 12, Forces only)

It was originally scheduled for six fortnightly editions with the option of a weekly series later in the year. After the fourth edition, ***It's That Man Again*** was abandoned owing to the outbreak of war.

Series Two (ITMA)

This was the start of ***ITMA*** proper, now virtually a different show; along with the BBC Variety Department it was now based in Bristol. A new cast was assembled from those available in the repertory department (the old cast had not been vetted by the Ministry of Information). The broadcasting ship had supposedly been commandeered and the only link with the first series was Handley's new secretary: Dotty (Vera Lennox) who was Cilly's sister. Handley himself had been drafted to ***ITMA***, a section within the department of fun.

Among the newcomers was the funny voice supremo Jack Train – once described as '25 voices under one hat'. He had originally applied to the BBC for an audition as a character actor (he was once stooge for the Crazy Gang duo Nervo and Knox); he was sent the wrong form and became a comedian. His famous creation, Funf the German spy, arrived in the second show. This mysterious, threatening character caught on with the public in a big way: 'This is Funf speaking'. To produce the voice Jack Train spoke sideways into a glass tumbler. Jack also played Fusspot, an extremely small-minded civil servant with the catchphrase 'Most irregular!' Apart from a period of illness, Train stayed for ***ITMA***'s entire run.

The first three shows still had the 'Guess Or No' feature, this time conducted by Vernon Harris. It was replaced by a regular Radio Luxembourg spoof, 'Radio Fakenburg'. The announcer was Maurice Denham, who would begin with, 'Mesdames et Messieurs, defense de cracher!' He would sign off with, 'Mesdames et Messieurs, vous pouvez cracher!'

Denham also played Vodkin (another Russian inventor) and Tommy's office char, Mrs Tickle (her first name was officially Lola – in the stage version of ***ITMA*** produced the following year, Tommy occasionally called her Tess). Sam Costa sang the 'Fakenburg' commercials selling unlikely ***ITMA*** products; he was also Lemuel, the office boy.

Early in the series Handley took over the Ministry of Fun, becoming the Minister of Aggravation and Mysteries c/o the Office Of Twerps (OOT). OOT was an over-zealous government department. At one time they even confiscated their own offices. The humour was a reaction to the wave of officialdom that swept Britain in the early days of the war.

> Good evening, Great Britain. As Minister of Aggravation it is my duty tonight on the umpteenth day of the war against depression to explain to you that I have 700 further restrictions to impose upon you. Here in the heart of the country I have been able to think out some of the most irritating regulations you've ever heard of (from Week 13 – 12 December 1939).

ITMA's style was now becoming fixed, with Handley as the central character trying to get on with his business, being continually interrupted by crazy characters and their catchphrases, either on the telephone or through the ***ITMA*** door. The show was also becoming increasingly topical.

The show went out during the 'phoney war'

(Series ended 5 August with 100th broadcast from the Grand Theatre, Llandudno)

Series 7 – (36 Weeks)

The Cast
Tommy Handley, Horace Percival, Fred Yule, Dorothy Summers, Sydney Keith, Dino Galvani, Bill Stephens, Bryan Herbert, Jean Capra, Jack Cooper (from Week 12), Paula Green (from Week 13), Diana Morrison (from Week 31), Marie Perrilli (from Week 31)

Music by
Charles Shadwell and the Variety Orchestra

7 October 1943–8 June 1944
Broadcast Thursdays 2030–2100
Broadcast on the Home Service (except Weeks 3 and 4, Forces only)

Special edition
Tom Marches Back
Cast as Series 7

12 June 1944
Broadcast 2120–2205
Broadcast on Home Service

Well for Santa Claus
Christmas Day edition

Cast included
Tommy Handley, Dorothy Summers, Fred Yule, Sydney Keith, Bryan Herbert, Ronald Chesney,

Barret and Max Field; storyteller: Derek McCulloch (Uncle Mac)

Music by
Charles Shadwell and the BBC Variety Orchestra

Produced by
Francis Worsley

25 December 1943
Broadcast 1720–1800
Broadcast on Home Service

Series 8 – (39 Weeks)

The Cast
Tommy Handley, Jack Train, Dorothy Summers, Horace Percival, Dino Galvani, Sydney Keith, Jean Capra, Diana Morrison, Paula Green, Fred Yule (from Week 3), Ann Rich (from Week 26), Charles Shadwell

Music by
Midland Light Orchestra conducted by Rae Jenkins

21 September 1944–14 June 1945
Broadcast 2030–2100 (except Weeks 10 and 36, broadcast 2130–2200)
Broadcast on the Home Service
Week 34 (10 May 1945) was a VE Day special called *V – ITMA*)

Series 9 – (39 Weeks)

The Cast
Tommy Handley, Jack

period. The blackout had begun and the government had closed all theatres and cinemas. This helped the show gain a massive audience.

In November, OOT was evacuated to a farmhouse in the country, where listeners met Farmer Jollop (Jack Train). By the end of the series the farm was commandeered by the army, and they were evacuated again.

Catchphrases for this series included:

'I wish I had as many shillings'

'I always do my best for all my gentlemen'

'Mine's a Persico'

'Friday! FRIDAY!'

'Well all right, all right!'

'What a common boy!'

The earliest ***ITMA*** recording dates from this series.

Series Three (It's That Sand Again – ITSA)

This short run began nearly eighteen months after the previous series because of the touring stage version. The Variety Department was now based in Bangor in North Wales. ***ITSA*** came from a converted chapel hall at Penrhyn. The setting was now the small seaside town of Foaming-at-the-Mouth, with Handley as the Mayor.

The cast were joined by Sydney Keith, Fred Yule, Horace Percival, Dino Galvani, Clarence Wright and Dorothy Summers.

Among the new characters were the Mayor's bodyguard, Sam Scram, played by Sydney Keith

('Boss, boss, sumpin' terrible's happened!'); Ali-Oop the pedlar, played by Horace Percival ('I go – I come back!'); Claude and Cecil, the polite broker's men who often spoke in rhyme ('After you, Claude' – 'No, after *you*, Cecil').

The Diver (Horace Percival) was based on a real character Handley remembered seeing at New Brighton during his childhood ('Don't forget the diver!' – 'I'm going down now, sir'). He was a melancholy character, always accompanied by the sound of bubbling. Jack Train played Lefty, the Chicago gangster ('It's my noives!') and Hari Kari, the Japanese Sandman, whose telephone conversations were total gibberish, understood only by Handley.

humphris

NO LIKEY?–OH, CRIKEY!'
8.30 p.m. Home Service

This series included a regular spoof film feature . . .

> Fog Bound Films Inc present an all-coughing, all-sneezing, all-spluttering epic, photographed in glorious khaki colour, entitled *Tom Marches On.*

The intellectuals now began to pick up on ***ITMA***, discovering it only two years after the general public did . . . !

Train, Clarence Wright, Fred Yule, Jean Capra, Carleton Hobbs, Hugh Morton, Mary O'Farrell, Lind Joyce, Michele dy Lys (replaced by Diana Morrison from Week 7)

Music by
Augmented BBC Variety Orchestra conducted by Charles Shadwell

20 September 1945–13 June 1946
Broadcast Thursdays 2030–2100
Broadcast on Home Service (except Week 33, broadcast on Light) (Week 23 was the 200th edition)

All-Star Party
Boxing Day edition

Written by
Louis Wigram and Jack Davies

Starring
Tommy Handley and Leslie Henson

Music by
Jack Payne and his Orchestra

Produced by
Michael North

Broadcast 1630–1700
Broadcast on Light Programme

Tommy's Handley's Bunk Holiday

Written by
Max Kester

Starring
Tommy Handley, Maudie Edwards, Frances Turner

Music by
The Squadronnaires Dance Orchestra, directed by Jimmy Miller
Produced by
Pat Dixon

Broadcast 5 August 1946, 2130–2200
Broadcast on the Light Programme

Can I Do You Now Sir?
Excerpt from the Combined Services Entertainment Show, from the Stage Door Canteen, London
Written by
Scruffy Dale
Featuring
Tommy Handley, Sidney James
Produced by
Tom Ronald

Broadcast 24 August 1946, 1800–1830
Broadcast on Light Programme

***Wither Tomtopia?* ('A Discussion on a Burning Topic')**
A microphone inquiry by experts into Handley's governorship of Tomtopia
Featuring
Tommy Handley, Sir William Darling MP (Chairman), Dilys Powell, Charles Hill (the Radio Doctor), A. G. Street, V. R. Kimmit

Broadcast 12 September 1946, 2030–2100

Series Four

This series reverted to the ***ITMA*** title. The show was now getting more than sixteen million listeners – the largest number then recorded by the Variety Department.

Handley was still the Mayor of Foaming-at-the-Mouth, with a new foreign secretary, Signor So-So (Dino Galvani), who could be heard saying, 'Notting at all! Notting at all!'

Other new characters were the Commercial Traveller (Clarence Wright) and Mrs Mopp, the corporation cleanser (Dorothy Summers), whose famous catchphrase was 'Can I do you now, sir?', originally 'Can I do for you now, Sir?'.

Her weekly meetings with Handley became a ritual. She always brought a gift of food, usually 'made out of my head', and always bade the Mayor a fond TTFN.

Her first gift was carrot jelly, which she'd strained through her jumper (this was a topical reference to the government's carrot campaign):

VOICE: **Do you know what you can do with a carrot?**
TOMMY: **Yes.** (Door closes)

The two ***ITMA*** char ladies, Mrs Mopp and Mrs Tickle, actually met in this series when Maurice Denham was on leave.

In the fifth programme, martial law was declared in Foaming-at-the-Mouth. This was the only ***ITMA*** to be faded out because of enemy action – a parachute mine exploded killing a BBC driver.

Series Five

Foaming-at-the-Mouth now had a munitions factory. Handley, sacked from his position as Mayor, was the manager. The characters all worked in the factory but what they actually produced was a mystery.

ITMA's topicality was now brought more to the fore. This meant that the script often had to be amended at the last minute.

New characters included Johann Bull, an extremely obvious German spy, and Norman the Doorman. Both were played by Fred Yule. There was also Jack Train as Bookham, the variety agent, while Clarence Wright played the Man from the Ministry, who always repeated the last word of his sentences.

The most celebrated of all ***ITMA*** characters arrived with Colonel Chinstrap (Jack Train). Apart from a brief spell on the wagon in the eighth series, he remained resolutely plastered throughout. He was a man whose idea of a gentleman was 'one who opens a bottle of whisky and throws away the cork'. This tipsy creation became a national institution, outliving ***ITMA*** and turning up on *The Goon Show*. He made his debut in a courtroom scene:

HANDLEY: **Didn't I meet you in Rumbellipore, sir?**

THE COLONEL: **You did not, sir, I was never there.**

HANDLEY: **Then you must have a double.**

THE COLONEL: **Thanks, I will.**

In November 1942, the show was relayed to the forces in the Middle East and West Africa (massing

Broadcast on Home Service

Series 10 – (39 Weeks)

The Cast
Tommy Handley, Jack Train, Diana Morrison, Hugh Morton, Fred Yule, Lind Joyce, Deryck Guyler, Tony Francis, Mollie Weir, Joan Harben (from Week 7)

Music by
BBC Variety Orchestra conducted by Rae Jenkins (replaced by Guy Daniels and the Augmented BBC Variety Orchestra from Week 25)

19 September 1946–12 June 1947
Broadcast Thursdays 2030–2100
Broadcast on the Home Service

The Private Life of Mrs Mopp

Written by
Ted Kavanagh

Featuring
Dorothy Summers

Produced by
Jacques Brown

25 November 1946–30 December 1946
Broadcast Mondays 1245–1300
Broadcast on the Home Service

Series 11 – (38 Weeks)

The Cast
Tommy Handley, Jack Train, Hugh Morton, Fred Yule, Lind Joyce,

Diana Morrison, Deryck Guyler, Joan Harben, Hattie Jacques
Music by
Augmented BBC Variety Orchestra conducted by Rae Jenkins

25 September 1947–10 June 1948
Broadcast Thursdays 2030–2100 (except Week 8, at 2115–2145, Week 14, at 2025–2055)
Broadcast on the Home Service
(Week 2 was broadcast from Radiolympia)

Series 12 – (16 Weeks)
The Cast
Tommy Handley, Jack Train, Hugh Morton, Fred Yule, Diana Morrison, Deryck Guyler, Joan Harben, Hattie Jacques
Music by
Handley's Kerbside Choristers, directed by George Mitchell, and the Augmented BBC Variety Orchestra conducted by Rae Jenkins
No. 6 of this series was the special 300th edition featuring Horace Percival, Clarence Wright, Dino Galvani, Sydney Keith, Dorothy Summers and Hugh Morton

23 September 1948–6 January 1949
Broadcast Thursdays 2030–2100

for El Alamein). It was the first time it had been broadcast specifically to the forces.

Series Six

It was decided that the munitions factory be relocated underground. On beginning to dig, Handley immediately encountered a spring, which, according to Sam Scram, 'shot a shower of spray, sky high, every seven seconds, spreading the smell of sulphur so strongly that it succeeded in sending the surrounding spectators semi-conscious.'

As a consequence, the factory became a health spa. The following week, listeners were introduced to Miss Pansy Cowe-Parsley, a fresh-air fanatic. Shortly afterwards, the spa became a holiday camp, was then taken over by the BBC, and was also descended upon by a circus and a zoo.

Clarence Wright left. New characters included Comical Chris (Bill Stephens), a non-stop joker who was known to possess a performing seal; the forgetful Mr Whatsisname (Horace Percival), whose conversation was peppered with 'whatsisname' and 'thingummybob'. He was based on a publican Handley had once known.

Vera Lennox and Dorothy Summers played two posh ladies; their conversation was strewn with 'dahlings' and always ended with the call, 'Taxi!'

Specially arranged musical items were now part of every show, often with words by Ted Kavanagh, which were relevant to the plot. From Week Four there were regular contributions from Peter Akister and the Jazz Ticulators.

Series Seven

The BBC Variety Department was now back in London and ***ITMA*** was broadcast from the Criterion Theatre. The show had now become so complicated that it needed at least six hours' rehearsal.

Jack Train left because of illness, and therefore Lefty was replaced by Sam Scram's brother, Butch (Bryan Herbert). It was suggested that another actor might play Colonel Chinstrap, but Handley would not hear of it. Jean Capra joined as Poppy Poopah.

Peter Geikie – a character in the long tradition of those that are talked about but never actually encountered – was first referred to in this series. He caught on in much the same way Funf had done. Peter Geikie gor the was blame for everything.

Diana Morrison (Aunt Sally) joined in the army edition.

By the Christmas edition Tommy had become a farmer and was now the Squire of Much-Fiddling.

> Now I'm the squire, I'd better get a new outfit. I shall want an old oak chest, a lot of snow to throw out my daughter into – and some whitewash so that she can't darken my doors again

This series included the famous special forces editions. In January, the team were invited by the Admiralty to the home fleet base at Scapa Flow. They gave fifteen performances in five days on ships and shore stations. An official show was recorded, the famous *HMS ITMA*, an edition that is still occasionally transmitted. It's worth hearing for the audience reaction alone.

A second version was recorded just an hour afterwards, which was even more enthusiastically

Broadcast on the Home Service

Postscript – ITMA Related Shows

Colonel Chinstrap and Major Mundy ('Cover Points at the Test Match')

Starring
Jack Train and Carleton Hobbs

27 June 1949
Broadcast Monday 1840–1845
Broadcast on the Home Service
(Jack Train also starred in *The Lives of Colonel Chinstrap* on BBC TV on 4 January 1952)

At Last! The True Story of Humphrey Chinstrap (Colonel, Retired)

Written by
Ted Kavanagh

Starring
Jack Train, Deryck Guyler, Horace Percival, Clarence Wright, Dino Galvani, Betty Hardy, Diana Maddox, Eric Whitley, Ted Kavanagh

Music by
Antony Spurgin

Produced by
Francis Dillon

received; overrunning by eight minutes, it was deemed too noisy for broadcasting.

An RAF edition followed, recorded back at the Criterion. An army edition was recorded at the Garrison Theatre, Woolwich. Here, Tommy's ideas for improving things included invisible cigarettes for ATS to smoke in the street!

Each of these specials was carefully researched. Handley, Kavanagh and Worsley visited the bases to 'pick up the gen'. These editions contain many 'in' jokes and authentic military slang. To tie in with the storyline, the shows coincided with Tommy's plans to convert the farm at Much-Fiddling Manor into military bases.

Series Eight

This series began with another special edition, this time for the war workers, recorded at the Wolseley car factory in Birmingham. Handley wasn't happy with the show, considering it a failure. ***ITMA*** didn't leave the studio again.

Throughout this series Handley was 'a man with a plan'. The plan always featured prominently in the storyline; it was always being discussed; it was frequently lost or stolen. But what it actually was remained a mystery.

ITMA now had the largest number of listeners of any radio comedy series: a massive worldwide audience. It was broadcast in Britain on Thursdays and repeated Sundays and Wednesdays. It was transmitted on the General Overseas Service, the Network of the Pacific Service (twice), the North American Service and the African Service. It was even listened to by many people in occupied Europe who didn't understand a word.

Jack Train returned with a new character, Mark Time, apparently 98 years old. His catchphrase was 'I'll have to ask me dad.' He spoke in a high-pitched (genuine) Devon accent. His entire family seemed to be incapable of independent thought. Diana Morrison was the formidable Miss Hotchkiss (Week 2), named after a machine-gun. She was rather fierce, but had a soft spot for Handley.

Francis Worsley was hospitalised for several months from the end of 1944. The ***ITMA*** script conferences took place at his bedside. Ronald Waldman took over studio production. Worsley returned to produce the Victory edition (***V – ITMA***) the following May.

CHINSTRAP: **How do you think I'm looking these days, sir?**

HANDLEY: **Well, I can't make up my mind whether you're floodlit or bloodshot.**

Series Nine

To avoid staleness the show was given a new format and an almost complete change of cast. Dorothy Summers, Sydney Keith, Horace Percival, Dino Galvani – (Mrs Mopp, Signor So-So, the Diver and Sam Scram) all left. They were replaced by Clarence Wright, Carleton Hobbs, Hugh Morton, Mary O'Farrell, Michele de Lys and the singer Lind Joyce.

Tommy became the Governor of Tomtopia, a far-flung and fairly insignificant part of the Empire. The Tomtopian situation gave Ted Kavanagh a chance to lampoon events in Britain.

The press now began to refer to Handley as 'the Governor' or 'His Excellency'. The move to

Tomtopia took six shows to complete: following the announcement, there was a fortnight's preparation followed by a month on board ship, where a whole set of new characters were introduced.

There was Carleton Hobbs playing Curly Kale, the chef who was sickened by even the thought of food. There was an anonymous character who ended all his conversations with 'Ain't it a shame, eh? Ain't it a shame?' George Gorge was a character whose attitude to food was just the opposite to Curly Kale's. He was played by Fred Yule ('Lovely grub!'). Then there was Sam Fairfechan (Hugh Morton), a Welshman who was subject to mid-sentence mood swings ('Good morning. How are you? – as if I cared!').

Mary O'Farrell played the bashful Lady Sonely and Nurse Riff-Rafferty. She was Handley's old nanny and had a large reserve of embarrassing anecdotes concerning his early childhood.

When the new Governor arrived at Tomtopia he was introduced to both the native and the British contingents, including Bigga Banga (Fred Yule), who spoke only Utopi, the local lingo; and Banjoleo (Lind Joyce), who spoke mainly Utopi but also a little English and acted as interpreter. Then there was Wamba m'Boojah (Hugh Morton), a native who spoke cut-glass BBC English, having once been an announcer in the Overseas Service.

Major Munday (Carleton Hobbs) and his daughter Naieve (Jean Capra) were imperial remnants about a hundred years behind the times.

A popular feature of this series was a weekly nostalgic chat between the Major and Colonel Chinstrap. In the weeks that followed, Tomtopia was descended upon by the determined culture-lover, Stella Stalls, who, with her drama company, was soon known and feared throughout the island.

In February an official enquiry team was sent by Her Majesty's Government to investigate the Tomtopian administration – among the officials were Lord Slough of Despond, Sir Alexander Palace and the Honourable Mrs de Point. This event inspired a real-life Tomtopian lunch at the Connaught Rooms, which was filmed for Pathe News. The lunch in turn inspired a one-off radio enquiry, *Wither Tomtopia?*

The series ended with the Governor leaving for England . . .

> Wait till I return to England a millionaire. I'll buy a tobacconist shop, lock the door, wait till there's a big queue and blow all the smoke through the keyhole.

Series Ten

Tommy was now living (as Mungo Mucklebairn) at Castle Weehouse, Dire Straights, Loch Tynn, 'somewhere in Scotland', where, with the assistance of an American publicity agent called Luke Slippy (Jack Train), he was attempting to build a moon rocket. The rocket was eventually built and launched, unfortunately falling short of its target; it landed back on Tomtopia.

Things had changed during Handley's absence: the island had a new Governor in Percy Palaver (Deryck Guyler), and the two did not get on.

Jean Capra had left. New characters included Mollie Weir as Tattie Mackintosh, Deryck Guyler as Dan Dungeon and the adenoidal Sir Short Supply of the Ministry. Joan Harben was the mournful Mona Lott ('It's being so cheerful that keeps me going').

Other additions to the Tomtopian scene included Hugh Morton's Basil Backwards and a character who always spoke in spoonerisms. Joan Harben's unnamed do-gooder spoke almost without pausing for breath. Her flow was interrupted only by the occasional cry of 'Down, Upsey!' to her pekinese.

There was the unlucky 'Ard Up And 'Appy, who always ended his frequent tales of woe with ' 'Ard up and 'appy, that's me.'

Sam Fairfechan now had a sister, Pam (Lind Joyce). Colonel Chinstrap had a nephew, Brigadier Dear – keen, young, abstemious and profoundly embarrassed by his uncle's super-sozzled lifestyle (Hugh Morton).

An interesting experiment was Reg Raspberry, the effects boy, played by Tony Francis, a young impressionist who specialised in 'noise impersonations'. He mimicked skidding cars, trains, galloping horses and crowded pubs; he used no dialogue. Although his skills were considerable, they held up the pace of the show and he didn't stay for long.

The popular song 'Open The Door, Richard' made its broadcasting debut in this series.

ITMA was moved to the Paris Cinema during this season. When the series ended, Handley, Worsley and Kavanagh visited America, mainly for a holiday but also partly for a fact-finding trip. This was a great success for Handley. Although he had not intended to broadcast, he did so three times, going over very well with American audiences. On one occasion his name was in lights on Broadway while he was a guest star in a show called *We The People* (described by Kavanagh as 'a high-powered *In Town Tonight*'). He turned down several offers to stay.

Series Eleven

Tommy returned from America and after calling at the labour exchange he found himself Industrial Adviser to His Majesty's Government. In the weeks that followed, he investigated Broadcasting House, became the Minister for Matrimony, ran a fuel-saving campaign and, following a direct order from Sir Stafford Cripps, organised a PR programme for England.

Hattie Jacques (the last member of the team) joined. At her audition she was so nervous that Handley held her hand. She played Sophie Tuckshop, the food-obsessed schoolgirl ('. . . but I'm all right now').

Deryck Guyler played Frisby Dyke, named after a

pre-war Liverpool department store. He's credited with being the first full-blown Liverpudlian comedy character. He engaged Handley in a battle of wits (and always won) each week. Hugh Morton played a man who started speaking in a whisper and ended up shouting at the top of his voice. Fred Yule was Atlas ('Me? In my state of health?').

A special edition, attended by the King and Queen as part of the BBC Silver Jubilee celebrations, came from the concert hall at Broadcasting House. The show was also televised and included a tour of the building, taking in a children's studio which displayed the notice, 'Twansmission in Pwogwess – Watch the Wed Light'.

By the end of the series, Handley's health was beginning to deteriorate. He had been overdoing it for some time; he was getting more than 1,000 fan letters a week and insisted on answering them all personally. His condition was causing concern among his friends. It was put to him that the next series should be postponed, but he pretended not to understand.

Series Twelve

Tommy was 'looking at life from the bottom of the ladder' – almost down and out and living at Henry Hall, the tramps' guesthouse. The proprietress was Miss Hotchkiss, who gave Tommy various jobs. In the 300th edition on 28 October 1948 he was given a job as night watchman at Madame Tussaud's Waxworks – 'Me, spend a night with Crippen and Stuart MacPherson? Not blinking likely!'

He found a door bearing the legend, 'The Hall of ***ITMA***'s past'. On entering he encountered a grand

ITMA reunion, meeting his old friends: Funf, Ali-Oop, the Commercial Traveller, Signor So-So, Sam Fairfechan, Sam Scram and Mrs Mopp.

There were only ten more shows. In the last, Handley was the proprietor of Uncle Tom's Cabin, a coffee stall. He was visited by all the current ***ITMA*** crew.

Three days after the recording, Handley died of a cerebral haemorrhage, suffering a stroke brought on by high blood pressure. News of his death reached the BBC while ***ITMA*** was being broadcast. It was announced to the public immediately after the 1730 repeat.

Straight after the show there was a heartfelt tribute by the Director General. The following week in the ***ITMA*** slot was a tribute show featuring a selection of Handley's favourite songs, sung by the cast, with narration by John Snagge. The show ended with the familiar ***ITMA*** door closing for the last time.

Tommy Handley's popularity was such that his death was the main item on the news and was seen almost as a national tragedy. Memorial services were held in Liverpool and St Paul's Cathedrals (a first for a comedian). Four thousand mourners crowded into St Paul's and the service was relayed to another 2,000 outside (it was also broadcast). There were an estimated 10,000 at the crematorium, with mourners lining the streets six deep.

Garrison Theatre

1939–1941

Transmission Details

Garrison Theatre

Series 1 – (23 Weeks)

Featuring
Jack Warner, Joan Winters, RSM (Major) Filtness, the Garrison Theatre Orchestra conducted by Charles Shadwell

10 November 1939–4 May 1940
Broadcast Saturdays (except first show, broadcast on a Friday)
2015 (or 2010)–2100 for first five shows, settling to a regular 2000–2100
Broadcast on the Home Service

Series 2 – (7 Weeks)

Featuring (variously throughout the series)
Personnel from first series along with Elsie and Doris Waters (Warner's sisters), Clapham and Dwyer, the Western Brothers, Norman Long, Adelaide Hall, Max Wall, Suzette Tarri, Nauton Wayne, Clarkeson Rose, Donald Peers, Wee Georgie Wood, Scott

The brainchild of Charles Shadwell, then director of the BBC Variety Orchestra, ***Garrison Theatre*** recreated the atmosphere of the troop shows of World War One; Shadwell had been entertainments officer in the West Yorkshire Regiment.

It was a very rowdy variety series, broadcast from Clifton Parish Hall in Bristol, mainly before an invited service audience, who were encouraged to join in the choruses, although they were warned that anyone singing rude words would be ejected. The show made Jack Warner a star. His portrayal of a disruptive cockney private was an immediate hit.

Jack had previously worked the West End cabaret circuit, performing comedy songs and impressions, accompanied by Jeffrey Darnell at the piano. Warner and Darnell made their radio debut in 1927 and were guests on *Music Hall* several times during the mid 1930s. The act broke up in 1937 and Jack went solo, specialising in dialect comedy. One of his prewar characterisations was Professor Schtopundschtart, a German academic who lectured on cricket, football and other English topics. His first radio success was impersonating Max Miller impersonating Maurice Chevalier.

Other ***Garrison Theatre*** regulars included the thunderous RSM Filtness, who kept order and was the genuine article, having been Charles Shadwell's major in World War One. He had rejoined the army but had been allowed to complete his BBC contract. Joan Winters (Shadwell's daughter) played the object of Private Warner's affections, a posh usherette ('programmes, chocolates, cigarettes') whom he always called his 'Littel Gel'. Their conversation became a very popular part of the show.

JACK: **Littel gel, excuse my familiarity, but was you ever in love with no one?**
JOAN: **As a matter of fact I was once – but it's all over now.**
JACK: **Oh – 'ow come ducks?**
JOAN: **Well I refused to marry him, and I'm afraid he's been drinking ever since.**
JACK: **'Ere, that's carrying a celebration *too* far you know!**

One week Jack supposedly entered the theatre riding a bicycle through the stalls, giving rise to the show's best-remembered catchphrase; 'Mind my bike!'

'When I dropped the phrase for two weeks, I had 3,000 letters from listeners asking why,' said Warner.

Other catchphrases included 'Blue Pencil', an allusion to wartime censorship ('not Blue Pencil likely!'); 'Veree Good Sir'; and 'De-da, de-da, de-da' (usually delivered in a sarcastic undertone).

Jack wrote all his own material, contributing comic songs and monologues such as 'My Bruvver in the Life Guards', 'Claude and his Sword', 'Sea-lions and Seals', 'Walking Hup and Dahn the Rawlway Laines' and a series of 'Funny Occupations' ('A Bunger-up of Rat 'oles', 'A Fumper and Flattener of Fevvers', 'A Caster-up of Alabaster Plaster' and many others).

He delivered lectures, in cockney dialect, on subjects such as ills (eels) and their significance in rill mills (real meals).

and Whaley, Arthur Askey and Richard Murdoch, Bennett and Williams and, on 24 February 1940, the music hall legend Florrie Forde

19 October 1940–30 November 1940
Broadcast Saturdays 2000–2100
Broadcast on Home and Forces

Stage Version
***Star Variety* (from the London Palladium)**
Featuring
Jack Warner, Joan Winters, Billy Cotton and his Band, Clifford and Marion, the Singing Marines, Sergeant Major Syd Railton, Lieutenant Charles Murray Winstanley Shadwell, Harry S. Pepper (compere)
Stage production
Robert Nesbitt

22 June 1940
Broadcast from the Palladium 1930–2015
Broadcast on Forces

Special editions
Excerpt from the stage show – from a Midland music hall, featuring the same cast

6 September 1940
Broadcast 2115–2200
Broadcast on Forces

From a northern theatre
2 October 1940
Broadcast 2115-2120
Broadcast on Forces

From a theatre in the south
Featuring
Jack Warner, Joan Winters, George Moon and Burton Brown, Vincent Tildsey's Mastersingers, Syd Crossley and the Garrison Theatre Band, Freddy 'The Funny Man' under the direction of Danny Walters
15 November 1941
Broadcast 1830–1900
Broadcast on Forces Network

Two records based on ***Garrison Theatre*** characters were made for Columbia in 1940: *What The Old Blue Pencil* (Jack Warner); *Littel Gel* by Leslie Sarony (Jack Warner and Joan Winters). Jack Warner also starred in *Saturday Social* with Billy Russell in 1942; *Jack's Dive* (1943); *Meet the Huggets* (1953–61) and *Motor Way* (1962).

A letter from 'My Bruvver Sid' was read each week; 'My Dear Jack, here I am again and I hope you are too –'. The punch line was always in the PS: 'PS: The boys would like to send you our regimental poker if you'll promise to make it – Blue Pencil – 'ot for 'Itler –'

A stage version of the show (which was also broadcast) toured until 1942. When Joan Winters took maternity leave, the 'Littel Gel' was played by the 20-stone compere Bryan Michie, in an ATS uniform.

THE 1940s

The 1940s

During the war and the period of austerity that followed, radio comedy's role as a morale-booster cannot be over-emphasised. When war broke out the schedules were abandoned while the BBC regrouped. In the disruption that followed the Variety Department was evacuated to Bristol and the airwaves were filled with news bulletins, organ music and propaganda talks. All cinemas and theatres were ordered to be closed immediately, and to compensate the government encouraged the BBC to broadcast more comedy and variety in the evenings.

Band Waggon was back on the air in a matter of weeks but this proved to be the final series. The show that really captured the imagination of the public was the revamped *ITMA* which satirised the growth of bureaucracy that characterised the period. Somewhat ironically the cast themselves had to work in conditions of strict surveillance. They were all vetted by government security and any departure from the written script would have resulted in the programme being taken off the air.

Other popular shows during wartime included *Garrison Theatre*, *Happidrome* and *Hi-Gang!* There were also shows aimed specifically at the services, such as *Ack-Ack-Beer-Beer*, for the personnel of the Anti-Aircraft and Balloon Barrage Commands. This provided early exposure for a young Kenneth Horne, as did another service show, *Merry-Go-Round*, which also featured Eric Barker, Richard Murdoch and Cheerful Charlie Chester.

After the fall of France, Bristol was no longer safe from enemy bombing, so the Variety Department relocated to Bangor in North Wales. The train from Weston-super-Mare carried 204 staff, one parrot, eight baby's cots, 40 bicycles, one small mangle, nine perambulators, three cats, two hat stands, 514 mixed cases, eight dogs and 175 trunks.

After the war *ITMA* remained enormously popular, but its impact was beginning to fade. The forces had proved to be a training ground for many writers and comedians; a new generation was knocking at the gates. Among the demobbed were: Frank Muir, Dennis Norden, Terry-Thomas, Spike Milligan, Peter Sellers, Dick Emery, Cardew Robinson, Tony Hancock, Frankie Howerd, Kenneth Williams, Harry Secombe and Jimmy Edwards. They gained early exposure in shows that were keen to promote fresh talent such as *They're Out* and *Variety Bandbox*.

The untimely death of Tommy Handley in 1949 marked the passing of an era; *ITMA* without Handley would have been unthinkable. *Take It From Here*, the most innovative and original of the post-war series, took over one of its repeat slots. This was a turning-point for the show. Listening figures increased dramatically; the new wave had arrived.

Elsie And Doris Waters

1940–1962

Elsie and Doris Waters were among the best-loved double acts in both radio and variety. Their classic Cockney characterisations of Gert and Daisy remained popular for more than 40 years.

GERT: **As a matter of fact I was weighed the other day – one of them weighing-machines that tell your fortune as well.**

DAISY: **Oo-er! What did it tell you?**

GERT: **Well, with me coat, I'm ten-stone-four, affectionate, clinging and easily led.**

DAISY: **Yes . . . ?**

GERT: **And without me coat I'm nine-stone-eight, domineering, ambitious and self-willed to the point of obstinacy.**

Elsie was Gert; Doris was Daisy. Their understated humour, coming from an era when overstatement was the norm, has not dated. Their act was naturalistic and conversational (with songs written by Elsie).

They wrote their own material and claimed never to have broadcast the same act twice throughout a long career, which also encompassed films and gramophone records.

After they'd studied piano at the Guildhall School of Music, their performing career began with masonics (after-dinner entertainment) followed by concert party. Their first broadcasts were in the late 1920s,

Transmission Details

Feed The Brute

11 Editions

Wednesday 9 April 1940–Saturday 20 April 1940
Broadcast 1815–1820
(No programme Sunday 19 April)

Gert And Daisy's Working Party

12 Weeks

Featuring
Elsie and Doris Waters with local talent from a different part of the country each week. Guests included Richard Murdoch, Peter Sinclair, Douglas ('Cardew') Robinson, Harry Hemsley, Peter Cavanagh, Stainless Stephen, Jack Warner (who was guest star in the first show, broadcast from London)

Produced by
Michael North or Brian Sears with a different co-producer for each show.

23 June 1948–15 September 1948
Broadcast Wednesdays 2115–2200

Broadcast on the Light Programme
(Shows came from London, Bristol, Belfast, Birmingham, Wales, Manchester, Northampton, Sunderland, Derby, Bradford)

Gert And Daisy's Christmas Working Party
Featuring
Elsie and Doris Waters, guest artist Harry Hemsley, Joan Hinde, the Odd Spots, Bernard Cleave, the Kordites, with the BBC Revue Orchestra conducted by Frank Cantell
Produced by
Michael North

25 December (Christmas Day) 1948
Broadcast 1615–1700
Broadcast on the Light Programme

Petticoat Lane (You Want It – We've Got It)
(23 Weeks)
Featuring
Elsie and Doris Waters and a variety of guest artists who were encountered as stallholders, street performers and local characters in Petticoat Lane

29 July 1949–28 December 1949

and the characters of Gert and Daisy arrived in 1930. Many guest spots followed, on shows such as *Henry Hall's Guest Night*, *Music Hall* and *Workers' Playtime*. Their brother, Jack, became famous as Jack Warner.

In April 1940 they starred in a series of five-minute programmes for The Ministry of Food called *Feed The Brute*, in which 'Mrs Waters' daughters', gave light-hearted advice on how to cope with wartime food restrictions. They were the first broadcasts ever donated by variety artists to a government department.

In the 50s, Gert and Daisy inherited a general store in *Floggit's*. These stories featured Joan Sims playing Emma Smeed and Greta of the Red Lion, and Iris Vandeleur, as Old Mother Butler. Names such as Anthony Newley, Ronnie Barker, Hugh Paddick and Ron Moody cropped up, too.

Floggit's
Series 1 – (16 Weeks)
Written by
Terry Nation, John Jenkin and Dave Freeman
Cast included
Joan Sims, Anthony Newley, Ronnie Barker, Hugh Paddick, Iris Vandeleur, Ron Moody, Doris Rogers, Peter Hawkins
Produced by
Alastair Scott-Johnson (except Weeks 6 and 7 which were produced by Bill Gates)

17 August 1956–30 November 1956
Broadcast Fridays 1930–2000
Broadcast on the Light Programme

Christmas edition

Tuesday 25 December 1956
Broadcast 2130–2200
Broadcast on the Light Programme

Series 2 – (18 Weeks)
Written by
Terry Nation, John Jenkin and Dave Freeman
Cast included
As Series 1
Produced by
Bill Gates

8 April 1957–5 August 1957
Broadcast Mondays 2015–2045 (except Weeks 13 and 14, at 2100–2130, and Week 18, at 2045–2130 (Bank Holiday Special))
Broadcast on the Light Programme

Hi-Gang!

1940–1949

This was a hugely popular wartime series, starring 'Hollywood's happiest couple', Bebe Daniels and Ben Lyon, and the violin-playing comedian Vic Oliver. The first comedy series to be broadcast by the BBC on Sundays, it was also the first BBC comedy show to run for 52 weeks without a break.

Hi-Gang! began with 'I'm Just Wild About Harry' from the Jay Wilbur Orchestra and was followed by the announcement, 'Coming to you from the heart of London'. This phrase was carefully chosen; Nazi propaganda had suggested that London was deserted and lay in ruins. ***Hi-Gang!*** was the only major comedy show actually broadcast from London at that time.

Fast-moving and slick, ***Hi-Gang!*** was fuelled by wisecracks and one-liners; its transatlantic style was a novelty to British listeners. Combinations of the three stars and a guest artist were interspersed with musical items. Ben Lyon was both master of ceremonies and target for much of the comedy:

VIC OLIVER: **I bet if Lady Godiva rode in here now, you'd be raving about the horse!**

There was a feature, 'If I Had The Chance', in which a guest artist would attempt to fulfil a secret ambition. On the first show the BBC organist Sandy MacPherson became a tap-dancer (falling into a drum kit in the process). Later in the series, the disc-jockey Christopher Stone became a comedian. And

Transmission Details

Rinso Radio Revue

30 Weeks

Written by
Robert O. Wilcoxon

Featuring
Ben Lyon (compere), Bebe Daniels and Tommy Handley with Sam Browne, Peggy Dell, the Henderson Twins, Bruce Trent, June Malo

Produced by
Stanley Maxted

11 September 1938–2 April 1939
Broadcast Sundays 1830–1900
Broadcast on Luxembourg from the Scala Theatre, London
(A poll conducted by the *Radio Pictorial* noted much enthusiasm for the show from working-class listeners, with criticism appearing further up the social scale)

Hi-Gang!

Series 1 – (52 Weeks)

Written by
Bebe Daniels and Ben Lyon

Additional material
Dick Pepper

Featuring
Bebe Daniels, Vic Oliver, Ben Lyon, with Jay Wilbur and his Orchestra, the Greene Sisters, Sam Browne

Produced by
Harry S. Pepper and Douglas Lawrence

26 May 1940–18 May 1941
Broadcast Sundays

Hi-Gang!

Series 2 – (26 Weeks)

Written by
Bebe Daniels and Ben Lyon

Additional material
Ray Sonin (Week 3 only)

Featuring
Bebe Daniels, Ben Lyon, Jay Wilbur and his Orchestra, Sam Browne (Week 1 only), the Radio Three

Recorded greetings came from
Hollywood stars Charles Boyer, Dorothy Lamour, Cary Grant, Judy Garland, Robert Taylor, Jeanette MacDonald, Tyrone Power, Claudette Colbert, Victor Maclagan and Ginger Rogers

Produced by
Douglas Lawrence and, from Week 7, Jacques Brown

Film Version

Written by
Val Guest, Marriott Edgar, J. O. C. Orton

in the 1949 revival Ronald Reagan gave a commentary on an English football match.

Bebe introduced a new song each week (including 'The White Cliffs of Dover'). Vic Oliver played the radio reporter Peep Keyhole and the show ended with a three-handed burlesque of an established genre, such as the western, pantomime, Shakespeare or the gangster movie.

There was a catchphrase – 'No, not you Momma – sit down!'

Vic Oliver (the Old Vic) was born Victor Oliver Samek in Austria to an aristocratic family. He was once billed as 'The Piano Playing Baron'. The young Vic studied piano and violin and emigrated to America, and by the mid 1930s he was an established comedian on both sides of the Atlantic. He became an American citizen in 1936 and, on marrying Sarah Churchill, became Winston Churchill's son-in-law from 1936–45. He took British citizenship in 1946.

In 1938 the Lyons starred with Tommy Handley in *The Rinso Radio Revue* for Radio Luxembourg. A forerunner to ***Hi-Gang!***, the show consisted mainly of wisecracking between the three stars with songs from Ben, Bebe, June Malo and Peggy Dell. The advantages of washing with Rinso were explained by a Mrs Goodsort.

The Lyons first starred at the BBC in a musical comedy by Raife Growener called *The Silent Melody* (7 July 1938).

Bebe and Ben approached Vic Oliver with the idea for ***Hi-Gang!*** in 1940. ('In this show we all appear as ourselves – I'll be the down-trodden one, you be the smart one, and Bebe will be on your side against me. We'll insult each other for all we're worth.')

Although the BBC were not that keen on the insult idea, a trial recording was made, which became the first of a projected series of six.

The first three shows were mediocre. By the fourth the formula had begun to gel; they pushed the insult technique as far as they could, even involving the guest artists. The identity of the guest star was always left as a surprise, as under wartime conditions, it was never absolutely certain that they would arrive. By the fifth edition, ***Hi-Gang!*** had become one of the BBC's most popular shows, ending only when Ben joined the USAAF.

Guest artists included: Laurence Olivier, Ralph Richardson, Valerie Hobson, Noël Coward, Jack Warner, Stanley Holloway, Christopher Stone, Robertson Hare, Alfred Drayton, Stanley Lupino, Florence Desmond, Georgie Wood, Geraldo, Evelyn Laye, Sarah Churchill, Jack Buchanan, Carroll Gibbons, Vera Lynn, Michael Redgrave, Robert Donat, Ivor Novello, John Gielgud, Fred Emney, Michael Standing (who sang).

Thanks to the Lyons' Hollywood connections, many American stars contributed to the show.

Hi-Gang! went out on Sundays, at 1800 to begin with, but was gradually pushed forward to 1600 because of air raids; the show was bombed out of the Maida Vale Studios and St George's Hall and eventually settled at the Paris Cinema in Lower Regent Street. A stage show, *Gangway* (at the Palladium in 1941), ran for 47 weeks, and there was a film version in the same year.

Bebe and Ben also broadcast to America. *Stars and*

and Howard Irving Young (from the radio series by Bebe Daniels and Ben Lyon)

Featuring
Graham Moffat, Moore Marriott, Jacques Brown, Sam Browne, Felix Aylmer, Georgina MacKinnon, Maurice Rhodes, Percy Parsons, Diana Beaumont, Mavis Villiers, the Greene Sisters, Jay Wilbur and his Band

Directed by
Marcel Varnel

Produced by
Edward Black (for General Film Distributors)

***Bebe, Vic And Ben* (follow-up to *Hi-Gang!*)**

12 Weeks

Written by
Ray Sonin

Featuring
Bebe, Vic and Ben, supported by the Debonnaires, Ian Sadler, Peter Cotes, Jay Wilbur and his Band

Produced by
Eric Spear

8 November 1942–24 January 1943
Broadcast Sundays 1830–1900
Broadcast on Forces Network
(A series called ***Hi-Gang! Memories*** – from gramophone records – was broadcast on the Home on Friday 18

January 1944, 1530–1600)

Hi-Gang! 1949

23 Weeks

Written by
Sid Colin

Also featuring
Benny Lee, George Mitchell's Hi Gangsters, the Dance Orchestra conducted by Stanley Black

Produced by
Tom Ronald

27 February 1949–4 August 1949 (no show 15 April)
Broadcast Fridays 2030–2100
Broadcast on the Home Service
(A special edition went out on Boxing Day, 1949, from 2130–2200) (See also *Life with the Lyons*)

Stripes in Britain was beamed from coast to coast and brought the voices of American service personnel to their families. The BBC's *Here's Wishing You Well Again* was dedicated to those in allied hospitals. Bebe also broadcast to America from the front line in Normandy – and was awarded the Medal for Freedom (the second highest civilian decoration).

Vic Oliver's other radio shows included *The Horlicks Picture House* (for Luxembourg 1937), *Happy Days* (with Sarah Churchill 1941), *Yankee Doodle Do* (1943), *Oliver Introduces* (1944), *Oliver's Twists* (1948), *Oliver Again* (1951). He was also master of ceremonies in *Variety Playhouse* (1953), and the castaway on the first edition of *Desert Island Discs* (29 January 1942).

Thanking Yew

1940–1945

Transmission Details

Thanking Yew

Series 1 – (6 Weeks)

Featuring
Cyril Fletcher, Pat Rignold, Bettie Bucknelle, Navan O'Reilly and Mr Malony (a ventriloquist), with the Dance Orchestra conducted by Billy

Cyril Fletcher was a concert party comedian with an extraordinary vocal range: '. . . from the depth of a Dogger Bank foghorn to a sound so high only dogs can hear it' (Bob Monkhouse).

Cyril Fletcher came to the radio via the Fol-De-Rols in 1936 and made many solo broadcasts, sometimes billed as 'The Utterly Refained Comedian', before being given his own series in 1940. He was the inventor of the 'Odd Ode', whose catchphrases included 'Pin back your lug 'oles', 'Dreaming of thee' and 'Yerse thankin' you.'

Often featuring his wife, the singer Betty Astell, his shows presented a gallery of eccentric characters, including Percy Parker the lanky lodger, Bob (Under the Bed) Tupp (a regular routine with the comedian Billy Russell) and Aggie the schoolgirl. His broadcasting career spanned over five decades, extending well into the television era with the long running show, *That's Life.*

The Radio Times said of Fletcher's show ***Thanking Yew***, 'He will do almost everything in it, from "Odd Odes" to "Thanking Yew", compering and playing innumerable small parts.'

Ternent (Week 3–6 featured Henry Hall and his Orchestra)

1 October 1940–5 November 1940
Broadcast Tuesdays 2000–2030 (except Week 1, at 2000–2035)
Broadcast on the Home and Forces Networks

Series 2 – (12 Weeks)

Written by
Dick Pepper

Featuring
Cyril Fletcher, Billy Russell, Betty Astell, Jack Cooper (singer), the BBC Variety Orchestra conducted by Charles Shadwell; guests throughout the series included Morton Fraser, Harry Parry, Stephane Grappelli

Produced by
Harry S. Pepper

Thanking Yew Tew

12 Weeks

Written by
Dick Pepper

Featuring
Cyril Fletcher, Dave Burnaby, Betty Astell, Jack Cooper, the BBC Variety Orchestra conducted by Charles Shadwell

Produced by
Harry S. Pepper

24 February 1946–12 May 1946
Broadcast Sundays 2130–2200
Broadcast on the Light Programme

Odes And Ends

12 Weeks

(In this series Cyril and Betty set up home)

Written by
Dick Pepper

Featuring
Cyril Fletcher, Betty Astell, Frederick Burtwell

Produced by
Ronnie Waldman

30 December 1941–17 March 1942
Broadcast Tuesdays 2125–2155
Broadcast on the Forces Network

Beggin' Yours

12 Weeks

Written by
Dick Pepper

Featuring
Cyril Fletcher, Betty Astell, Jack Cooper, Davy Burnaby, the BBC Variety Orchestra conducted by Rae Jenkins (Week 7 featured Charles Shadwell and his Orchestra)

Produced by
Harry S. Pepper

7 October 1946–23 December 1946
Broadcast Mondays 1945–2015
Broadcast on the Light Programme

Fletcher's Fare

6 Weeks

Written by
Bob Monkhouse, Denis Goodwin

Featuring
Cyril Fletcher, Betty Astell, Bob Monkhouse, Denis Goodwin, Bob Sharples and his Music

Produced by
Leslie Bridgmont

7 August 1952–11 September 1952
Broadcast Thursdays 1930–2200
Broadcast on the Light Programme

Series 2 – (10 Weeks)

16 February 1953–20 April 1953
Broadcast Mondays 1930–2000
Broadcast on the Light Programme

Not To Worry (1964)

Written by
Alistair Foot and John Cleese

Send For Doctor Dick

1940–1941

This series of adventures of a bogus doctor was scripted by *ITMA*'s Ted Kavanagh. Dick Francis played the doctor, wreaking havoc upon his unsuspecting patients.

His quick-thinking assistant was played by the musical comedy star Sonnie Hale, while his ever-reliable secretary was Patricia Leonard.

It was a variety show in the *Band Waggon* mould, with regular features such as 'Show Piece' (series works of dance band composers), 'Doctor Dick's Recoveries', 'Melody Special' and 'The Clubmen'. It was devised by Ted Kavanagh and Michael North.

Transmission Details

Send For Doctor Dick

Series 1 – (7 Weeks)

Written by
Ted Kavanagh

Featuring
Dick Francis, Sonnie Hale, Patricia Leonard, Ralph de Rohan, Helen Clare, Jacques Brown (from 27 November 1940), BBC Variety Orchestra conducted by Charles Shadwell

Produced by
Vernon Harris

23 October–11 December 1940
Broadcast Wednesdays 2020–2100
Broadcast on Forces

Series 2 – (12 Weeks)

Written by
Ted Kavanagh

Featuring
Dick Francis, Sonnie Hale, Doris Hare, Paula Green, Ian Sadler, Bettie Bucknelle (singer), the Male Voice Quartet, Alan Paul, Ivor Dennis, the BBC Variety Orchestra conducted by Charles Shadwell (leader, Frank Cantell)

Produced by
Vernon Harris

18 June 1941–3 September 1941
Broadcast Wednesdays 2020–2100
(except Weeks 7–12, at 2120–2200)
Broadcast on Forces

The Happidrome

1941–1947

The imaginary Happidrome Theatre was 'leased, with a view to giving the public the very cheeriest entertainment.'

The show was broadcast live from the Grand Theatre in Llandudno on Sunday evenings, before an audience of war workers and service personnel. Each edition boasted a strong line-up of established variety acts, linked by the antics of a trio of resident stars.

Harry Korris played Mr Lovejoy, the Happidrome proprietor, while Cecil Frederick was Ramsbottom, the stage manager. Robbie Vincent was Enoch, the call boy. Together they performed sketches and routines (written by Korris) and original songs.

Ramsbottom was basically the straight man, each week providing the exasperated Mr Lovejoy with gags, which invariably backfired when used on the gormless Enoch. Firmly rooted in the northern music hall tradition, the three had met while working in Blackpool a few years earlier, with Ernest Binn's Arcadian Follies.

The Happidrome's most famous catchphrase was Enoch's authoritative 'Let me tell *you*!' – usually greeted with a groan from the proprietor. It was even turned into a song in 1943.

Others included Korris's weary 'If ever a man suffered' and 'Take him away, Ramsbottom.'

Through nearly 150 editions, Mr Lovejoy was never able to get the better of Enoch . . .

Transmission Details

The Happidrome

Series 1 – (53 Weeks)

Featuring
Harry Korris, Cecil Frederick, Robbie Vincent with first-show guests Murray and Mooney, Rupert Hazell and Elsie Day, Lily Morris, Sidney Burchall, Tommy Handley, Renara, the Happidrome Orchestra and Chorus (the child impersonator Harry Hemsley's famous character Horace made his broadcast debut on the 4 January 1942 edition)

Produced by
Ernest Longstaffe

9 February 1941–8 February 1942
Broadcast Sundays 2000–2100 (except Week 7, at 1315–1415, and Week 28, at 2200–2300)
Broadcast on Forces

Just What The Doctor Ordered (Happidrome)

Featuring
Harry Korris, Robbie Vincent, Cecil

Frederick and other members of the company, who were entertaining patients and staff of a military hospital somewhere in the north

Presented by
Victor Smythe

Tuesday 9 September 1941
Broadcast on Forces Network

Series 2 – (52 Weeks)

7 March 1943–27 February 1944
Broadcast Sundays 1910–2000 (except Week 4, at 1915–2000, and Week 52, at 2015–2100)
Broadcast on Forces

***Happidrome* (Film Version) (Released April 1943)**

Written by
Tom Arnold and James Seymore, from the radio series by Harry Korris

Featuring
Harry Korris, Robbie Vincent, Cecil Frederick, Bunty Meadows, Lisa Lee, Jennie Gregson, Joss Ambler, Valentine Dunn, Muriel Zillah, Connie Creighton, Marie Lawson, Olga Stevenson, Arthur Hambling, Bombardier Billy Wells, Leslie Hutchinson and the Cairoli Brothers

Directed by
Phil Brandon

ENOCH: **D'you know, these trousers fit me tighter than me skin?**

MR LOVEJOY: **Now don't be daft – your trousers can't be tighter than your skin.**

ENOCH: **They are! I can sit down in me skin.**

MR LOVEJOY: **You'll have to smarten yourself up a bit. Look at your neck – why don't you wash it?**

ENOCH: **I haven't any soap.**

MR LOVEJOY: **Soap – well you've got a tongue in your head, haven't you?**

ENOCH: **Yes, but it won't reach the back of me neck!**

All artists wore full costume and make-up. Ramsbottom dressed fairly conventionally; the portly Mr Lovejoy sported a loud check suit and undersized bowler; the diminutive Enoch wore a small peaked cap, a dog-eared and ancient black bowtie, grey shirt and extremely baggy trousers.

The show's theme was:

We three in Happidrome –
Working for the BBC –
Ramsbottom – and Enoch – and me

. . . and it was sung to the tune of the Ink Spots' hit, 'We Three – My Echo, My Shadow and Me'.

The show was hugely successful. The first series was originally scheduled to run for six weeks, with the option of another six. It ran for 53 editions! ***The Happidrome*** spawned stage and film versions and several gramophone records were issued.

RAMSBOTTOM: **Tell me, Governor, do you know anything about love?**
MR LOVEJOY: **Well I ought to – I drove a taxi for three years.**

Among the artists who featured as guests throughout the entire successful run of ***The Happidrome*** were: Bennet and Williams, Clapham and Dwyer, Robb Wilton, Betty Driver, Wee Georgie Wood and Dolly Harmer, Issy Bonn, Scott and Whaley, Norman Long, Ronald Chesney, Charles Penrose, Revnell and West, Harry Hemsley, Nosmo King and Hubert, The Roosters Concert Party, Cyril Fletcher and Betty Astell, Harry Champion, G. H. Elliot, Nellie Wallace, Claude Dampier and Billie Carlyle, Tessie O'Shea, Hetty King, George Lacy, Jimmy James, Morris and Cowley, Cavan O'Connor, The Two Leslies, Suzette Tarri, Renee Huston and Donald Stewart, Stanelli, Charlie Chester, Billy Bennett, Dorothy Ward, Alice Lloyd, Clarice Mayne, Clarkson Rose, Turner Layton, Caryll and Mundy, Jack Train, Hatton and Manners, Charlie Kunz, Dave Willis, Billy Russell, Max and Harry Nesbitt, Hutch, George Robey, Jack Warner, Naughton and Gold, Peter Sinclair, Ted Ray, Rawicz and Landauer, Sandy Powell, Flotsam and Jetsam, Beryl Orde, Wilfred Pickles, Nat Mills and Bobbie, Jewel and Warriss, the Western Brothers, Norman Evans, Hal Monty, Gillie Potter, Zeigler and Booth, Teddy Brown, Lucan and McShane, Murgatroyd and Winterbottom, Adelaide Hall, Haver and Lee, Max Bacon, Paddie O'Neil, Forsythe, Seamon and Farrell, Billy ('Uke') Scott, Harold Berens, Margery Manners, Terry-Thomas, Leon Cortez, Leonard Henry, Peter Brough, Joseph Locke, Percy Edwards,

Produced by
Harold Boxall, Jack Buchanan and Tom Arnold, for Aldwych (MGM) (Harry Korris and Robbie Vincent also supported Frank Randle in the films *Somewhere in England* (1940), *Somewhere in Camp* and *Somewhere on Leave* (both 1942)

Round The Halls
An excerpt from ***The Happidrome*** called *Northern Music Hall* from the Palace Theatre, Halifax

Featuring
Harry Korris, Robbie Vincent, Pat Lennox and Sylvia, the Four Charladies, Hal Swain and his Swing Sisters and full company

Wednesday 24 January 1945
Broadcast 2115–2145
Broadcast on GFP

Series 3 – (37 Weeks)

Featuring
The full company, with Terry-Thomas, who made his broadcast debut on the edition of 12 November 1946

8 October 1946–18 June 1947
Broadcast mainly Tuesdays, and included editions on Boxing Day and New Year's Eve, various times between 1915 and 2115 but mostly from 2015–2115. Most shows were an hour's duration

Specials

November 14 1947
A BBC Silver Jubilee special

Featuring
Alec Pleon, Joseph Locke, Suzette Tarri, the Radio Revellers and Colinson and Breen, Les Perry's Vaudeville Orchestra, the BBC Revue Chorus conducted by Ernest Longstaffe

Beryl Reid, Vic Oliver, Davey Kaye, Winifred Atwell, Eddie Reindeer, Cardew Robinson, Bob and Alf Pearson, Jeanne de Casalis, Albert Whelan, Harry Lester and his Hayseeds and Peter Cavanagh.

Produced by
Ernest Longstaffe and Peter Duncan

14 November 1947
Broadcast 2000–2100
Broadcast on the Light Programme

Boxing Day 1947

Also featuring
Ribton and Richards, Percy Edwards, Vic Oliver, BBC Variety Orchestra conducted by Ernest Longstaffe

Produced by
Ernest Longstaffe

Broadcast 1300–1400
Broadcast on the Light Programme

The Laugh Trail

February–March 1941

Transmission Details

The Laugh Trail

Featuring
Harry Scott, Eddie Whaley

Music by
BBC Variety Orchestra, conducted by Charles Shadwell; music written by Hero de Rance

Produced by
Harry S. Pepper

Episode List
The First Clue; Late at the Prompt Corner; Seeing Stars at the Film Studio; The Clue of the Kit Bag; Guess Night; The Man in Box A

12 February 1941–19 March 1941
Broadcast Wednesdays 2020–2100 on the Home Service

The Americans Harry Scott and Eddie Whaley first worked together in 1901, entertaining the customers while they were barmen in Pennsylvania. They came to Britain before the First World War, and, after toning down the Americanisms in their act, they became very popular with the British public, making Britain their home in the early 1920s.

They first broadcast in a weekly series of fifteen-minute shows from Savoy Hill in 1926 and found greater radio fame in the 1930s as Cuthbert and Pussyfoot – regular comic relief in the *Kentucky Minstrels*.

The Laugh Trail was a comedy thriller and represented a slight change of style, in that Cuthbert and Pussyfoot (the human bloodhounds) were now detectives. The series was scripted by Con West, the writer of their *Kentucky Minstrels'* material. The music was written by Hero de Rance.

Old Mother Riley

1941–1948

There were two series built around Arthur Lucan's whirlwind washerwoman: *Old Mother Riley Takes the Air* and *Old Mother Riley and Her Daughter Kitty*.

Both variety series co-starred Kitty McShane as Mother Riley's daughter.

Lucan and McShane (who were husband and wife) tackled their radio performances in the same spirit as their live shows ('How can I be that wild Old Mother Riley if I have to hold a script in my hand all the time?')

They learned their parts, performing with full costumes, make-up and props, before a studio audience:

RILEY: **What did you go into a museum for? Was it raining?**

KITTY: **No, darling, it wasn't raining: I went to see an ancient curiosity.**

RILEY: **An ancient curiosity?**

KITTY: **An ancient curiosity.**

RILEY: **And you had to go out to a museum to see an ancient curiosity! Why didn't you come home to see your mother?**

Transmission Details

Old Mother Riley Takes the Air

14 Weeks

Written by
Arthur Lucan, Kitty McShane

Devised by
Harry Alan Towers

Featuring
Arthur Lucan, Kitty McShane, Rex Ramer, Doris Nicholls, Ben Beaumont, Clifford Bean, Hugh Morton; guests throughout series included: Syd Walker, Adele Dixon, Vera Lennox, Jessie Matthews, Jack Train, Dorothy Ward, Murray and Mooney, Jeanne de Casalis, Sonnie Hale, Bobbie Comber, Charlie Clapham, Claude Hulbert, Nettlerash, Turner Layton, Lionel Gamlin, Frank Titteron, Bobby Howes, Harry Hemsley, Max Bacon, Wee Georgie Wood, Dolly Harmer, Tommy Handley

Music by
The Augmented Dance Orchestra and Revue Chorus directed by Billy Ternent (Hyam

Greenbaum in Week 11)

Compere
Norman Shelley, Hugh Morton or Lionel Gamlin

Produced by
Tom Ronald

21 June 1941–20 September 1941
Broadcast Saturdays 2015–2100 on Home and Forces

Old Mother Riley's Christmas Party (Special For Christmas Day)

Written by
Arthur Lucan

Featuring
Arthur Lucan, Kitty McShane, Billy Bennett, Dorothy Carless, Forsythe, Seamon and Farrell, Tommy Trinder

Music by
Geraldo and his Orchestra

Produced by
Tom Ronald

25 December 1941
Broadcast 1935–2050 on Home Service

Old Mother Riley And Her Daughter Kitty

Series 1 – (10 Weeks)

Written by
Arthur Lucan

Featuring
Arthur Lucan, Kitty McShane, Michael Lynd (compere); guests throughout series included Tommy Handley, Jeanne de Casalis, Harry Hemsley, Max and Harry Nesbitt, Murray and Mooney, Forsyth, Seamon and Farrell, Robb Wilton, Beryl Orde

Music by
BBC Revue Chorus and Augmented Dance Orchestra directed by Billy Ternent

Produced by
Tom Ronald

6 June 1942–8 August 1942
Broadcast Saturdays 2015–2100
Broadcast on Home and Forces (except Weeks 3, 6, 7, Forces only)

Series 2 – (6 Weeks)

Written by
Kitty McShane, Ronnie Taylor

Featuring
Arthur Lucan, Kitty McShane, Willer Neal, Oliver Burleigh, Rhoderick Walker, Kenneth Morgan

Music by
BBC Revue Orchestra conducted by Frank Cantell

Produced by
Tom Ronald

20 September–25 October 1948

Hogsnorton

1941–1943

Transmission Details

Hogsnorton Hob Nobbing

4 Weeks
Presented by the Department of National Service Entertainment (NAAFI)

Featuring
Joyce Grenfell, Nora Savage, Roderick

'Good evening England, this is Gillie Potter speaking to you in English.'

An eccentric and highly individual performer, Gillie Potter made his radio debut in the early 1930s with an occasional series of talks, usually lasting ten or fifteen minutes. They were delivered in a steady, unhurried manner, reminiscent of a sermon.

The programmes were mainly, though not always, concerned with the 'general situation' in the rural backwater of Hogsnorton. They also gave an account of the doings of its extraordinary inhabitants (who are credited with being the first fictitious community in the history of broadcasting), among them Lord Marshmallow MFH, Canon Fodder, the Rev T. Cake and General Sir Stimulant Maudlin-Tite of 'The Tankards', Great Boosey.

> I came across his Lordship superintending the draining of the duck pond, which had already brought to light a missing tweeny maid and the euphonium which was lost last August Bank Holiday, when the Temperance Band got so very drunk.

There were reports from the Hogsnorton Hunt, the Hogsnorton Goose Club, the Point-to-Point and the nightly ceremony of 'Tavern Turn Out'. One broadcast provided details of Hogsnorton's heroic wartime resistance.

Titles included *The Hogsnorton Show*, *Yoiks And All That*, *Historic Hogsnorton*, *Heigho For Hogsnorton* and *Epithalamium Hogsnortonium Marriage*, wherein the wedding of the season was described by the fourth of the bride's fifteen fiances.

Although he never abandoned the 'instructive talk' format Gillie Potter also broadcast as a solo turn in variety programmes and was the star of several series. He enjoyed great success in variety, his career continuing well into the 1950s.

Hogsnorton Hob Nobbing was an edition of *ENSA Half Hour* – the only variety show to star 'the Sage of Hogsnorton'.

Other series titles included ***Here at Hogsnorton***, described as 'a scintillating survey of hebdomadal hearsay by England's egregious patrician philosopher'

Jones, Harry Hudson
Music by
The Great Boosey Temperance Band (alias the ENSA Variety Orchestra) under the direction of Geraldo

1 October 1941–22 October 1941
Broadcast Wednesdays 1830–1900
Broadcast on Forces

Here At Hogsnorton
8 Weeks

8 October 1943–25 November 1943
Broadcast Fridays 2000–2015
Broadcast on the Home Service

Heard At Hogsnorton
10 Weeks

17 January 1946–6 June 1946
Broadcast Thursdays 2000–2010 (except Week 6, at 2020–2030, Week 7, at 1955–2005, Week 8, at 2005–2015; no show on 14 February)

Mr Gillie Potter The Sage Of Hogsnorton
13 Weeks

6 January 1952–6 April 1952
Week 6 had to be rescheduled owing to the death of King George VI

and ***Heard at Hogsnorton***: 'a series of fortnightly forthrightly talks on national news by England's patrician philosopher Gillie Potter'.

Meet Our Joe/Over The Garden Wall

1942–1950

Transmission Details

Meet Our Joe
6 Weeks
Written by
Clifford Lewis
Featuring
Norman Evans, Billy Scott Comber, Wilfred Pickles, Jeanette Jacks, Johnny Rosen and his Swing Spotters
Produced by
Richard North

6 June 1942–11 July 1942
Broadcast Saturdays 1900–1930
Broadcast on Home and Forces (except Weeks 2–4, Forces only)

Over The Garden Wall
Series 1 – (6 Weeks)
Written by
Ronald Taylor

Rochdale-born Norman Evans was considered to be the greatest pantomime dame since Dan Leno. He was also a great star of variety, appearing in sketches such as 'At The Dentist's', in which he played both dentist and patient, appearing in silhouette behind a screen. The most notable sketch, however, was 'Over the Garden Wall', which was the name of the programme itself after a series of ***Meet Our Joe***, and ran for three series altogether.

In the early 1930s, he was an amateur performer but turned professional in 1934 after being encouraged to do so by Gracie Fields. By 1937 he was a bill-topper.

Meet Our Joe was a variety-based series featuring an Evans character called Joe Ramsbottom. ***Over The Garden Wall*** was built around his most celebrated character, the gossipy Fanny Fairbottom. Evans's original stage sketch was basically a backyard conversation with imaginary neighbours. In the radio version the neighbours were brought to life – they included little Willie, the lodger and, most notably, Mrs Ethel Higginbottom.

You know Ethel Higginbottom? Aye, she's had

her face lifted . . . It's not safe to leave anything lying about these days, is it?

The second series concentrated mainly on the two neighbours, Fanny and Ethel, and the various scrapes they got into: on joining the police, on trying to become radio performers or simply as guests at a wedding. The show broadcast on 23 December 1948 concerned their attempts at cooking a Christmas turkey.

Featuring
Norman Evans, Ethel Manners, Mary Naylor, Percy Garside, Arthur Arnold, Peter Broadbent, Richard Valery and his Concert Orchestra
Produced by
Bowker Andrews
from the NAAFI Club in Manchester

10 February 1948–16 March 1948
Broadcast Tuesdays 1930–2000 (except Week 3, at 2030–2100
Broadcast on Light Programme

Series 2 – (12 Weeks)
Written by
Ronald Taylor
Featuring
Norman Evans, Ethel Manners, Doreen Lavender, George Baines, Herbert Smith, Peter Broadbent, the Northern Variety Orchestra conducted by Toni
Produced by
Bowker Andrews

7 October 1948–23 December 1948
Broadcast Thursdays 1930–2000
Broadcast on the Light Programme

Series 3 – (11 Weeks)
Written by
Ronald Taylor and Eddy Maguire
Featuring
Norman Evans, Betty Jumel, Lee Lawrence, Herbert Smith, Peter Broadbent, Norma Evans and the Maple Leaf Four, Ray Martin and his Orchestra
Produced by
Bowker Andrews

4 November 1949–20 January 1950
Broadcast Fridays 2030–2100 (from Week 9, at 2100–2130; no programme on 30 December)
Broadcast on the Light Programme
Also broadcast on the North of England Home Service

How

1942–1962

This was a satire series broadcast occasionally between 1942 and 1962, the work of Stephen Potter and Joyce Grenfell – 'as demonstrated by the distinguished members of the ***How*** Repertory Company . . .'

The ***How*** series had no set format during its 20-year run but usually dealt with 'How to' and 'How not to' topics.

Transmission Details

Notable *How's* included:

How To Look At A Town
Written by
John Betjeman, who narrated

Produced by
Douglas Cleaverdon

Broadcast 6 July 1943
Re-broadcast 9 January 1946 on the Home Service 2200–2230

How To Deal With Christmas

Featuring
Celia Johnson

19 December 1945
Broadcast on the Home Service

How To Move House

4 April 1946
Broadcast 2000–2030
Broadcast on the Home Service

How To Listen
This included not only how to, but how not to, how they *used* to and how you *must*. First edition to be broadcast on the Third Programme

29 September 1946
Broadcast 1800
Broadcast on the Third Programme

How To Cope With Christmas
(Enlarged edition of *How to Deal with Christmas*)

Featuring
Robert Donat and Celia Johnson

The scripts were based on improvisations, captured with the help of a shorthand writer. The earlier shows were broadcast live.

Potter's and Grenfell's original intention was to give the listeners a glimpse of 'the arts made and in the making'. There were 29 ***Hows*** in all, including several revised revivals.

FIRST MAN: **That man really writes those poems about the lake of longing and the garden of recollection . . . ?**
SECOND MAN: **Yes – even the back of his head is fascinating.**
FIRST MAN: **Let's *stare* at the back of his head.**

From *How to Give a Party*.

22 December 1946
Broadcast 1800–1845
Broadcast on the Third Programme

How To Give A Party

Featuring
Deryck Guyler, Roy Plomley and Carleton Hobbs

26 March 1950
Broadcast 1815–1845
Broadcast on the Third Programme

How To Appreciate Shakespeare

20 April 1946
Broadcast 1800–1830
Broadcast on the Third Programme

How To Travel

Featuring
Deryck Guyler, Roy Plomley and Carleton Hobbs

19 July 1950
Broadcast 2155–2225
Broadcast on the Third Programme

How To Go To The Theatre

29 December 1950
Broadcast 2000–2040
Broadcast on the Third Programme

How To Broadcast

29 September 1951
Broadcast on the Third Programme

Variety Bandbox

1944–1953

This was billed as the show that presented 'the people of variety to a variety of people', and was for many years the BBC's weekly variety highspot. It was conceived as *Bandbox Variety* and re-christened by a typing error.

Variety Bandbox was first transmitted on the General Overseas Programme in December 1942, moved to the General Forces Programme in March 1944 and ended on the Light Programme after nearly 500 editions in September 1953.

Originally an entertainment for forces overseas, the show opened with a snatch of 'I Love to Sing' by the band and ended with the audience singing, 'Let's Have Another One'. Earlier editions were dedicated to overseas newspapers such as the *Ceylon Review*, and the *Basrah Times* and were introduced by a Mistress of Ceremonies, usually a glamorous film actress such as Margaret Lockwood, Frances Day or Googie Withers. Later editions were introduced by Philip Slessor.

Fast-moving, with the minimum of announcements, ***Bandbox*** had a high comedy content (the show featured a resident comedian), adapting to changes in public taste with its policy of finding fresh talent and building new stars.

'If an artist is unknown to me, I give him or her the usual routine audition, and if it turns out well I include the act in a short audition programme in front of the ***Bandbox*** audience and before the ***Bandbox*** broadcast begins. That puts the artist in

Transmission Details

Variety Bandbox

Series 1 – (373 Weeks)

Featuring
John Blore and his Dance Orchestra, Charles Shadwell and the BBC Variety Orchestra, Eric Winstone and his Orchestra, the BBC Revue Orchestra conducted by Frank Cantell, the Billy Ternent Orchestra

Producers included
Philip Brown, Cecil Madden, Stephen Williams, Bryan Sears, Joy Russell-Smith, Tom Ronald, John Foreman

Locations
Queensbury All-Services Club, Camberwell Palace, People's Palace at Mile End, Hippodrome at Golders Green, Cambridge Theatre, Kilburn Empire

27 February 1944–29 April 1951
Broadcast Sundays 1730–1815 (repeated Wednesdays)
Exceptions were:
Week 6 (1800–1845), Weeks 12–18 (1800–1900), Weeks 19–29 (Tuesdays, 1400–1500;

repeated in usual Sunday slot), Weeks 30–57 (Tuesdays, 1300–1400), Weeks 58–72 (1400–1500), Weeks 73 and 74 (1300–1400), Weeks 75–84 (Sundays, 1700–1800, Light Programme), Weeks 85–110 (1800–1900), Weeks 111–135 (1815–1900), Weeks 136–147 (1800–1900), Christmas Day Special 1946 (1630–1730, Wednesday, Light), Weeks 148–158 (1700–1800), Weeks 159–162 (1800–1900), Weeks 163–179 (1600–1700), Weeks 180–192 (1800–1900), Weeks 193–214 (1700–1800), Christmas Day Special 1947 (1700–1800, Light), Weeks 215–246 (2000–2100), Weeks 247–266 (2100–2200), Weeks 267–295 (1930–2030), Weeks 296 to end of series (2100–2200), Christmas Day Special 1949 (1300–1400)

Series 2 – (44 Weeks)

Featuring
Jimmy Handley (introducing the first seven shows), Cyril Stapleton and his Orchestra, Woolf Phillips and the Skyrockets, Al Read, Arthur English, Reg Dixon, Harry Locke, Richard Murdoch, Bernard Miles; guests on first show included

his right element and we find out what he can really do' (Bryan Sears, producer, 1949).

Among the ***Bandbox*** discoveries were: Tony Hancock, Reg Dixon, George Williams, Dick Emery, Derek Roy, Robert Moreton, Harry Secombe and Douglas ('Cardew') Robinson.

Beryl Reid was the first comedienne to be given a regular spot from 9 March 1952.

The most successful of all the ***Bandbox*** discoveries was a nervous young Yorkshireman, who auditioned for the producer Joy Russell-Smith in 1946. With previous experience in an army concert party, he actually auditioned for the demob show *They're Out.* He was almost paralysed by nerves. Russell-Smith claimed she had never heard anything like it in her life.

He was booked for three shows. Billed as 'The Borderline Case', his first broadcast was 1 December 1946. *The Radio Times* for that week described him as 'a comedian who is really different in that he doesn't tell a single gag', going on to say that the producer 'wouldn't let us into the secret of Frankie Howerd's humour because it might take some of the surprise from the first show.'

'I was on the air for seven minutes,' he said, 'and they were seven minutes of sheer torture. I spluttered and stammered, unconsciously pulling faces and running my hand through my hair.'

Within weeks Frankie was a huge success, his hesitant, stream-of-consciousness style was then devastatingly new. Although giving the impression of disorder, his act was carefully rehearsed down to the last comma. Soon after his debut Frankie virtually re-invented his technique, specifically for the radio, deliberately mispronouncing certain words and making full use of his remarkable vocal range:

'Ladies and gentle*men* – I was a-*mazed!*'

'The dial and the vocal chords just don't go together. A lot of people, I am told, expect to find that I'm about fifty, short and fat and wearing a spiv suit!' (1950 interview).

At one time he was billed as 'Francis Howerd – Baritone (the lowest of the low)' in a series of appalling mock operas within the ***Bandbox*** show.

'And the best of luck!'

'There are those amongst us tonight whom I shall "do".'

He became resident comedian almost immediately, broadcasting on alternate weeks with Derek Roy, with whom he established a mock rivalry. Soon he was doing three solo spots instead of the usual one. Frankie stayed until 20 March 1949. He became resident again (this time in tandem with Reg Dixon) from 16 October 1949 to 2 April 1950, taking part in 60 shows in all.

One regular spot of 1950 invited the listener into the consulting-room of the eminent philosopher Professor Francis Howerd; his clients were famous stars who came seeking advice. Among them were Dirk Bogarde (who, since appearing in the film *The Blue Lamp*, had a compulsion to rob everybody he met at gunpoint; the Professor's advice was to leave the gun at home); Margaret Lockwood, Richard Burton, Robert Newton, Tony Hancock, Richard Attenborough and Gilbert Harding.

When he finally left on 2 April 1950 (he made a

the Beverly Sisters, George Williams and Arthur English; guests on last show included Stan Stennett, George Williams, Rawicz and Landauer, Billy Ternent, Frankie Howerd

8 October 1951–28 September 1952
Broadcast Mondays 2100–2200 for first eight programmes, then Sundays 2100–2200
Broadcast on the Light Programme

few more broadcasts as a guest, including the last ***Bandbox*** of all on 28 September 1952), he was replaced by a show within a show, *Blessem Hall*, a hotel sitcom in which the entire cast were Peter Sellers and Miriam Karlin. Between them they played Major Manoeuvre (the manager), Giuseppe Chipolata (the head waiter), 'erbert Perks (the night porter), Mrs Bucket (the char) and Mrs Snitchpuffle (a foreign refugee). They even impersonated famous artists in the hotel cabaret.

There was an advance visit to *Blessem Hall* on 26 March 1950, and the series proper began on alternate weeks from 16 April 1950 to 21 July 1950. From 28 May 1950 Jimmy Handley joined the cast. There were nine editions in all.

The first resident comedian was Hal Monty, followed by Derek Roy, Albert Modley, Reg Dixon and Arthur English. At the beginning of 1951, there were four resident comedians broadcasting on a rota system: Tony Hancock, George ('I'm not well') Williams, Vic Wise and Bill Kerr.

The second series began on 8 October 1951. The resident comedians were Al Read, Arthur English, Reg Dixon, Harry Locke, Robert Moreton and Bernard Miles.

As well as variety turns, there were features such as 'Composer Cavalcade', 'Continental Corner', 'Songs of Yesterday', 'The Middle Eight' and 'Ring in the New'.

Bandbox regulars included: Issy Bonn, the Western Brothers, Avril Angers, Tessie O'Shea, Vic Oliver, Jewel and Warriss, Violet Carson, Ivy Benson, Jack Warner, Pat Kirkwood, Geraldo, Edmundo Ross, Olive Groves, Flotsam and Jetsam, Bruce Trent, Petula Clark, Adelaide Hall, Dorothy Squires, Peter Cavanagh, Cyril Fletcher, Billy ('Uke') Scott, Peter Brough, Max and Harry Nesbitt, Peter Sinclair, Sandy Sandford, Rita Williams, the Beverly Sisters, Billy Milton, Max Bacon, Clapham and Dwyer, Ivor Moreton and Davy Kaye, Forsythe, Seamon and Farrell, Ronald Chesney, Felix Mendelssohn's Hawaiian Serenaders, Jeanne de Casalis, Terry-Thomas, Victor Seaforth, Harry Hemsley, Hutch, Ronnie Ronalde, Max Wall, Beryl Orde, Donald Peers, Nat Mills and Bobbie, Ted Ray, the Three Monarchs, Harry Secombe, Douglas ('Cardew') Robinson, Bill Waddington, Rudy Starita, Anona Winn, the Radio Revellers, Percy Edwards, Dick Bentley, Ronald Frankau, Robert Moreton, Albert and Les Ward, Bill Kerr, Bob Monkhouse, Janet Brown, Eric Woodburn, Max Bygraves, Michael Howerd, Charlie Kunz, Tony Hancock, Joe Church, Jack Watson, Beryl Reid, George Williams, Benny Hill, Terry Scott, Reg Dixon, Joan Hinde, Alfred Marks, Dick Emery, Suzette Tarri, Betty Driver, Ted and Barbara Andrews (and Julie), Jimmy Wheeler, Arthur English, Miriam Karlin, Leon Cortez, Harold Berens, Mrs Shufflewick, Stephane Grappelli, Claude Hulbert and Enid Trevor, Al Read, Charlie Chester, Margery Manners.

Merry-Go-Round/ Waterlogged Spa

March 1944–June 1948

Transmission Details

Merry-Go-Round

Series 1 – (125 Editions)
Called ***Merry-Go-Round*** from Programme 37 on 3 November 1944. From Programme 103, all shows came from *HMS Waterlogged* – series 'demobbed' and first civvy show was in February 1946. First broadcast from *HMS Waterlogged* was on 10 August 1945 in 26th edition of *Merry-Go-Round*. Show broadcast every third week after that until 15 February 1946 (103rd *Merry-Go-Round*), when it came to be broadcast every week.

Featuring
Sub Lt Eric Barker, Pearl Hackney, Lt Jon Pertwee (from 14 December 1945), the Blue Mariners Dance Band conducted by George Crow, 'Double or Quits' cash quiz conducted by Lt Harold Warrender RNVR

This was a service show, previously called *Mediterranean Merry-Go-Round* and *Middle East Merry-Go-Round*, catering for the army, air force and navy in weekly rotation. It was first broadcast on 3 March 1944. 'Week by week the Merry-Go-Round goes around the services, bringing music and fun to boys and girls in khaki and two shades of blue.'

The earlier shows featured artists such as Buddy Featherstonehaugh and his Radio Rhythm Club Sextet, Ralph Reader and a regular variety show called 'Café de NAAFI'.

The series gave rise to three radio classics: *Much-Binding-in-the-Marsh* with Richard Murdoch and Kenneth Horne (air force edition – 31 March 1944), *Stand Easy* with Charlie Chester (army edition – 5 October 1945) and ***Waterlogged Spa/Merry-Go-Round*** with Eric Barker (navy edition – 10 August 1945).

By 21 September 1945 the three shows were being broadcast in rotation, under the ***Merry-Go-Round*** banner. From 15 February 1946 the show became the sole property of Eric Barker in a continuation of the naval edition. After a further two series, it was re-christened ***Waterlogged Spa***, with the series beginning on 17 September 1948.

Before the series proper, Eric Barker had broadcast on ten of the earlier ***Merry-Go-Round*** programmes, both alone and with Pearl Hackney. He wrote a script for the show, which eventually evolved into the ***Waterlogged Spa*** series. The first show to come from *HMS Waterlogged* was broadcast on 10 August 1945 (the 95th edition of ***Merry-Go-Round***).

HMS Waterlogged was a naval shore base at Sinking-in-the-Ooze, under the command of the anxiety-prone skipper Eric ('Heart-throb') Barker, with Pearl Hackney (Mrs Barker) and music by George Crow. Jon Pertwee joined the show on 14 December 1945. At the time he was a special lieutenant who was present at rehearsals, as a representative of the Admiralty, to ensure that the programme didn't go too far. In one show an extra voice was needed to shout from the audience, 'Why keep pickin' on the poor perisher?'; Pertwee volunteered. Eric Barker said in 1956, 'The moment he spoke it was apparent that here was a new personality. Lieutenant Jon Pertwee joined our team and stayed with it for five years.'

His character, Able Seaman Pertwee, spoke in a high-pitched cockney squawk.

The show began with the ***Merry-Go-Round*** theme, 'The Army, the Navy and the Air Force', whistled by the audience. Then there would be an introductory monologue from Barker. His signature tune was 'All the Nice Girls Love a Sailor'. This would be followed by scenes and sketches depicting life at *HMS Waterlogged*. There was always a scene between Eric Barker and Pearl Hackney . . .

HACKNEY: **You're not a man at all.**
BARKER: **Really? Why doesn't somebody tell me these things. What am I?**
HACKNEY: **Do you ever go to the ballet?**
BARKER: **No, it's too rough.**

Produced by
Leslie ('Burgomeister') Bridgmont

3 March 1944–19 July 1946
Broadcast Fridays
From Programme 1, 2000–2100; from Programme 5, 1915–2015; from Programme 31, 1900–2000; from Programme 45, 2130–2200; from Programme 58, 1915–2000; from Programme 73, 1815–1915; from Programme 75, 2000–2100; from Programme 80, 2100–2200
Broadcast on General Forces Programme

Series 2 – (45 Editions)
All came from *Waterlogged Spa* at Sinking-in-the-Ooze

Written by
Eric Barker

Featuring
Eric Barker, Pearl Hackney, Jon Pertwee, Cherry Lind, Richard Gray, Humphrey Lestoqu, Barbara Sumner, George Crow and his Blue Mariners Dance Band; 'Double or Quits' quiz conducted by Bill Gates, but from Programme 20 by Joe Linnane

Produced by
Leslie Bridgmont

6 September 1946–11 July 1947

Broadcast Fridays 2100–2200
Broadcast on the Light Programme
(Programme 39 was on a Sunday, 1400–1500, rescheduled because of Queen's birthday)
There was a Christmas Day edition, 1300–1400, Light Programme

Series 3 – (41 Editions)
Same credits, except that Harold Warrender conducted the 'Competitive Cash Quiz' – the cast versus the visitors

19 September 1947–17 June 1948
Broadcast Fridays 2100–2200; from Programme 18, Thursdays 1930–2030
Broadcast on the Light Programme
Programme 15 was a Christmas edition, broadcast 1300–1400

Merry-Go-Round Melodies
9 Editions
Tunes from ***Merry-Go-Round*** played by the Blue Mariners Dance Orchestra conducted by George Crow, sung by Barbara Sumner

Produced by
Leslie Bridgmont

4 October 1947–29 November 1947
Broadcast Saturdays, varying times
Broadcast on the Light Programme

The second half of the programme was taken up by the 'Double or Quits Cash Quiz', hosted by Harold Warrender (later Bill Gates). The contestants were all navy personnel. The quiz was dropped when the show became ***Waterlogged Spa*** in 1948.

In 1946 the series was 'demobbed', when *HMS Waterlogged*'s three Nissen huts and a shed became ***The Waterlogged Spa***, with Barker as manager. The show became faster and more complex, and many new characters were introduced. The later series seem to occupy a territory midway between *ITMA* and *The Goon Show*. There were still plenty of eccentric characters with catchphrases coming in and out of the door, but the show had certainly become more surreal.

Waterlogged Spa had its own indiscreet secret police (two in number) who continually marched around to their own bugle and cymbal accompaniment. The *Spa* boasted an amateur dramatic society and a glee party, which also formed the nucleus of a women's territorial reserve.

Other characters included Flying Officer Keen (Howard Marion-Crawford). His catchphrase was 'I'm mad Keen'. He spoke so quickly that at times he was virtually incomprehensible. Then there was Lord Waterlogged (later Baron Waterlogged), a guttural cockney played by Richard Gray. His first name was Albert, and he was on first-name terms with the PM, but his politics were a mystery. 'Bob's your flippin' uncle' was his catchphrase.

His daughter, the Honourable Phoeb, was often referred to but never heard. The barmy Dr Oliver Dither (Eric Woodburn) would say, 'I'll be very surprised if you feel a thing – in fact, the last man I tried it on still can't feel a thing.' Jon Pertwee played Joe the postman (with a voice similar to his later Worzel Gummidge TV characterisation) – 'What does it matter what you do as long as you tear 'em up?'

He also played Svenson the Norwegian stoker, who was understood only by WREN Hackney ('Neggardy crop du bombit') and ex-secret serviceman Commander Highprice – 'Hush! Keep it dark!'

The most popular character was Flying Officer Kyte (Humphrey Lestoqu), a demobbed airman who spoke almost entirely in RAF slang.

Waterlogged Spa became the BBC's top-rated show in 1947. There were 252 editions in all.

Eric Barker

Eric Barker had had an early career as a writer, followed by a long stint as a comedian at the Windmill Theatre. He first broadcast for the BBC in 1933 in *First Time Here* – described as 'a teatime programme for beginners'. By the outbreak of war he was an established BBC cabaret artist.

In 1940 he was one of the three principal artists in *Howdy Folks*, a satirical revue, comprising sketches and music. Barker wrote two sketches for each show. Devised and produced by Leslie Bridgmont, it also starred the impressionists Nan Kenway and Douglas Young, with Jacques Brown, Clarence Wright and Helen Clare.

When Barker joined the navy he was replaced by Cyril Fletcher. There was a second series (with Barker) in 1944.

Later in 1940 he starred in four editions of *Wait for It*, playing the Honourable Godfrey Crumpet, private detective. The show was also produced by Leslie Bridgmont.

Waterlogged Spa
42 Editions
Written by
Eric Barker
Featuring
Eric Barker, Pearl Hackney, Jon Pertwee, Richard Gray, Sylvia Robin (newcomer singer); others featured in the series: Eric Woodburn, Howard Marion-Crawford, Cherry Lind and, from Programme 40, Jack Watson and Terry Scott; also the *Waterlogged Spa* Glee Party and George Crow and his Blue Mariners Dance Orchestra
Produced by
Leslie Bridgmont

17 September 1948–29 June 1949
Broadcast Fridays 1930–2000; from Programme 17, Wednesdays 1930–2000
Broadcast on the Light Programme

Puffney Post Office
14 Editions
Based on Jon Pertwee's postman from *Waterlogged Spa*, set in rural community of Puffney. No studio audience; no music

21 April 1950–21 July 1950
Broadcast Fridays 1930–2000 (except Programmes 5, 8, 10, at 1915–1945; and Programme 6, at 1900–1930)

Broadcast on the Home Service

The series was revived in 1944, with Kenway and Young added to the cast.

Much-Binding-In-The-Marsh

1947–1953

Transmission Details

Much-Binding-In-The-Marsh

One-off specials

Christmas Day 1944
Broadcast Monday 2000–2055
Broadcast on General Forces Programme

21 July 1945
Broadcast Saturday 2100–2115
Broadcast on General Forces Programme

Christmas Day 1945
Broadcast Tuesday 1015–1045
Broadcast on General Forces Programme

Series 1 – (38 Weeks plus a Bank Holiday special)

Also featuring
Marylin Williams, the Augmented Dance Orchestra conducted by Stanley Black, Maurice Denham (from Programme 7), Vivien Chatterton and Dick Griffin (from Programme 27), Billy

In the early 1940s Kenneth Horne was doing some shows for the BBC's overseas recorded broadcasting service as compere/announcer. In one show he introduced Richard Murdoch as 'the station commander of ***Much-Binding-in-the-Marsh***'. They later shared an Office at the Air Ministry and developed the theme further. Listeners were first introduced to the RAF station in *Laughter Command* on 31 March 1944 when ***Much-Binding-in-the-March*** was broadcast as the Air Force edition of the service show *Merry-Go-Round.* Flight Lieutenant Richard Murdoch was the OC and Wing Commander Kenneth Horne was the AOC. LAC Sam Costa would join later.

H: **Why has this chap Costa been allowed to meddle with the accounts?**
M: **Well Sir, we thought he was the ideal man to deal with figures, on account of his peacetime occupation.**
H: **Oh and what was his peacetime occupation?**
M: **Stagehand at the Windmill Theatre.**

There was an all-star RAF Orchestra directed by Sidney Torch and Ronnie Waldman (later Harold

Warrender) conducting a quiz called 'Double or Quits'.

It was produced by David Manderson and later by Leslie Bridgmont.

Guests in this first run included Joyce Grenfell, Dorothy Carless, Joan Winters and Binnie Hale.

The next edition was six weeks later on 12 May 1944, and the next was twelve weeks after that. Ralph Reader and his Gang Show and 'Café de NAAFI' were also broadcast as the air force edition of *Merry-Go-Round.*

From the fourth programme on 27 October 1944 (and the 36th *Merry-Go-Round*) the show was broadcast every six weeks – still sharing with Ralph Reader and 'Café de NAAFI' – until it became the only air force edition broadcasting every three weeks from 19 October 1945 until their last show on 1 February 1946. There were 20 in all.

The Radio Times said of the first series on 27 December 1946, 'Richard Murdoch has decided to convert his once famous aerodrome into a roadhouse and from what we remember of the flying field this can be used as the bathing pool – a building permit won't be necessary.'

The show became a series in its own right in January 1947. In the seventh show the cast were joined by Maurice Denham (once described by Richard Murdoch as a vocal chameleon). The other members of the cast played themselves, more or less, but Denham took on more than 60 roles, playing just about everybody else on the show, including Gregory the sparrow, Nigel the silkworm, Group Captain Funnybone, Mr Blake (an almost totally incomprehensible rustic) and Ivy Clingbine. His main character was the cheerful Dudley Davenport ('Dudley Davenport at your service, sir!'). His catchphrase was 'Oh I say, I am a fool!'

Ternent and his Orchestra (from Programme 37)

2 January 1947–18 September 1947
Broadcast Thursdays 1930–2000 (except Week 25, 2030–2100; Bank Holiday edition of 4 August 1947, broadcast 1330–1400; Programme 32, 2030–2200; Programme 37, 2215–2245; Programme 38, 2130–2200)
Broadcast on the Light Programme

Series 2 – (30 Weeks plus a Bank Holiday special)

Also featuring
Janet Davis, Maurice Denham, Augmented Dance Orchestra conducted by Stanley Black. Barbara Valerie and Gwen Catley featured in Programme 2, and Janet Davis substituted for Gwen Catley in Programme 3; vice-versa in Programme 4; Sylvia Robin stood in for Gwen Catley in Programmes 29 and 30.

26 November 1947–16 June 1948
Broadcast Wednesdays at varying times between 1930–2200; Bank Holiday edition, 29 March 1948, 1400–1430
Broadcast on the Light Programme

'MUCH-BINDING-IN-THE-MARSH'

Series 3 – (43 Weeks)
Also featuring Maurice Denham, Maureen Riscoe, Helen Hill, the Dance Orchestra conducted by Stanley Black

21 September 1948–12 July 1949
Broadcast Tuesdays 2000–2030 (series ended with 113th post-war edition)
Broadcast on the Light Programme

Christmas Special (Christmas Day 1949 – Sunday)
Featuring Usual cast plus Charles Shadwell and his Orchestra

Broadcast 2130–2200
Broadcast on the Light Programme

Series 4 – (27 Weeks)
Also featuring Maurice Denham, Diana Morrison, Barbara Leigh, the

Other catchphrases included: 'Not a word to Bessie about this, Murdoch'; 'Have you read any good books lately?'; 'Good morning sir, was there something?' (Sam Costa); 'These sets take a long time to warm up'; 'Good old Char-lee!'

Sam Costa would often refer to a character called Charlie Farnsbarns, but he was never heard from.

In the early 1950s the show defected to Radio Luxembourg for a series sponsored by Mars Bars.

'It wasn't really a great success – even my mother said it was rotten, and she was my greatest fan' (Richard Murdoch).

When they returned to the BBC in 1951 the series was rechristened *Over To You*.

There were also 20 episodes of a series called *Much Murdoch* made for the Australian Broadcasting Company, seven of them with Kenneth Horne.

In the final 1953–54 series Richard Murdoch inherited a newspaper called *Sticklecrumpets Weekly*. The circulation consisted of two elderly gentlemen who had forgotten to cancel their subscriptions. The paper's name became *The Weekly Bind*. The cast were joined by Dora Bryan as Mrs Plum, the woman's expert.

Dance Orchestra conducted by Stanley Black

15 March 1950–13 September 1950
Broadcast Wednesdays 2000–2030 (except Weeks 18 and 19, broadcast at 2015–2045)
Broadcast on the Light Programme

***Over To You* (the successor to Much-Binding-In-The-Marsh)**

28 Weeks

Written by
Richard Murdoch, Kenneth Horne and Anthony Armstrong

Additional material
Talbot Rothwell

Featuring
Richard Murdoch, Kenneth Horne, Sam Costa, Maurice Denham, Diana Morrison, the Dance Orchestra conducted by Stanley Black

Produced by
Leslie Bridgmont

30 September 1951–14 April 1952
Broadcast Sundays 1530–1700 (Weeks 1–13); 1830–1900 (Weeks 14–25); 1945–2015 (Weeks 26–28)

Much Binding

35 Weeks

Written by
Richard Murdoch and Kenneth Horne

Featuring
Richard Murdoch, Kenneth Horne, Sam Costa, Maurice Denham, Dora Bryan (as Miss Plum), the BBC Men's Chorus (Chorus Master Leslie Woolgate), BBC Variety Orchestra conducted by Paul Fenoulhet (Weeks 1, 2, 10–35), BBC Revue Orchestra conducted by Harry Rabinowitz (Weeks 3–9); Nicholas Parsons replaced Maurice Denham in Weeks 24–35

Produced by
Leslie Bridgmont

21 July 1953–23 March 1954
Broadcast Fridays 2130–2200 (except Week 5, at 2225–2255 and Week 7, at 2220–2250 (from the National Radio Show at Earls Court)
Broadcast on the Home Service

The Forces Show

Written by
Bob Monkhouse, Denis Goodwin

Featuring
Richard Murdoch, Kenneth Horne, Sam Costa, the Peter Knight Singers, Leslie Welch (the Memory Man), the Augmented Dance Orchestra conducted by Stanley Black, Lana Morris (from Programme 19); guest comedians throughout the series included Bill Kerr, Cyril Fletcher, Max Bygraves, Max Wall, Terry-Thomas, Peter Cavanagh, Dick Emery, Benny Hill, Bob Monkhouse, Jon Pertwee, Denis Goodwin, Jimmy Wheeler, Stan Stennet, Jack Train. From 30th show: presented by Jewel and Warriss with Betty Driver

Special features included
'The Singers', 'Guest Comedian', 'Show Time' (one week, featuring excerpts from the soundtrack of *The Sound Barrier*), 'Novelty Corner' and 'Solo Pianist'

Produced by
Leslie Bridgmont and Frank Hooper

30 September 1952–24 March 1953
Broadcast Tuesdays (fortnightly from Show 23) 2000–2100
Broadcast on the Light Programme

Christmas Crackers on Christmas Day 1953 (1310–1400, Home Service) featured a *Much Binding* segment with Richard Murdoch, Kenneth Horne, Sam Costa and Maurice Denham, among others. There were also contributions from *The Goon Show*, *Bedtime with Braden*, *A Life of Bliss*, *Variety Playhouse* and *Ray's a Laugh*.

Richard Murdoch And Kenneth Horne Talking It Over

5 Editions

20–25 December 1954
Monday to Friday 1830–1835
Broadcast on the Home Service

Chatter about everything and anything. The five-minute programme also contained a 'crazy Crossword' with clues that were answered the following evening, and a topical version of the *Much Binding* theme.

Stand Easy

1946–1949

Transmission Details

Stand Easy

Series 1 – (54 Weeks)

Written by
Charlie Chester

Featuring
Cheerful Charlie Chester with his Crazy Gang of Arthur Haynes, Ken Morris, Len Martin, Louise Gainsborough, Ramon St Clair, Norma Clarke, Diana Whitburn, the Blue Rockets Dance Orchestra conducted by Eric Robinson (the last two programmes featured the Sky Rockets directed by Benny Daniels)

Produced by
Leslie Bridgmont

11 February 1946–17 February 1947
Broadcast Mondays 1915–1945 (except Weeks 11–25, at 2130–2200, Weeks 26 and 27, at 2000–2030, Week 29, at 1945–2015, Week 38, at 1915–1945, Week 39, at 2135–2200)
Broadcast on the Light Programme

Cheerful Charlie Chester made his radio debut in 1937 in an edition of *Music Hall*, sharing the bill with Tommy Handley. Known at one time as the boy yodeller from Eastbourne, during the war, while serving with the Irish Fusiliers, Chester was ordered by the War Office to write an army contribution to the services show *Merry-Go-Round.* The resulting show, *Studio Stand Easy*, was a frantic mixture of high-speed gags, sketches, songs and sentiment. In 1946 it became ***Stand Easy***, a series in its own right.

Enormously successful, it had among its regular features a popular song 'murdered' at the piano: '– the mind of the arch criminal Chester puts to paper the evidence that is destined to condemn . . . Professor Ken Morris.'

There were regular serials, including 'Tarzan of the Tapes' featuring the jungle trio, Sarah Nade, Wanna Wash (the native outcast) and little Stabu the elephant boy (the serial was interspersed by 'native chants' from the savage Spiveroo tribe). There was also 'The Amazing Adventures of Whippet Kwick, the Cat Burglar'. These serials pioneered the interruption technique so beloved of later shows like *I'm Sorry, I'll Read That Again.*

There was also 'The Riddle of the Middle', again with Professor Ken Morris at the piano. Three melodies were played, but with the wrong middles: 'Can you guess the Riddle of the Middle?' Then there was 'What's cooking?', a regular recipe for housewives by the Eminent Indian cook Singh Jit: 'If you take cranberries and stew 'em like apple sauce it tastes much more like prunes than Rhubarb does – how do I do it?'

Edwina Caroll brought greetings to hospital patients in 'Harmony for Hospitals'. There were songs from 'The Voice' (Frederick Ferrari), and comedy songs from the gang, written by Charlie ('The Old Bazaar in Cairo').

Each show contained a high-speed stand-up spot from Cheerful Charlie:

> And fat! She's so fat, I took her into a restaurant one day, she bent down to do her shoelace up – they flung a table-cloth over her and laid tea!

Among the regular characters were the two spivs, Tish and Tosh (Chester and Len Martin); Hiram Cheap, the producer of the Hambone Repertory Company, Ivor Complaint, the union official (Arthur Haynes), and Ray Ling, the Chinese fence.

Catchphrases included: 'I say. What a smasher!'; 'Oh yes, you will, oh no, you won't'.

The show invariably ended with a sentimental harmony number from the entire gang. In the earlier *Merry-Go-Round* editions (which lasted one hour), the second half of the show was taken up with the 'Double or Quits Cash Quiz', conducted by Will Hay.

After five series ***Stand Easy*** evolved into another crazy show – *Keep Smiling* (1950). Ken Morris, Len Marten and Frederick Ferrari were kept from the old gang. Newcomers were Deryck Guyler, Molly Weir (both recently from *ITMA*) and the character actress Edna Fryer.

Chester was a regular contributor to *Workers' Playtime*, *Midday Music Hall* and *Calling All Forces*, where he was heard opposite Tony Hancock.

Charlie Chester's Christmas Party

Featuring
Same gang

Broadcast Boxing Day 1946 (Thursday)
1915–1945
Broadcast on the Light Programme

Stand Easy (Bank Holiday Edition)

Featuring
Charlie Chester with his Crazy Gang of Arthur Haynes, Ken Morris, Len Marten, Louise Gainsborough, Ramon St Clair and Norma Clarke, with Eric Robinson and his Dance Orchestra

Produced by
Leslie Bridgmont and Ian C. Messiter

Monday 4 August 1947
Broadcast 2130–2200
Broadcast on the Light Programme

BBC Jubilee Edition

Featuring
The gang, with other credits the same

Monday 10 November 1947
Broadcast 1930–2000
Broadcast on the Light Programme

Series 2 – (22 Weeks)

Featuring
Charlie and the gang: Ken Morris, Len Marten, Arthur Haynes, Mary Lou, Ramon St Clair, the Melody Maids,

Frederick Ferrari, the Augmented BBC Revue Orchestra conducted by Frank Cantell

Produced by
Leslie Bridgmont

22 December 1947–16 May 1948
Broadcast Mondays 2130–2200 (except Week 6, at 2015–2045)
Broadcast on the Light Programme

Series 3 – (13 Weeks)

Featuring
Cheerful Charlie and the gang: Ken Morris, Len Marten, Arthur Haynes, Henry Lytton, Edwina Caroll, Frederick Ferrari, the Henry Hall Orchestra conducted by Frank Chacksfield

Produced by
Leslie Bridgmont

21 June 1948–13 September 1948
Broadcast Mondays 2130–2200
Broadcast on the Light Programme

Series 4 – (14 Weeks)

Featuring
Charlie with Ken Morris, Arthur Haynes, Len Marten, Edwina Caroll (as Charlie's dizzy secretary), Frederick Ferrari, the Singing Silhouettes

3 January 1949–4 April 1949

Studio Stand Easy was first broadcast as the army edition of *Merry-Go-Round* (5 October 1945) – you were invited to meet Cheerful Charlie Chester and the happy band of 'other cranks' from 'Stars in Battledress', Sergeant Arthur Haynes, Corporal Ken Morris, Driver Joe Giggs, Ramon St Clair and Corporal Sally ('Click-Click') Rogers, with the Blue Rockets conducted by Eric Robinson.

The second half of the programme was taken up by Question-master Will Hay and the 'Double or Quits Cash Quiz'. There were seven editions in all (one every third week); the last show to be broadcast as part of *Merry-Go-Round* was on 8 February 1946. It had started 12 September 1945.

By the time we get to *That Man Chester* in 1959, we see Charlie supported by Pat Coombs, Jimmy Lavall, Bill Pertwee and the Maple Leaf Four with Bob Sharples and his Orchestra. Bernard Botting and Charles Hart wrote the scripts and split the show in two.

The top half was largely taken up with a new radio family called the Dregs, who were a nightmare answer to the Glums in the long-running *Take It From Here*. Myrtle and Alf Dreg lived somewhere in King's Cross with their children, Veronica and Monty.

The second half of the show was different in that it was an ongoing serial, unusual for this kind of show. It was called *The Quite-a-Mess Saga*, and featured Deryck Guyler and Professor Quite-a-Mess (think of Quatermass), who, with Chester's help, tried to cope with a malignant plant that was strangling London.

That Man Chester lasted only one series, and was replaced by another Leslie Bridgmont production, *The Charlie Chester Show*, which had among its cast

Dick Emery, Maggie Fitzgibbon and Peter Twine. This had a much looser format and was written largely by Gene Crowley with additional material by David Climie. The BBC Revue Orchestra with Malcolm Lockyer and the Quartetto Italiano provided the music.

This series ran for thirteen weeks from 29 May 1961.

Broadcast Mondays 2130–2200 (except Week 6, at 2030–2100)
Broadcast on the Light Programme
Stand Easy was televised in January

Series 5 – (26 Weeks)

Featuring
Charlie plus Ken Morris, Arthur Haynes, Len Marten, Edwina Caroll, Henry Lytton, Frederick Ferrari, the ***Stand Easy*** Orchestra conducted by Frank Chacksfield (from Week 4 it was called the ***Stand Easy*** Dance Orchestra)

Produced by
Alick Hayes (Frank Hooper from Week 15)

6 July–29 December 1949
Broadcast Wednesdays 1930–2000
Broadcast on the Light Programme

***Keep Smiling* (Christmas Day Special)**

Featuring
Charlie Chester and his Crazy Gang: Ken Morris, Len Marten, Molly Weir, Deryck Guyler, Edna Fryer, Frederick Ferrari, the Mitchell Maids, the BBC Revue Orchestra conducted by Robert Busby

Produced by
Leslie Bridgmont

Keep Smiling

25 Weeks

Featuring
The usual gang plus Henry Lytton in Weeks 15–21

3 January 1951–27 June 1951
Broadcast Wednesdays 1930–2000
Broadcast on the Light Programme
(*The Charlie Chester Show* was televised in 1951)

Come to Char-lee
Situation series set in Charlie's flat

Written by
Pat Dunlop and Maurice Drake (from Week 5, by Pat Dunlop, Maurice Drake and Charlie Chester)

Featuring
Charlie Chester, Michael Bentine (his neighbour), Cardew ('The Cad') Robinson (Charlie's valet) – the trio were described in *The Radio Times* as 'the nose, the teeth and the beard'; also with Dora Bryan and Patricia Cutts (as the 'love interest'); from Week 9, Dora was replaced by Edna Fryer. Each show featured songs from both David Hughes and the Radio Revellers.

Produced by
Leslie Bridgmont

26 February 1953–14 May 1953
Broadcast Thursdays 1930–2000
Broadcast on the Light Programme

The Charlie Chester Show

Featuring
Charlie Chester, Len Marten, Arthur Haynes, Ken Morris, Edna Fryer, The Littlewoods Girls' Choir

Introduced by
Alan Clarke

Produced by
Eric Miller

4 January 1955
Broadcast Tuesday 1900–1930
Broadcast on the Home Service

***Ring That Bell* (3 Programmes)**

Personnel as above

22 February 1955, 15 March 1955 and 5 April 1955
Broadcast Tuesdays 1900–1930
Broadcast on the Home Service

Good Old Charlie/A Proper Charlie

Series 1 – (10 Weeks)

Written by
Charles Hart and Bernard Botting

Featuring
Deryck Guyler, Edna Fryer, Len Lowe, Marion Miller, the Radio Revellers

Produced by
Leslie Bridgmont

17 April 1956–17 July 1956 (called ***A Proper Charlie*** from Week 2)

Broadcast Tuesdays 2000–2030
Broadcast on the Light Programme
(No show on 5 June 1956 or 19 June 1956)

One-off

From National Radio Show at Earls Court
28 August 1956
Broadcast Tuesday 1930–2000
Broadcast on the Light Programme

Series 2 – (16 Weeks)

Written by
Charles Hart and Bernard Botting

Featuring
Deryck Guyler, Len Lowe, Pat Coombs, Marion Miller, The Stargazers, BBC Revue Orchestra, conducted by Harry Rabinowitz

Produced by
Leslie Bridgmont (Frank Hooper from Week 6 onwards)

23 April 1957–6 August 1957
Broadcast Tuesdays 1930–2000
Broadcast on the Light Programme

That Man Chester

14 Weeks

Written by
Charles Hart and Bernard Botting

Featuring
Charlie Chester, Deryck Guyler, Pat Coombs, Jimmy Lavall and Bill Pertwee

Music by
The Maple Leaf Four and Bob Sharples and his Orchestra

Produced by
Leslie Bridgmont

12 June 1959–11 September 1959
Broadcast Fridays 2030–2100 (repeated the following Wednesday, 1930)
Broadcast on the Light Programme

The Charlie Chester Show

13 Weeks

Written by
Gene Crowley and David Climie

Featuring
Charlie Chester, Dick Emery, Maggie Fitzgibbon and Peter Twine

Music by
The BBC Revue Orchestra with Malcolm Lockyer and the Quartetto Italiano

Produced by
Leslie Bridgmont

29 May 1961–21 August 1961
Broadcast Mondays 2100–2130
Broadcast on the Light Programme

The Will Hay Programme

1944–1945

Transmission Details

The Diary Of A Dominie
A one-off General Forces Programme show

Written by
Max Kester and Con West

Music by
Stanley Black and the

Practically two situation comedies in one, starring Will Hay as Doctor Muffin, the renowned headmaster of St Michael's School for boys. The first half of the programme was set in the bijou semi-detached villa of the volatile Mrs Potts (Beryl Riggs), where Dr Muffin was installed as paying guest. Mrs Potts was impressed by the doctor's academic standing and fell easy victim to his flattery. She possessed a precocious and argumentative son, Alfie (a rather mature sounding Clarence Wright), who, in spite of his tender years, was just as corrupt as Dr Muffin:

DOCTOR MUFFIN: **You'd even twist your own mother!**

ALFIE: **What do you think *you're* doing?**

DOCTOR MUFFIN: **Well she's not my mother *is* she?**

Another resident was Mr Brown (Dick Francis). He was not on such friendly terms with the landlady: 'If I had my way I'd sew the old sausage up in a sack and sling her in the canal.'

The second half of the show was based on Hay's old stage routines; following a number from Stanley Black and the Dance Orchestra, the scene changed to that of 'the studious and cloistered quiet' of the schoolroom at St Michael's. Here Dr Muffin presided over: D'Arcy – swot, groveller, sneak and know-it-all, from whom the doctor gleaned most of his information (he was played by twelve year old John Clark); Smart (Charles Hawtrey) who was both aggressive and disrespectful ('If you're so clever – why do you always correct D'Arcy's book first?'); and Beckett, an ancient of days, so backward that he had never been allowed to leave school (Billy Nicholls).

The series drew one of the largest audiences then known by the BBC. The third series was scheduled for six shows; five are listed in *The Radio Times*, but only three were ever transmitted. Hay considered the scripts to be below standard and refused to broadcast. He found no fault with the scriptwriters themselves but was deeply dissatisfied with the way in which they had to work.

The show was by no means topical but the writers

Dance Orchestra
Produced by
Alick Hayes

Friday 21 July 1944, 2115–2145

The Will Hay Programme or Diary Of A Schoolmaster

8 Weeks

Written by
Max Kester and Con West

Also featuring
Clarence Wright, Arthur Young, Franklyn Bellamy, Charles Hawtrey, Babs Valerie, Derek Lansiaux, Cyril Gardener, Marjorie Mars, Beryl Riggs, Billy Nicholls, John Clark

Music by
The Dance Orchestra conducted by Stanley Black, who arranged incidental music

Designed by
Will Hay

Produced by
Alick Hayes

18 August 1944–6 October 1944
Broadcast Fridays 2115–2145 (except Week 5, at 2200)
General Forces Programme

Series 2 – (6 Weeks)

Written by
Will Hay, Max Kester and Alick Hayes

Also featuring
Clarence Wright, Beryl Riggs, Dick Francis, Charles

Hawtrey, Billy Nicholls, John Clark
Music by
The Dance Orchestra conducted by Stanley Black, who also arranged incidental music
Produced by
Alick Hayes

20 December 1944–24 January 1945
Broadcast Wednesdays 2130–2200
Broadcast on the Home Service

(Will Hay Celebrates) Victory at St Michael's
One-off
Written by
Will Hay, Max Kester and Alick Hayes
Music by
The Dance Orchestra conducted by Stanley Black
Produced by
Alick Hayes

were required to meet an unnecessary weekly deadline. Hay could see no sense in this arrangement, instead preferring the scripts to be written well in advance. In an article in the *Daily Mail* he said, 'It took me twenty years to build up the reputation I have. It could be torn down in two broadcasts.'

He continued his radio career as part of *The Brains Trust* and as the question-master in 'The Double-or-Quits Cash Quiz' section of *Merry-Go-Round*, but ***The Will Hay Programme*** was never resumed.

Broadcast Friday 11 May 1945, 2030–2100
Broadcast on the Home Service

Series 3 – (3 Weeks)
Written by
Max Kester
Also featuring
Dick Francis, Beryl Riggs, Eileen Way, Graeme Muir, Michael Hunt, Peter Byrne, Billy Nicholls
Music by
St Michael's Choir trained and conducted by Harold Noble, John Blore and his Theatre Orchestra
Designed by
Will Hay
Produced by
Alick Hayes

31 July 1945–14 August 1945
Broadcast Tuesdays 2030–2100
Broadcast on the Home Service

Tom Arnold's Hoop-La!

1944–1945

A lively variety series which took place in a fairground. The setting allowed the programme, which was a succession of sketches, musical items and individual acts, to flow without interruption from an announcer or compere. The various sections were either simply encountered by the listener or introduced very quickly by barkers.

Regular features included 'The Pin-Up Parlour', 'The Dancing Booth', 'The Juke Box' (a musical guest spot) and Robb Wilton in his familiar Mr Muddlecombe character, as the flustered fairground manager: 'I want a bandage for a sore throat.' 'How long?' 'I want it now!'

In the second series Jack Train was the double-dealing Cheapjack Train from Petticoat Lane: 'What can't speak can't lie!'

Stall holder Max Wall was patronised by the impossibly 'refained' Guy and Auntie (later to evolve into the Duchess and Humphrey), who visited the fairground each week in their capacity as students of human nature. Played by Doris Nichols and an almost unrecognisably cut-glass Harold Berens, their sole purpose in ***Hoop-La!*** was to be insulted:

GUY: **Oh Auntie, this boorish fellow is positively revolting!**

MAX: **You know sir, I like you. I do really. I should like to have two of you for our mantelpiece.**

Transmission Details

Tom Arnold's Hoop-La!

Series 1 – (8 Weeks)

Written by
Max Kester and Howard Barnes (from Week 2)

Featuring
Robb Wilton, Max Wall, Freddie Forbes, Polly Ward, the RAF Dance Orchestra conducted by Jimmy Miller; guests through series included Cavan O'Connor, Revnell and West, Geraldo and his Orchestra, Hutch, Harry Korris and Enoch, Kenway and Young, Hatton and Manners, Jewel and Warriss, Cicely Courtneidge, Nat Mills and Robbie, Teddy Brown

Produced by
Pat Dixon

Features included
'The Pin-Up Parlour', 'The Juke Box', 'The Dancing Booth', 'The International Palace of Varieties'.

10 October 1944–28 November 1944
Broadcast Tuesdays 1915–2000
A General Forces Programme

Series 2 – (18 Weeks)
Written by
Max Kester
Featuring
Robb Wilton, Max Wall, Jack Train, Harold Berens, Doris Nichols, Benny Lee, Big Bill Campbell and his Rocky Mountaineers or Harry Lester and his Hayseeds, Debroy Summers Orchestra conducted by Bobby Howell; guests throughout series included Vic Oliver, Hal Monty, Claude Hulbert and Enid Trevor, the Western Brothers, Revnell and West, Jewel and Warriss, Murgatroyd and Winterbottom, Richard Murdoch, Forsyth, Seamon and Farrell, Nat Mills and Bobbie, Clapham and Dwyer, Hatton and Manners
Produced by
Pat Dixon

9 February 1945–29 May 1945
Broadcast Tuesdays 1915–2000
General Forces Programme

GUY: **Look here sir – I don't want to have to get ugly!**
MAX: **If I may say so sir, a blow in the face with a meat axe would improve your appearance.**

Max would also regularly steer the conversation around to a favourite subject, 'Our Shed'.

MAX: **You'll never get there in a thousand years.**
AUNTIE: **Where?**
MAX: **Our shed.**

In a small boy's voice he would then talk about 'the horrible creatures and creepy-crawly things' that lived in his garden shed and of the mischief that he got up to with his 'dim brother'.

MAX: **They told him to get back where he came from.**
AUNTIE: **And where's that?**
MAX: **Our shed.**

There were three numbers from Big Bill Campbell's Rocky Mountain Rhythm, or on alternate weeks Harry Lester and his Hayseeds. The final part of the show was 'The International Palace of Varieties', an extended guest spot and miniature variety show in itself.

Hoop-La! inspired two other series, *Our Shed* and *Petticoat Lane.*

Our Shed

July–September 1946

This was an off-beat series scheduled to bridge the gap between two series of *ITMA*. ***Our Shed*** spun off from Max Wall's solo contributions to *Hoop-La!* Some familiar characters and situations were featured. There were more tales of Max's dim brother, and amateur psychiatrist and snob Auntie, together with her toffee-nosed sidekick, Humphrey (formerly Guy), returned to be insulted yet again.

'Just the phrase, "Oh *look*, here's Humphrey, everybody!" used to get a belly laugh, as audiences were waiting for me to say it,' said Wall.

Other characters included The Voice (Arthur Rigby), Ma (a lady over-fond of milk stout, played by Doris Nichols), and a character played by Wall who was obsessed with his fiancee and continually thwarted in his attempts to buy her a present or to be alone with her. *The Radio Times* also listed a spiv character called Mr Mosseltoff (Harold Berens), but he was dropped at the last minute.

Our Shed ran for just ten editions, but it obviously had an impact on some listeners. 'Unfortunately it never came back,' said Max Wall in 1975, 'which I thought then and still think was a pity. It is amazing the number of

Transmission Details

Our Shed

10 Weeks

Written by
Max Wall (scripts shuffled and cut by Pat Dixon)

Featuring
Harold Berens, Doris Nichols, Arthur Rigby, Hamish Menzies ('the maestro of the joanna'), Marion Pola, Kenneth Blain, Patricia Hayes, Reg Leopold's ***Our Shed*** Saloon Orchestra

Petticoat Lane (You Want It, We've Got It)

23 Editions

Featuring
Elsie and Doris Waters, Michael Howerd, Max Wall, Benny Hill, Maurice Keary, Joan Young, Albert and Les Ward, Benny Lee, Peter Sellers (who replaced Benny Hill in Programmes 17–23)

Music by
BBC Variety Orchestra, directed by Rae Jenkins

Produced by
Pat Dixon (except Programmes 2–7, produced by Charles

Chilton, and Programmes 17–23, produced by Tom Ronald)

29 July 1949–28 December 1948
Broadcast Fridays 2130–2215 (Programmes 1–8), Wednesdays 1900–1945 (9–21), 1830–1915 (22), 1915–2000 (23)
Broadcast on the Home Service

people who remember ***Our Shed*** and think that it ran for months. It must have had something.'

No recordings of ***Our Shed*** are known to exist.

Humphrey and Auntie surfaced again in *Petticoat Lane*, a vehicle for Elsie and Doris Waters. It was broadcast live from the People's Palace in the Mile End Road. Harold Berens had other commitments, so Humphrey was played by the singer Benny Lee, and the cast included Benny Hill.

Ignorance Is Bliss

1946–1953

Transmission Details

Ignorance Is Bliss
(All shows featured Harold Berens, Michael Moore and Gladys Hay, with Stewart MacPherson as quizmaster unless otherwise stated)

Series 1 – (12 Weeks)
Featuring
Sid Millward and the Nitwits
Produced by
Gordon Crier (by arrangement with Maurice Winnick)

26 July 1946–9 October 1946
Broadcast Fridays 2130–2200 (except Weeks 8–12,

This was first broadcast on April Fools' Day in 1946. It was a British version of an American show called *It Pays to be Ignorant.*

Although carefully scripted, this anarchic antidote to *The Brains Trust* gave the impression of being completely spontaneous. The quizmaster was an apparently sophisticated Canadian, Stewart MacPherson, 'the man who thinks the most beautiful words in the English language are "You have been listening to ***Ignorance is Bliss***".'

By contrast, the permanent panel of hand-picked halfwits were fairly unsophisticated, consisting of 'Silly ass' Michael Moore – 'a man whose hobby is setting fire to police stations'; the Cockney character comedian Harold Berens (catchphrase: 'Wot a geezer!'), who was said to be '... a man who always counts his money in front of a mirror – he doesn't even trust himself'; and the ever so slightly more refined Gladys Hay – 'a woman so big that before she was born her mother must have been frightened by the Albert Hall'.

During the show they were asked to answer a selection of the most blindingly obvious questions (two of which were drawn out of a dunce's cap by members of the studio audience). Examples are, 'Who wrote the diary of Samuel Pepys?', 'How many rings in a three-ring circus?' and 'A car is travelling at fifty miles an hour – how fast is another car going at the same speed travelling?'

The questions were avoided, digressed from or disregarded, but never answered. The programme always seemed one step away from degenerating into an unruly slanging match. There was much beating about the bush, many appalling jokes and a great deal of shouting, often from Stewart MacPherson as he attempted to keep order . . .

BERENS: **I was in a picture recently – I was in *The Razor's Edge*. I was a gay young blade. A regular cut-up!**

MOORE: **Oh, you're sharp tonight, Mr Berens!**

BERENS: **I know, I know, I strop at nothing!**

MacPHERSON: **Will you two cut that out before I work myself up into a lather! Now SHAADAAP!**

The comic momentum was kept up by two excruciating contributions from the resident band. The first was the legendary Sid Millward and the Nitwits, arguably the world's finest comedy showband. Later

broadcast Wednesdays 2000–2030)
Broadcast on the Light Programme

Series 2 – (34 Weeks)
Professor Crock and the Crackpots took over from the Nitwits from Programme 14; the New Foulharmonic Orchestra conducted by Mynheer Hal Evans took over from the Crackpots from Programme 28

Produced by
Pat Dixon

9 December 1946–28 July 1947
Broadcast Mondays 1915–1945 (from Week 14, broadcast 2130–2200)
Broadcast on the Light Programme

Special BBC Jubilee Edition

Also featuring
The Revellers

10 November 1947
Broadcast 2100–2130
Broadcast on the Light Programme

Series 3 – (10 Weeks)

Written by
Sid Colin

Produced by
Pat Dixon

23 November 1947–25 January 1948
Broadcast Sundays 2130–2200
Broadcast on the Light Programme

Series 4 – (14 Weeks)
Written by
Sid Colin
Musical indiscretions supplied by
Albert and Les Ward and Mynheer Hal Evans and the Foulharmonic Orchestra
Produced by
Pat Dixon

15 March 1948–14 June 1948
Broadcast Mondays 2130–2200 (except Week 7, broadcast at 1900 because of the royal silver wedding)
Broadcast on the Light Programme

Series 5 – (24 Weeks)
Written by
Ronnie Hanbury and George Wadmore from Week 12
Featuring
The Foulharmonic Orchestra directed by Jack Coles; the Soupstains replaced Albert and Les Ward
Produced by
George Inns (from Week 19 by Neil Tucson)

6 May 1949–21 October 1949
Broadcast Fridays 1930–2000
Broadcast on the Light Programme

shows included contributions from Professor Crock and the Crackpots, the New Foulharmonic Orchestra and the Soupstains. Sid and the Nitwits returned for the final series in 1953.

A quotation from Stewart MacPherson:

> To give you an idea of what kind of musician Dr Crock is – before he formed his band he couldn't even get a job wetting the thumb of the man who turns over the music for the triangle-player in Spike Jones's City Slickers.

Stewart MacPherson was replaced by Eamonn Andrews in the seventh series (1950) and he in turn was replaced by Patrick Burns in the eighth (1953).

There was a stage version at the London Casino (now the Prince Edward Theatre).

BERENS: **I'm going to give up smoking too – it's getting too blinking dangerous.**
MacPHERSON: **Dangerous?**
BERENS: **Yerse – three times since Tuesday I've had my fingers trod on!**

Series 6 – (13 Weeks)
Written by
Ronnie Hanbury
Also featuring
Eamonn Andrews, who replaced Stewart MacPherson
Music by
The Dixielanders and the Cherokeys with Frank Baron
Produced by
Tom Ronald

27 February 1950–22 May 1950
Broadcast Mondays 1930–2000
Broadcast on the Light Programme

Series 7 – (13 Weeks)
Written by
Ronnie Hanbury and George Wadmore
Also featuring
Patrick Burns (sports commentator from Canada) replaced Eamonn Andrews; Richard Gray played Berens's brother from the audience
Music by
Sid Millward and the Nitwits with Wally Stewart and Cyril Lagey
Produced by
George Inns
19 August 1953–10 November 1953

Broadcast Wednesdays 1930–2100
Broadcast on the Light Programme

Nitwit Serenade

Written by
Sid Colin

Described as 25 meaningless minutes in the company of the Nitwits with Sid Millward and Wally Stewart, Cyril Lagey, Roger Smith's Talking Guitar, Marion Sanders and Enso Toppano, Biff Byfield

Produced by
John Foreman

23 March 1950–1 June 1950
Broadcast Thursdays 1820–1845
Broadcast on the Light Programme

Up The Pole

1947–1952

One of the greatest of all variety double acts, Jewel and Warriss first worked together in 1934. They broadcast occasionally on variety shows and in 1941 there were two editions of their own show *Carry On 'Arry* (named after a catchphrase). In 1946 they hosted thirteen editions of the service show *Navy Mixture* (subtitled *The Jewel and Warriss Showboat of the Air*).

'*Navy Mixture* was no great success but it gave Ben and me essential experience,' said Jewel.

The producer George Inns put them into a new show, ***Up the Pole***. In this series the characters of Jewel and Warriss (as proprietors of an Arctic trading post) became more clearly defined: Ben was the fast-talking, bullying, straight man and Jimmy elicited sympathy as the gullible victim. As a live act they made full use of elaborate props, bizarre sketches and situations. The comedy of ***Up the Pole*** was firmly rooted in the northern music hall tradition:

BEN: **We won't run away like common thieves!**

Transmission Details

The Navy Mixture presents *The Jewel And Warriss Showboat Of The Air*

36 Weeks
An entertainment designed for the Royal Navy

Written by
Eddie Maguire (Weeks 15 and 16 co-written by Ronnie Hanbury)

Featuring
Jimmy Jewel and Ben Warriss, Henry Lytton (as Rappaport the butler), Benny Lee (singer, doubling as McKay, the caretaker), Betty Paul (Olga), the Radio Three, Charles Smart (organ), Charmian Innes, Maurice Denham, the Song Pedlars and the Showboat Serenaders; Gaby Rogers came along later in the

series; Week 15 came from the Naval Barracks, Petersfield, featuring the BBC Revue Orchestra conducted by Frank Cantell

Produced by
George Inns

27 July 1946–29 March 1947
Broadcast Saturdays 2130–2200 (except Weeks 19, 36, at 1930–2000; Weeks 20–24, 27–35, at 1915–1945)
Broadcast on the Light Programme

Up The Pole

Series 1 – (45 Weeks)

Written by
Ronnie Hanbury and Richard and Brian Rowland

Featuring
Jewel and Warriss, Claude Dampier, Jon Pertwee, Valerie Tandy, Sydney Simonè and his Orchestra; guests throughout series included Todd Slaughter, Valentine Dyall, Bernard Miles, Leslie Perrins, Maurice Denham, Dino Galvani, Sam Costa, Stanelli, Benny Lee, Arthur Haynes (three times in a row), Harold Berens, Cardew Robinson, Dick Francis, Fred Yule and, from Week 9, Stanley Black and the Dance Orchestra

Produced by
George Inns

JIMMY: **No – we'll take a taxi like posh thieves!**

Claude Dampier ('You'll never guess') played the dithering Horace Hotplate, the Mayor of the North Pole, Jon Pertwee played the crooked Mr Burp, and Betty Paul was the girlfriend.

BETTY: **Oh Jimmy! Where did you learn to kiss like that?**
BEN: **Syphoning petrol!**

The unusual setting (it lasted only for the first series) was used to mirror the current situation in Britain (there was also an employment problem at the North Pole). For the second series the action was moved to a rural police station, with Horace Hotplate as the superintendent and Jimmy and Ben as constables. In the third series Jimmy and Ben lived in a flat above a disused fire station.

Each show featured a special guest star. The first was legendary barnstormer, Todd Slaughter, who recreated his murderous role as Sweeney Todd the demon barber. ***Up the Pole*** was a great success, scoring a big hit with the family audience. Jimmy Jewel said, '***Up the Pole*** had done more for us

in a month than all the years of working on stage. We had become national names.'

Between the third and fourth series Jewel and Warriss starred in a comedy thriller entitled *Jimmy and Ben*. There were two separate adventures, *Corn in Egypt* and *Up and Atom*.

In 1951, Jewel and Warriss were the stars of Britain's first regular TV comedy series, *Turn it Up*. It attained the highest ratings of any light entertainment show up to that time.

Music by
The BBC Variety Orchestra conducted by Rae Jenkins (Week 3: BBC Variety Orchestra only; from Week 4: Variety Orchestra conducted by Paul Fenoulhet)

Produced by
George Inns

Corn in Egypt – 6 episodes

3 November 1950–8 December 1950

Up and Atom – 7 episodes

15 December 1950–26 January 1951
Broadcast Fridays 1930–2000
Broadcast on the Light Programme

Broadcast Mondays 1930–2000 (except Week 1, at 1915–1945; Week 8, a Sunday, at 1200–1230; Week 14, a Tuesday; Weeks 19 and 20, Tuesdays, 2100–2130; Week 37, at 2100–2130)
Broadcast on the Light Programme

Series 2 – (26 Weeks)

Written by
Ronnie Hanbury

Also featuring
Claude Dampier, Jon Pertwee, Betty Paul, the Five Smith Brothers, Roger Snowdon (Weeks 2–5), Stanley Black and the Dance Orchestra

Produced by
George Inns

1 November 1948–24 April 1949
Broadcast Mondays 1930–2000 (except Weeks 16–19, 2000–2030; Week 20, Thursday, at 2100–2130; Weeks 23–26, Sundays, 1630–1700)
Broadcast on the Light Programme

Series 3 – (26 Weeks)

Written by
Ronnie Hanbury

Also featuring
Claude Dampier, Jon Pertwee, Betty Paul, Bertie Hare (Doris's brother – character parts), the Five Smith Brothers, the Dance Orchestra conducted by Stanley Black and, in Weeks 18 and 19, Leon Cortez

Produced by
George Inns

21 October 1949–14 April 1950
Broadcast Fridays 1930–2000
Broadcast on the Light Programme

Series 4 – (13 Weeks)

Also featuring
Jon Pertwee, Claude Dampier, Josephine Crombie (as the new girlfriend), Fred Yule (new character man – in Week 10 Bertie Hare replaced Fred Yule), BBC Revue Orchestra conducted by Robert Busby (from Week 3, Frank Chacksfield and his Orchestra and the Taverners)

20 June 1952–12 September 1952
Broadcast Fridays 2045–2115
Broadcast on the Light Programme

***Jimmy And Ben* (*Corn In Egypt/Up And Atom*)**

Comedy thrillers – 13 editions

Written by
Ronnie Hanbury

Featuring
Jewel and Warriss, Harold Berens, Leon Cortez, Miriam Karlin, Eric Phillips, Stephen Jack, Arthur Haynes

The Forces Show

18 Editions

Written by
Ronnie Hanbury and George Wadmore

Featuring
Jewel and Warriss, Betty Driver, Michael Miles with 'The Forces Quiz'; guests included Winifred Atwell and the Three Monarchs. From 30 June 1953, feature: 'Can You Beat . . .' – Pharos and Marina provided 'quick questions and apt answers' (mindreading act)

Music by
Woolf Phillips and the Sky Rockets

Produced by
Jacques Brown and Trafford Whitelock (except first show, produced by Bill Worsley)

7 April 1953–8 September 1953
Broadcast Tuesdays 2000–2100
Broadcast on the Light Programme

Looking For Trouble

11 Editions

Written by
Len Fincham and Laurie Wyman

Featuring
Jimmy Jewel and Ben Warriss with Betty Paul, John Blythe, Michael Shepley, Jean Anderson and in Edition 5 (30 May 1955) Arthur Lowe

Produced by
Jacques Brown

2 May 1955–11 July 1955
Broadcast Mondays 2030–2100 on the Home Service

Series 2 – (12 Editions)

Featuring
(as above)

Written by
Len Fincham and Laurie Wyman

Produced by
Jacques Brown

7 March 1956–23 May 1956
Broadcast Wednesdays 1900–1930
Broadcast on the Home Service

The Jewel And Warriss Show

13 Weeks

Written by
Sid Green and Dick Hills

Featuring
Jewel and Warriss, Peter Butterworth, Jack Watson, Graham Stark, Barbara Young

Produced by
Tom Ronald

26 November 1958–18 February 1959
Broadcast Wednesdays 2000–2030
Broadcast on the Home Service

Take It From Here

1948–1960

Transmission Details

Navy Mixture
25 Editions
A blend of comedy, novelty and music introduced by Joy Nichols

Featuring
The Song Pedlars, 'Professor' Jimmy Edwards (with a light-hearted lecture), Leslie Welch ('Ask the Memory Man' – questions on sport), Vic Oliver, the BBC Revue Orchestra conducted by Frank Cantell (Programme 8:

'***Take It From Here*** was completely post-war in its attitudes and it recognised the literacy of the listener' (Dennis Norden).

In the austere post-war years, radio was at its most influential. Shows that had grown up with the war, like *ITMA*, continued to attract huge numbers of listeners, but their content remained largely unchanged. The first brand-new comedy to emerge from this period was ***Take It From Here***. Fast-paced and gag-fuelled, it owed something to revue and much to the American style of radio comedy. For half a decade no other show matched it for originality. In the overall picture of post-war radio comedy

Take It From Here ranks alongside *The Goon Show* as one of the most influential post-war programmes.

The writers, Frank Muir and Dennis Norden, became two of the best-known names in comedy. Both were part of Ted Kavanagh Associates, a production stable set up by the writer of *ITMA* to promote fresh talent and new ideas. Muir started his comedy career writing for radio in Iceland, where he was stationed during the war as a photographer for the RAF. After the war he wrote regularly for the BBC, his work including a series of comic lectures, entitled *You May Take Notes* for Jimmy Edwards, as part of the service show *Navy Mixture*.

Norden also served in the RAF, as a wireless operator, at the same time writing sketches for concert party and revue. After the war he provided material for more than 150 variety comedians, including Nat Mills and Bobbie and Billy Caryll and Hilda Mundy. He also contributed gags to *Navy Mixture*.

The hostess of *Navy Mixture* was the Australian singing star Joy Nichols (she also provided character voices for the Edwards lecture items). Dick Bentley, another Australian (he had made his British radio debut in 1939), had been a guest comedian on two broadcasts.

The producer was Charles Maxwell. He had worked for Radio Luxembourg before the war; and it was he who brought Muir and Norden together. He had originally wanted to team Edwards and Nichols; Norden was then writing for Bentley, and the idea was extended to team all three.

'We were offered the chance of writing a whole half-hour and there was no cop-out. If it failed it was because of us,' said Dennis Norden. Frank Muir described it as 'a three-handed show with a very loose

BBC Variety Orchestra conducted by Rae Jenkins); guests in series included Suzette Tarri, Adelaide Hall, Benny Lee, the Western Brothers, Ted Ray, Forsythe, Seamon and Farrell, Peter Brough and Archie Andrews, Claude Hulbert and Enid Trevor, Jeanne de Casalis, Jack Warner, Dorothy Squires, Avril Angers, Cardew Robinson, Ted Ray, Paddie O'Neil, Jack Watson, Dick Bentley

Features also included 'Picture in Song' – with a different singer each week

5 July 1947–22 December 1947

Broadcast varying times and days

Broadcast on the Light Programme (except Programme 4 – Home Service)

Take It From Here

Series 1 – (29 Weeks)

Featuring

Joy Nichols, Dick Bentley, Professor Jimmy Edwards, Wilfred Babbage (replaced by Clarence Wright after 5th show), Alan Dean (announcer), the Keynotes, the Augmented BBC Revue Orchestra conducted by Frank Cantell (in addition the unknown but ubiquitous Herbert

Mostyn regularly got a listing; Herbert was Frank Muir's middle name and Mostyn was Dennis Norden's)

Produced by
Charles Maxwell

23 March 1948–5 October 1948
Broadcast Tuesdays Weeks 1–17 1930–2000; Weeks 18–26 2000–2030; Week 27 2215–2245; Weeks 28 and 29 2100–2130

Series 2 – (37 Weeks)

Featuring
Joy Nichols, Dick Bentley, Professor Jimmy Edwards, Wallas Eaton, Alan Dean and the Keynotes, BBC Revue Orchestra conducted by Frank Cantell

Produced by
Charles Maxwell

28 December 1948–28 June 1949
Broadcast Tuesdays 2100–2130 (except Weeks 24 and 26, at 2130–2200; Week 25, at 1930–2000)
Programme 23 (22 March 1949) was recorded at the Naval Barracks, Portsmouth
Broadcast on the Light Programme

Series 3 – (35 Weeks)

Featuring
Joy Nichols, Dick Bentley, Jimmy Edwards with Wallas Eaton, Alan Dean and the Keynotes and the

framework so that the format can bealtered if it doesn't click at the beginning.'

The first edition of ***Take It From Here***, soon known as ***TIFH*** (pronounced Tife), was broadcast on 23 March 1948. The opening scene was a broadcasting studio, with the cast about to go on the air without a script or producer. Muir and Norden were writing specifically for the cast, exaggerating their real personalities.

The early shows began with dialogue between the three stars, followed by topical sketches, songs from Joy Nichols and the Keynotes; and usually ended with a burlesque of a film or play:

EDWARDS: **This here's my chief reporter, Ace Bentley – he's got a big nose for a scoop.**

NICHOLS: **He looks more like he's got a big scoop for a nose!**

The writers had a fondness for pastiche. ***TIFH*** specialised in spoof dramas that were packed with appalling puns and unashamedly bad jokes, in much the same way that *Round the Horne* and *I'm Sorry, I'll Read That Again* would do a decade and a half later.

After the first six shows the feedback was less than enthusiastic. However Muir and Norden were reshaping the show after each broadcast. This new partnership was keen to tap into audience reaction. The BBC were quick to criticise, claiming that they were overestimating audience intelligence.

Wallas Eaton joined the cast for the second series. He was a versatile performer who was particularly adept at providing different voices and accents.

The real turning point came after the sudden

death of Tommy Handley in January 1949. The show was promoted to the coveted Saturday lunchtime slot, vacated by one of *ITMA*'s three repeats. Listening figures began to improve significantly. In 1949 ***Take It From Here*** won the Best Radio Show of the Year in the *Daily Mail* National Radio Awards. They won the award again in 1951.

A successful stage version ran between 1950–51, playing the Victoria Palace and the Prince of Wales Theatres in London and the Winter Gardens Blackpool. The show was eventually called *Take It From Us.*

In the third series there was more emphasis on topicality with 'Mirror of the Week', a satirical commentary on the happenings of the day.

Joy Nichols left at the end of the fifth series in 1953 (she starred in her own musical series *Shout For Joy* in 1955). She was replaced by June Whitfield and Alma Cogan. The opening dialogue was now between Edwards and Bentley . . .

EDWARDS: **Oh Bentley for goodness sake; all day long you've had your nose stuck in that book – why?**

BENTLEY: **I lost my book mark. I don't want to lose my place Jim; these stories are real spine tinglers – see 'Strange Tales of the Orient'.**

Augmented BBC Revue Orchestra conducted by Frank Cantell

11 October 1949–30 May 1950
Broadcast Tuesdays 2000–2030 (except Week 4, at 2030–2100)
Broadcast on the Light Programme

Series 4 (27 Weeks)

Featuring
The *Take It From Here* team with Joy Nichols replacing Sally Rogers from Weeks 11–19

4 December 1951–3 June 1952
Broadcast Tuesdays 2100–2130 (except Week 11, rescheduled owing to the death of King George, broadcast instead on Sunday 17 February; Week 15, at 1930–2000; Week 25, at 2015–2045; Week 26, at 2045–2115)
Broadcast on the Light Programme

(On Sunday 2 March 1953 the team entertained from the Coliseum Theatre as part of the National Radio Awards – 2100–2200, Light Programme)

Series 5 – (26 Weeks)

Featuring
Joy Nichols, Dick Bentley, Professor Jimmy Edwards, Wallas Eaton and the Keynotes, the

EDWARDS: **I didn't know you were interested in football!**

Take It From Here will always be remembered for a sketch idea that grew into a long-running sitcom within the show, *The Glums*. They were first heard as 'a typically British family' in ***TIFH*** Talking Point; they soon took over the second half of the show. Jimmy Edwards was the boozy, overbearing Mr Glum; Dick Bentley was his dim-witted son and June Whitfield was Ron's protective fiancée Eth.

ETH: **Look Ron, when you go up for an interview, what exactly do you *say* to them?**

RON: **Nothing they could take offence at, Eth. Just – 'Good afternoon; my name's Ron Glum; good afternoon'.**

ETH: [repeats thoughtfully] **'Good afternoon; my name's Ron . . .' Why do you add that second 'good afternoon'?**

RON: **Well, I'm generally on my way out by then.**

The scene was always set by Mr Glum talking (over a scrounged brown ale at closing time) to Ted, the landlord of the local. Alma Cogan made occasional noises off (a thud or a muffled scream) as Mrs Glum, but never actually spoke. An antidote to 'nice' radio families such as the Huggetts, the Lyons and the Archers, the Glums soon became the most popular part of the show.

MR GLUM: **One thing you can say about that boy of mine is that nothing ever goes wrong with him *physically*. How can there, when there's no moving parts?**

Augmented BBC Revue Orchestra in Weeks 1–12; BBC Variety Orchestra in Week 20; Harry Rabinowitz in Weeks 13–16, 19, 23, 26; BBC Variety Orchestra conducted by Paul Fenoulhet in Weeks 18, 21, 24, 25

Produced by
Charles Maxwell
(Week 24 came from *HMS Indefatigable* at Spithead)

5 January 1953–29 June 1953
Broadcast Mondays 2130–2200
Broadcast on the Light Programme

Series 6 – (26 Weeks)
(First series with June Whitfield, first series featuring the Glums)

Featuring
Dick Bentley, Professor Jimmy Edwards, Wallas Eaton, Alma Cogan, June Whitfield, the Keynotes, Augmented BBC Revue Orchestra conducted by Harry Rabinowitz

Produced by
Charles Maxwell

(The team also broadcast in the *Daily Mail* National Radio Awards on Sunday 31 January 1954, 2100–2200 on the Light. Same credits. *Take It From Here* was joint winner with *The Archers* for 'most entertaining programme')

Like most great situation comedies, *The Glums* seemed almost true to life. This was Muir's and Norden's real talent, an ability to mirror everyday life; it gave Ron, Eth and Mr Glum a universality previously unknown in radio comedy. The inspiration for the original *Glums* sketch arose when the writers were considering the absurdity of the engagement ritual. For Ron and Eth, this condition was permanent, which lead to an ever-rising tide of tension within the Glum household:

'There was something very sexual lurking behind it, though it could never be made explicit in those days,' said Norden.

MR GLUM: **Ron's a boy who needs his father's care. Big as he is, he still comes into my bedroom of a morning for cuddles.**
ETH: **Cuddles!**
RON: **That's the name of my new tortoise, Eth. He sleeps under Dad's bed.**

12 November 1953–6 May 1954
Broadcast Thursdays 2130–2200
Broadcast on the Light Programme

Series 7 – (26 Weeks)
(First show was the 200th edition)

Featuring
The *TIFH* team as Series 6

9 December 1954–2 June 1955
Broadcast Thursdays 2130–2200
Broadcast on the Light Programme

Series 8 – (26 Weeks)

Featuring
The *TIFH* team as Series 6 and 7

11 October 1955–4 April 1956
Broadcast Tuesdays 2000–2030
Broadcast on the Light Programme

Series 9 – (20 Weeks)

Featuring
The *TIFH* team but without Alma Cogan

2 January 1957–15 May 1957
Broadcast Wednesdays 2000–2030
Broadcast on the Light Programme

Series 10 – (20 Weeks)

Featuring
The *TIFH* team plus the Keynotes and the BBC Revue Orchestra with Harry Rabinowitz

Produced by
Charles Maxwell

8 January 1958–21 May 1958
Broadcast Wednesdays 2130–2200
Broadcast on the Light Programme

Series 11 – (16 Weeks)

Featuring
Usual team plus the Keynotes, the BBC Revue Orchestra with Harry Rabinowitz
Produced by
Charles Maxwell

27 November 1958–12 March 1959
Broadcast Thursdays 2100–2130
Broadcast on the Light Programme

Series 12 – (20 Weeks)

Written by
Eric Merriman and Barry Took

Featuring
Usual team plus Toni Eden, Sid Philips and his Orchestra, the Polka Dots (after Week 9), the BBC Revue Orchestra with Harry Rabinowitz

Produced by
Charles Chilton

22 November 1959–3 March 1960
Broadcast Thursdays 2100–2130
Broadcast on the Light Programme

Gently Bentley

Series 1 – (12 Weeks)

MR GLUM: **Ron won't have him in his own room because in the middle of the night he crawls around the floor looking for bits of food. And that disturbs the tortoise.**

The Glums scripts were adapted for television by LWT in 1979. Jimmy Edwards recreated his role as Mr Glum; Ron was played by Ian Lavender and Eth by Patricia Brake.

(When Joy Nichols took maternity leave early in 1952 her vocal spot was taken over by Dick Bentley. This was in addition to his own series of song-based shows. The title was a catchphrase of Jimmy Edwards)
Featuring
Josephine Crombie, Alma Cogan, Frank Cordell and his Orchestra

Produced by
Roy Speer

11 August 1952–7 November 1952
Broadcast Mondays 1930–2000 (except Week 8, 3 October, broadcast Friday at 2045–2115)
Broadcast on the Light Programme

Series 2 – (8 Weeks)

Featuring
Dorothy Carless, Pearl Carr, Malcolm Lockyer and his Orchestra (Carless and Cogan were Bentley's 'singing girlfriends' – this series led to Cogan's joining *TIFH*)

Produced by
Roy Speer

20 July–7 September 1953
Broadcast 2000–2030 on the Light Programme

Listen My Children

8 Weeks
(Experimental series described in *The Radio Times* as 'gently satirical' – also billed as 'a new cure for insomnia' and 'a bedtime story for adults'. Featured same cast each week, but there were no identifiable characters, no guest, no studio audience)

Writers included
Frank Muir and Dennis Norden
Featuring
Robert Beatty, Benny Lee, Jon Pertwee, Harry Secombe, Peter Watson, Patricia Hayes, Carole Carr, Benny Hill, Vic Lewis and his Orchestra

Produced by
Pat Dixon

Broadcast 1 June–20 July 1948
Tuesdays 2030–2100 on the Home Service

***Third Division* (Some Vulgar Fractions)**

6 Weeks

Written by
Frank Muir and Dennis Norden
Additional material by
Paul Dehan

Featuring
Robert Beatty, Benny Lee, Bruce Belfrage, Patricia Hayes, Harry Secombe, Peter Sellers, Michael Bentine, Benny Hill, Carole Carr, Margaret Lindsay, Robert Moreton, the George Mitchell Choir, Vic Lewis and his Orchestra (strings under Reg Leopold)

26 January 1949–2 March 1949
Broadcast Wednesdays 2000–2030 (except Week 5, at 2055–2130)
Broadcast on the Third Programme

Ray's A Laugh

1949–1961

'When the Music-hall tradition died, comedian Ted Ray arrived on Radio and TV, bringing with him a charming manner that was in danger of being forgotten.' – Anthony and Deborah Hayward.

One of Britain's all-time great comedy performers who topped the bill in theatres for many years was the biggest radio star during the 1950s and made a successful foray into television. Peter Sellers cited Ted Ray as his major influence on his career and Sellers himself was part of the long-running radio series ***Ray's A Laugh*** along with Kenneth Connor, Kitty Bluett and Patricia Hayes.

Ted Ray was born Charles Olden in Wigan in 1906 but grew up in Liverpool where, during the early 1920s, he played violin in dance bands. He formed a double act with the pianist Charlie Wardle, who had moderate success. After an amicable split, the young Olden went solo, playing song parodies in a seedy costume and going under the name of Hugh Neek. His agent at the time advised him not to speak and his act changed once more to just violin-playing and dancing. His name this time was Nedlo the Gypsy Violinist, and on one occasion, while playing in Sunderland, he had to cover for a comic and reintroduced the patter into his act. In time the Nedlo act disappeared and the young Ted Ray began to adopt a casual style that worked with audiences. The name Ted Ray was chosen

Transmission Details

Ray's A Laugh

Series 1 – (64 Weeks)

Written by
Ronnie Hanbury (Weeks 1–15); Ronnie Hanbury and Eddie Maguire (Weeks 16–25); Ted Ray and Eddie Maguire (Weeks 26–64)

Additional material by
George Wadmore (Until Week 34)

The Cast
Ted Ray, Kitty Bluett, Fred Yule, Peter Sellers, Bob and Alf Pearson, Beaux and the Belles, Patricia Hayes and Leslie Perrins (from Week 14)

Music by
Stanley Black and the BBC Dance Orchestra

Produced by
George Inns

Monday 4 April 1949–Tuesday 27 June 1950
Weeks 1–8 every Monday at 1930; Weeks 9–37 every Tuesday at 2000; Week 38 (27 December 1949)

Tuesday at 2030; Weeks 39–43 every Tuesday at 2130; Weeks 44–64 every Tuesday at 1930 Broadcast on the Home Service

Series 2 – (44 Weeks)

Written by
Eddie Maguire and Ted Ray

Additional material by
George Wadmore

The Cast
Ted Ray, Kitty Bluett, Patricia Hayes, Fred Yule, Peter Sellers, Bob and Alf Pearson, Leslie Perrins and Beaux and the Belles

Music by
Stanley Black and the BBC Dance Orchestra

Produced by
George Inns except Weeks 22–27; produced by Roy Speer

Thursday 21 September 1950–Thursday 26 July 1951 Weeks 1–44 transmitted at 2030 except Week 31 – Friday 27 April 1951 at 2015; Week 32 – Monday 30 April 1951 at 1945; Week 36 – Wednesday 30 May 1951 at 2030 Broadcast on the Home Service

Ted And Kitty's Christmas

Written by
Eddie Maguire and Ted Ray with additional

from a list of past winners of the Open Golf Championship.

Between 1931 and 1939 Ted Ray was becoming well known on the live circuit but couldn't appear on radio because of a non-broadcasting clause in his music-hall contracts. Eventually he appeared on *Music Hall*, *Dance Cabaret* and the weekly revue, *On The Dot*. His first solo series, *Just Fooling*, fell victim to the outbreak of war and only one episode was broadcast. But Ray became a household name as the leading artist in *Calling All Force*, which ran concurrently with the legendary ***Ray's A Laugh*** showing the immense popularity of this entertainer. Various titles were considered for his first 'name' series, among them *Hoo-Ray For Fun* and *Hip-Hoo-Ray*.

Beginning in 1949, ***Ray's A Laugh*** was the direct successor to *ITMA*, which had ceased broadcasting because of the death of its star, Tommy Handley.

'When it began, ***Ray's A Laugh*** slipped neatly into the traditional *ITMA* spot in programmes. Ted was often regarded as the only comic who could follow Tommy Handley, but if the microphone hadn't been invented Ted Ray would still have been at the top of the

Variety profession' (*The Radio Times*, 1958).

The programme began its life as more of a sketch show with a large cast. Kitty Bluett, a young Australian actress, was cast as Ted Ray's wife. Bluett was born in London into a stage family and made her name in radio plays before becoming part of the ***Ray's A Laugh*** team. The double act Bob and Alf Pearson appeared every week in the show with their familiar musical numbers. Bob Pearson also played Mrs Hoskin to Ray's Ivy, who together were doddery old ladies inspired by real-life characters Ray met in Morecambe. Mrs Hoskin was a rather fat lady with a never-ceasing range of ailments ('Ee, it was agony') and Ivy was her squeaky-voiced friend forever talking about the never-seen Dr Hardcastle.

MRS HOSKIN: **I sent for young Dr Hardcastle.**

IVY: **He's loo-vely Mrs Hoskin . . . he's loo-vely!**

The singer Fred Yule, who had been a bass with the Kentucky Minstrels, played Nelson, Ted's brother-in-law, in domestic scenarios and would enter most scenes with the line, 'I heard you say that, Teddy Boy!'

Regular parts of these early shows included a domestic scene and George – 'the Man With the Conscience'. Leslie Perrins played Ted Ray's conscience, a very far-out idea for a show that was broadcast soon after the war. George, played by Ray, was initially a reporter for the *Cannon Enquirer* before moving to the *Daily Bugle*, which was edited by Mr (Old Man) Rivers.

Patricia Hayes was a team regular and provided the voices for many parts including the Mayfair Girl.

material by George Wadmore

Cast
Ted Ray, Kitty Bluett, Patricia Hayes, Fred Yule, Peter Sellers, Leslie Perrins, Betty Hardy

Music by
Stanley Black and the BBC Dance Orchestra

Produced by
George Inns

Transmitted on Monday 25 December 1950 at 1630
Broadcast on the Home Service

Series 3 – (37 Weeks)

Written by
Eddie Maguire, George Wadmore and Ted Ray

The Cast
Ted Ray, Kitty Bluett, Patricia Hayes, Peter Sellers, Jack Watson, Charles Leno, John Hanson and the Kingsmen (Graham Stark appeared in Weeks 12, 13, and 17)

Music by
Stanley Black and the BBC Dance Orchestra

Produced by
George Inns

Thursday 1 November 1951–Thursday 17 July 1952
Weeks 1–37 broadcast at 2030 (except Week 4 at 1900)
Broadcast on the Home Service

Series 4 – (27 Weeks)

Written by
Eddie Maguire, George Wadmore and Ted Ray
The Cast
Ted Ray, Kitty Bluett, Patricia Hayes, Peter Sellers, Patricia Gilbert, Charles Hawtrey (Fred Yule appeared in Week 25)
Music by
Paul Fenhoulet and the BBC Variety Orchestra
Produced by
George Inns

Thursday 25 December 1952–Thursday 25 June 1953
Week 1 broadcast at 2115; Weeks 2–27 broadcast at 2030
Broadcast on the Home Service

Ted And Kitty's Easter Outing
Written by
Eddie Maguire, George Wadmore and Ted Ray
The Cast
Ted Ray, Kitty Bluett, Peter Sellers, Bob Pearson, Patricia Hayes and Graham Stark
Produced by
George Inns

Broadcast on Easter Monday 6 April 1953
Transmitted at 1945
Broadcast on the Home Service

Ray's A Laugh
(one-off show from the National Radio Show)
Written by
Eddie Maguire, George Wadmore and Ted Ray
The Cast
Ted Ray, Kitty Bluett,

Her recurring catchphrase was 'Yes, but not until after six o'clock!' which was her inevitable reply to a question from Ray.

The other main actor of the ***Ray's A Laugh*** team was the 23-year-old Peter Sellers who, apart from a few appearances on variety shows like *Show-Time*, was making his radio debut. Sellers had broken into radio by phoning up the producer Roy Speer and pretending to be Kenneth Horne. He kept insisting that Sellers was a wonderful new performer and then 'Richard Murdoch' came on the line to put in a few good words.

Sellers came clean at the end of the conversation, once Speer had been taken in, and was immediately granted an audition. Sellers' characters on ***Ray's A Laugh*** included Soppy, a small boy with the catchphrase, 'Just like your big red conk!' and also a fruity old girl who would start her sentences with giggles before going on to say, 'My name's Crystal Jollibottom, you saucebox!'

Other musical content was provided by Beaux and the Belles and it was produced by George Inns who had previously worked with Ted Ray on *Henry Hall's Guest Night.* The first fifteen shows were written by Ronnie Hanbury with Eddie Maguire co-writing the next ten. The remainder were written by Eddie Maguire and Ted Ray. Additional material was penned by George Wadmore (until show 34).

Initially the show went very badly, despite being well received by the studio audience. In a 1949 interview Ray describes how the team avoided disaster:

'We faced up to it and reorganised the show, and I just kept my fingers crossed, hoping that we'd survive the thirteen weeks of that first contract.'

The thirteen weeks turned into a record 65 weeks.

Finally the first series ended on 27 June 1950 and by 21 September of the same year the second series had started. This was also exceptionally long-running with 44 shows broadcast. There were no major changes to the personnel except that Roy Speer stepped in to produce weeks 22 to 27. At the time of this series Ted Ray was also starring in *Calling All Forces.*

A special one-off Christmas episode was broadcast on Christmas Day 1950, called *Ted and Kitty's Christmas.* The cast comprised Ted Ray, Kitty Bluett, Fred Yule, Peter Sellers, Leslie Perrins, Patricia Hayes and Betty Hardy. The scripts were once again written by Eddie Maguire and Ted Ray, with additional material by George Wadmore, and George Inns produced it.

Series three saw the first big cast changes. Charles Leno was brought in to play 'Dear old Dad' who had previously appeared in a very modest way in a script. Jack Watson joined the cast, John Hanson and the Kingsmen provided the music and Graham Stark appeared in three episodes. The greater part of the half-hour was now taken up with Ted's and Kitty's domestic situation. Ray seemed continually to browbeat his wife and she would more often than not give as good as she got. A constant store of ammunition in this war of cross words was Kitty's mother:

TED: **You are in love with Trumble. [His boss] Just like he is.**

KITTY: **Don't be so silly. Mr Trumble is old enough to be my father.**

TED: **But not stupid enough to be. He's seen your mother.**

KITTY: **Ted! There you go again poking fun at my mother.**

Peter Sellers, Charles Hawtrey, Patricia Hayes and Kenneth Connor

Music by
BBC Revue Orchestra with Harry Rabinowitz

Produced by
George Inns

Broadcast Thursday 3 September 1953
Transmitted at 1930
Broadcast on the Home Service

Series 5 – (31 Weeks)

Written by
George Wadmore and Ted Ray

The Cast
Ted Ray, Kitty Bluett, Patricia Hayes, Peter Sellers, Charles Hawtrey and Kenneth Connor

Music by
Paul Fenhoulet and the BBC Variety Orchestra

Produced by
George Inns

Thursday 25 September 1953–Thursday 29 April 1954
Weeks 1–31 broadcast at 2030
Broadcast on the Home Service

Series 6 – (31 Weeks)

Written by
Sid Colin, Talbot Rothwell and George Wadmore

The Cast
Ted Ray, Diane Hart, Patricia Hayes, Alexander Gauge, Kenneth Connor and

Pamela Manson
Produced by
Roy Speer

From 13 October 1955
Broadcast on the Home Service
Series 7 – (26 Weeks)
Written by
Charles Hart and Bernard Botting
The Cast
Ted Ray, Kitty Bluett, Laidman Browne, Kenneth Connor, Fred Yule and Elsie Palmer
Produced by
Leslie Bridgmont

From 25 October 1956
Broadcast on the Home Service
Series 8 – (26 Weeks)
Written by
Charles Hart and Bernard Botting
The Cast
Ted Ray, Kitty Bluett, Laidman Browne and Kenneth Connor
Produced by
Leslie Bridgmont
From 4 October 1957
Broadcast on the Home Service
Series 9 – (26 Weeks)
Written by
Charles Hart and Bernard Botting
The Cast
Ted Ray, Kitty Bluett, Laidman Browne and Kenneth Connor
Produced by
Leslie Bridgmont

TED: **I'm sorry darling, I was only teasing. Next time I see her I'll try poking bananas.**

The real comedy in the series happened with the injection of a new character into a scene. Sellers and Kenneth Connor had a flabbergasting range of voices, which added much-needed colour to a series that was in danger of becoming bland. The former continued his tradition of taking the parts of females and teamed up with Patricia Hayes as the two aged old ladies from across the road, Gertrude and Wilomena Fitz.

GERTRUDE: **It's about Wilomena again. She wants to take a part time job in the refrigerator factory. But she thinks it might be too cold.**
KITTY: **Cold?**
WILOMENA: **Yes, they want me to work in short shifts.**

Sellers was excelling himself as a master of voices and the character of Serge Suit was introduced. He was a friendly Russian: 'I lerewike to hear Tchaikerowovsky's *Serewugar Plerewum Ferewairy*.'

The fourth series introduced Charles Hawtrey into the cast and also Patricia Gilbert. By now the number of episodes had been trimmed down to 27, still high by today's standards. The series began on Christmas Day 1952 and ran until 25 June 1953. There were two special shows, one on Easter Monday (6 April) called *Ted and Kitty's Easter Outing* and one broadcast on 3 September from the National Radio Show at Earls Court, which introduced Kenneth Connor into the cast.

Series five started on 25 September 1953 and Kenneth Connor joined the cast, which now had Ted Ray, Kitty Bluett, Peter Sellers, Patricia Hayes, Charles Hawtrey and Kenneth Connor. George Wadmore and Ted Ray wrote the scripts and George Inns continued to produce the show.

Connor's best-known character was the grumpy, nasally-voiced Sidney Mincing, who told the longest jokes on radio. He cropped up in a variety of settings, always playing the same part. In one episode from 1958, Mincing is the managing director of a cigarette factor called Wheezes. Ray visits to purchase 80,000 cigarettes in order to claim his free set of golf clubs:

MINCING: **Perhaps you'd like to look around the theatre where we make our cigarettes**
KITTY: **Yes, I would. [Double take] Theatre! For making cigarettes?**
MINCING: **Well you see, Mr Ray, we've found a way to increase production you see. We get all our staff working in the theatre and every half an hour a comedian comes on the stage and tells them funny stories.**
TED: **I get it, Mincing. And that way you get all your staff rolling in the aisles.**
MINCING: **Oh that's most unfair that is.**
TED: **Why?**
MINCING: **I particularly wanted to say that.**

Hayes adopted the persona of the domineering charwoman Mrs Easy and Mrs Benson, the woman

From 29 September 1958
Broadcast on the Home Service

Series 10 – (26 Weeks)
Written by
Bernard Botting and Charles Hart
The Cast
Ted Ray, Kitty Bluett, Laidman Browne and Kenneth Connor
Produced by
Leslie Bridgmont

Friday 11 September 1959 to Friday 4 March 1960
Weeks 1–26 transmitted at 2000
Weeks 1–26 repeated on the following Sunday at 1415
Broadcast on the Light Programme

Series 11 – (20 Weeks)
Written by
Bernard Botting and Charles Hart
The Cast
Ted Ray, Kitty Bluett, Laidman Browne, Kenneth Connor and Pat Coombs
Produced by
Leslie Bridgmont

Friday 2 September 1960 to Friday 13 January 1961
Weeks 1–20 transmitted at 1930
Weeks 1–20 repeated on the following Sunday at 1415
Broadcast on the Light Programme

***The Spice of Life* (26 Weeks)**
Written by
Gene Crowley
The Cast
Ted Ray, June Whitfield, Deryck Guyler, Gene Crowley and Therese Burton
Music by
BBC Revue Orchestra
Produced by
Roy Speer
8 October 1956–1 April 1957
Broadcast Mondays 2015–2100
Broadcast on the Home Service

***Ted Ray Time* (25 Weeks)**
Written by
George Wadmore
The Cast
Ted Ray, June Whitfield, Harold Berens, Kenneth Connor, Audrey Jeans, Don Peters (Peter Sellers and Joan Sims in Weeks 10–14)
Music by
BBC Variety Orchestra
Produced by
George Inns
25 October 1954–18 April 1955
Broadcast 2030–2100 (except Week 6, 1930–2000)
Broadcast on the Home Service

***Ted Ray Christmas Time* (One-off)**
Written by
George Wadmore

next door. Mrs Easy was a modern-day Mrs Malaprop and her choice of certain words or phrases was a constant fount of laughs. In a 1954 episode she is resigning after her husband has come into some money:

MRS EASY: **I must hask you to accept my resitation.**
TED: **What are you talking about?**
MRS EASY: **Well Mr Easy has come into money.**
KITTY: **What's that?**
MRS EASY: **He's had a windball of £3,000.**

Series five ended on 29 April 1954 after 31 editions and was followed with a one-off show called *The Ted Ray Show*, which starred Harold Berens, Kenneth Connor and Audrey Jeans. This show was broadcast from the National Radio Show on 3 September at 9.45 p.m. Peter Sellers left after this series to work solely on *The Goon Show*, which was now very popular, and to pursue what was to be a rapidly expanding film career.

There was then a gap between the fifth and sixth series, which was the longest so far. During that time Ted Ray appeared in *Ted Ray Time*, which broadcast from 25 October 1954. Starring alongside Ray was the same cast of *Ted Ray Time*: Harold Berens, Kenneth Connor, Audrey Jeans and Don Peters. Music was by Beaux and the Belles and the script was by Ted Ray, George Wadmore and Sid Colin, with George Inns producing.

The biggest change to the sixth series line-up was the absence of Kitty Bluett, who was replaced by Diane Hart as Mary, Ted Ray's wife. Kenneth Connor became the brother-in-law Harold, and

Alexander Gauge his boss, Mr Faraday. Patricia Hayes was Mrs Chatsworth and Pamela Manson joined the team playing Jane Foster. The series switched to a more domestic situation and the scripts were now being written by Sid Colin, George Wadmore and Talbot Rothwell, who went on to write most of the *Carry On* films. This series began on 13 October 1955.

In October of 1956 the seventh series began with the return of Kitty Bluett. Another big change occurred with the partnership of Charles Hart and Bernard Botting writing the scripts and Leslie Bridgmont producing. Kenneth Connor now played Herbert Toil, the odd-job man, and the character actor Laidman Browne joined the cast as Mr Trumble, Ted Ray's boss. His opening words were, 'Ray, step into my office a minute!' and this became his catchphrase.

Running concurrently with ***Ray's A Laugh*** was a series called *Spice of Life*, described as 'a carefree mixture of comedy and music'. This began on 8 October 1956 and starred, alongside Ray, June Whitfield, Deryck Guyler, Gene Crowley and Therese Burton. The scripts were written by Ted Ray, Sid Colin and George Wadmore.

Other series began on 4 October 1957, 26 September 1958 and 4 September 1959, with the final series on 2 September 1960. The final series, number 11, introduced Pat Coombs as the home help Miss Ursula Prune, who has an unrequited love for Ted. Another addition to the cast was Percy Edwards who added an assortment of noises to the proceedings.

The whole domestic scenario was something of its time. In an interview with *The Radio Times* in 1957, Ted Ray said, 'I like to feel when Kitty and I are

The Cast
Ted Ray, June Whitfield, Peter Sellers, Harold Berens, Don Peters and Joan Sims

Music by
BBC Variety Orchestra

Produced by
George Inns

27 December 1954
Broadcast Monday 2030–2100
Broadcast on the Home Service

doing one of our sketches that all over the country married couples are looking at each other and saying: "But darling, that's exactly what happened to us the other day!" ' He described the show as having a 'rationale of tediousness' at its core. It was the additional characters that broke the threatening tedium.

Ted Ray And The Tuba

October–November 1962

Transmission Details

Ted Ray And The Tuba

Series 1 – (12 Weeks)
(Cast and music refer to ***Ted Ray and The Tuba*** and not to the other episodes)

Written by
Laurie Wyman

The Cast
Ted Ray, Paul Whitsun-Jones, David Nettheim, Barbara Mitchell, John Baddely, Susan Burnet

Music by
The Ken Moule Septet (tuba played by Jim Powell) and the Polka Dots

Produced by
Trafford Whitelock

Thursday 4 October 1962 – Thursday 20 December 1962
Weeks 1–12 transmitted at 1931;
Weeks 1–12 repeated on the following

In 1962 the *Navy Lark* writer Laurie Wyman wrote a series of twelve half-hour comedies centred around Ted Ray. This deviated from the tried and tested domestic setting with his on-air wife of Kitty Bluett. Instead Ted was teamed up each week with an object ranging from a tuba to a cat's whisker. In an article in *The Radio Times* of 27 September 1962 Tony Asplin writes, 'The question in scriptwriters' minds now is *what* and not *who* makes people laugh.'

For this series Laurie Wyman was very much influenced by the work of the American humorists Bob Newhart and Shelly Berman. Rather than relying on quick-fire gags, the humour emerges instead from the overall comic situation. In his own words, Wyman's idea was 'to take a strange object and treat it as a normal thing.'

In the first episode Ted is teamed up with a tuba, which he loses on the Underground. He then becomes a plunger-fitter and valve-maker in a tuba factory before playing the part of a music tutor attempting to rid a timid lady of her inhibitions when it comes to playing 'this man-eating instrument of burnished brass.'

Scott and Whaley – American cross-talk double act. Photo taken late 1920s. Starred in BBC radio minstrel show, *Kentucky Minstrels*, and as characters, Cuthbert and Pussyfoot in *The Laughter Trail. (Lew Lane Collection)*

Elsie and Doris Waters as Gert and Daisy. Photo taken 1934 when they appeared as guests on *Henry Hall's Music Night* and *Worker's Playtime*. *(Lew Lane Collection)*

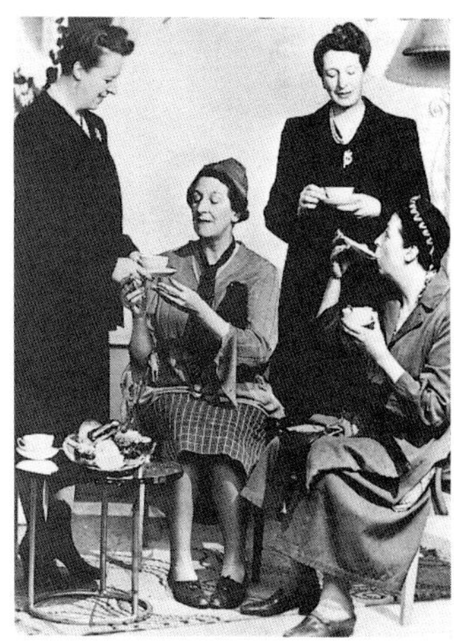

A cunningly devised shot featuring Elsie and Doris having Gert and Daisy to tea. Photo taken 1940. *(Lew Lane Collection)*

Tommy Handley circa 1935/6 before his ITMA days. *(Lew Lane Collection)*

A rare shot of George Formby with his wife, Beryl taken in 1938. *(Lew Lane Collection)*

Norman Evans as Fanny Fairbottom in a pre-war 'over the garden wall' shot. This photo was taken in the 1930s prior to his radio show which began in 1942. *(Lew Lane Collection)*

Happidrome 1941 featuring Robby Vincent, Harry Korris and Cecil Frederick. *(Lew Lane Collection)*

ITMA 1942 featuring Fred Yule, Tommy Handley and Jack Train. Jack Train is making the 'funf' noise sideways into a glass. *(BBC Photograph Library and Archives)*

14-year-old Eric Morecambe and Ernie Wise in 1942 as newly-formed double act. *(Lew Lane Collection)*

Eric Morecambe and Ernie Wise thirteen years later in 1955. *(Lew Lane Collection)*

The cast of *Our Shed* 1946 featuring Patricia Hayes in the front. *(BBC Photograph Library and Archives)*

Charlie Chester - photo taken late 1940s. *(Lew Lane Collection)*

Showboat of the Air 1946 featuring Ben Warriss and Jimmy Jewel. *(Lew Lane Collection)*

Arthur Askey 1946. *(Lew Lane Collection)*

The cast of *Up the Pole* 1947. *(BBC Photograph Library and Archives)*

Much-Binding-in-the-Marsh 1947 featuring clockwise from top left, Richard Murdoch, Sam Costa, Maurice Denham and Kenneth Horne. *(BBC Photograph Library and Archives)*

Sunday at 1400
Broadcast on the Light Programme

Episodes:
1. Ted Ray and the Tuba; 2. Ted Ray and the Elephant; 3. Ted Ray and the Rabbit Suit; 4. Ted Ray and the Fence; 5. Ted Ray and the Squeak; 6. Ted Ray and the Square; 7. Ted Ray and the Cat's Whisker (with Henry Hall); *8. Ted Ray and the Frame; 9. Ted Ray and the Trailer; 10. Ted Ray and the Fiddle; 11. Ted Ray and the Dummy; 12. Ted Ray and the Card*

How's Your Father?

from April 1964

In 1964 Ted Ray was cast in a new series called ***How's Your Father?***, 'a new series in which Ted Ray squares the family circle.' For this short-lived series he was joined by Thora Hird as Mrs Bender the housekeeper, Elanor Summerfield as his sister Ethel, Annette Andre as Angela – Mrs Bender's daughter – and his real-life son Robin as his radio son.

Also in the cast were Pat Coombs, Terence Alexander and Isabel Rainie. The script was by Bob Monkhouse's partner, Denis Goodwin, and the show was produced by Trafford Whitelock.

Transmission Details

How's Your Father?

Cast
Ted Ray, Thora Hird, Elanor Summerfield, Annette Andre, Robin Ray, Pat Coombs, Terence Alexander, Isabel Rainie

Written by
Denis Goodwin

Produced by
Trafford Whitelock

Fridays from 10 April 1964 at 1930

THE 1950s

The 1950s

The 1950s was truly a golden decade for radio comedy. The plethora of long-running and consistently funny shows reflected the kind of mood and optimism inherent in the nation at this time.

With the war over and rationing soon to come to an end there was an ever-increasing feeling of hope. The implementation of a welfare state saw that more of the population were housed, educated and cared for. Rebuilding a nation damaged by war created more jobs and resulted in a recovering economy.

By the mid 1950s the war seemed firmly in the past and this was reflected in a change in radio programming. The number of forces-related programmes, rife in the mid to late 40s, was significantly lower. A younger generation of comedians were now finding a platform to flex their creative muscle. These performers had often been part of concert party units, be it Ralph Reader's RAF Gangshow or ENSA; and, while they were undeniably influenced by their performing apprenticeship in warzones, their comedy was forward-looking and fresh. *The Goon Show* was certainly one such show.

Spike Milligan was deeply marked by his war experience and while his writing was often very nihilistic it had a fantastic childlike quality that removed it from reality. This desire to form a unique and bizarre world to escape into was eventually shared by the nation, who relished their weekly helping of Goonish goings-on. At first *The Goon Show* was almost too bizarre for its audience – it was so unlike anything that had preceded it. But perseverance paid off and within three series, Eccles, Bluebottle, Neddie and Henry Crun were as well known as Sellers, Secombe and Milligan.

While *The Goon Show* was the shining example of originality in this decade, there were other shows that captured the affection of the listening public. *Ray's A Laugh* was a vehicle for its star Ted Ray. Ray's rise to fame happened at the very end of the 40s after the death of Tommy Handley in 1949. While Handley could not have been replaced, the BBC made *Ray's A Laugh* a direct successor to *ITMA* in the schedules. For the whole of the 50s it was at the top of the ratings and helped to launch the career of a young Peter Sellers.

Educating Archie was a show that saw many stars come and go as tutor to the irrepressible Archie Andrews. It is odd to think that one of the biggest stars of radio in this decade was a dummy operated by Peter Brough. Tony Hancock, Bernard Bresslaw, Bruce Forsyth, Max Bygraves all served time as tutor. This was a show that appealed to several generations, and this is a rarity, for many shows are loved by young people and snubbed by older folk or vice versa. The one tutor to go on to much bigger things was Tony Hancock.

Hancock was a star shaped by radio. Once the writers Galton and Simpson had found what they considered to be the right kind of vehicle for this rising star, Hancock's ascent to fame was rapid. Although essentially a sitcom, *Hancock's Half Hour* reflected the change and mood happening in Britain at that time. This was communicated by a comic creation that mixed humour with pathos to devastating effect so that he virtually became a mouthpiece for the nation. Hancock went on to a successful TV career but the pressure of fame led to his suicide. He was irreplaceable, and *Hancock's Half Hour* remains one of the great shows of all time.

Domestic sitcom was popular in the 50s. One could cite the housing boom and the launch of the consumer age as reasons for the rise in this kind of comedy. It is fair to say that no sitcom changed the face of radio. It was not the most original kind of format but the popularity of shows like *Life With The Lyons*, *Meet The Huggetts* and *A Life Of Bliss* meant that these shows cannot be ignored. Their fictional family set-ups were so familiar after a few years that they became less sitcom and more fly-on-the-wall programmes.

There has always been a desire among the British to watch or listen to other people's tragedies or mundane lives. Soap operas like *EastEnders* and *Brookside* are filled with suffering and tedium and yet are still top of the ratings. In the 50s, domestic scenes were very popular and comedy was rife within them. One show launched a family who were as familiar as the royals. *Take It From Here* was made up of sketches written by two young writers called Frank Muir and Dennis Norden. One of these sketches was the recurring saga of *The Glums* with Mr Glum, Ethel and Ron. Ethel and Ron were the perpetually engaged couple whose lives seemed to be governed by the presence of Ethel's father Mr Glum. Through this family the rapid change going on in the country was reflected.

Comedy has always been a powerful weapon that can be used to devastating effect in the hands of great writers. Galton and Simpson, Muir and Norden and Spike Milligan all made names for themselves as writers of great repute during the 50s. Often the writer is overlooked, but these people invented characters that were invited back into the home week after week, often for the best part of a decade.

Radio in this decade truly made stars out of many comics. The variety circuit was still alive in the 50s and, when artists like Ted Ray and the Goons appeared live, they were virtually mobbed by fans. Mass media weren't part of everyday life, television was still a privilege for the rich and radio was the main entertainment in the home. More and more radios were being manufactured and technology saw a reduction in the size of radiograms from sideboards the size of Essex to boxes that could sit on top of a mantelpiece. In the 50s it was more common for a family *not* to possess a radio.

By the end of the decade American influences had crept into British culture with the rise of rock'n'roll and the birth of the teenager. Many regard this as the end to a golden era when the family would sit and listen to radio shows together. Soon television would take over and many of radio's stars would move, tempted by more money and greater security. But there were some memorable radio comedies yet to be broadcast, none more so than in the 1950s.

The Bradens

1950–1956

Transmission Details

Leave Your Name and Number

14 Weeks

Written by
Eric Nichol

Featuring
Miriam Karlin, Stephen Jack, Lyn Evans, Norman Shelley, Stanley Black and the Dance Orchestra

Produced by
Ian Messiter

28 April 1950–28 July 1950
Broadcast Fridays 2015–2045
Broadcast on the Light Programme

Mr and Mrs North

8 Weeks
(Comedy Thriller following on directly from *Leave Your Name and Number*)

Written by
Frances and Richard Lockridge and freely adapted by Bernard Braden

Produced by
Ian Messiter

Episode List
Murder by Experiment; Murder in Mink; The Silent Partner; The Uncertain Lady; The Hangman's Noose; Double Trouble

The Bradens (Bernard Braden and Barbara Kelly) were well known in their native Canada. They first broadcast as part of *Show Parade* in a playlet called 'Sweet Corn' by Robert Stannage. This was broadcast on the Light Programme on Monday 16 May 1949 from 1930 to 2000, and produced by Ian Messiter.

Their next broadcast – this time taking up all of *Show Parade* – was just a fortnight later on 30 May.

The title, *Leave Your Name and Number*, was taken from the traditional farewell at the end of an audition. The plot concerned two Canadians trying to make their way on the English stage, and featured Robert Farnon and his Orchestra. It was written by Braden and Kelly and produced by Ian Messiter with Reginald Purdell.

This one-off was developed into a series between April and July 1951, with the Bradens seemingly always looking for a chance to put on their act. In the cast were Miriam Karlin, Stephen Jack, Lyn Evans and Norman Shelley.

Following this, in August and September 1950, was *Mr and Mrs North*, described as a comedy thriller, with episode titles such as *Murder by Experiment* and *Murder in Mink*.

Meanwhile, back in January had begun a pioneering morning comedy show called *Breakfast with Braden* – an informal mix of songs, sketches and chat. There was no studio audience, but laughter was supplied by Nat Temple and his Orchestra. *Breakfast* became *Bedtime with Braden* later in the same year. Features included 'The Life Story of Lovely Barbara Kelly' and extracts from the *Encyclopaedia Bradennica.* The producer, Pat Dixon, incidentally, had been responsible for *It's A Pleasure*, written by and starring the American Dick Dudley, which was the BBC's first ever breakfast comedy show, going out in 1944.

In 1953, the Bradens also had their own programme of gramophone records – *A Record Wrangle* – which went out on Saturdays.

4 August 1950–15 September 1950
Broadcast on the Light Programme

Bedtime with Braden

Series 1 – (14 Weeks)

Written by
Eric Nichol

Featuring
Bernard Braden, Barbara Kelly, Benny Lee, Pearl Carr, Nat Temple and his Orchestra

Produced by
Pat Dixon

19 September 1950–29 December 1950
Broadcast Tuesdays 2130–2200 (from Week 10 Fridays) on the Home Service

Series 2 – (27 Weeks)

Featuring
Bernard Braden, Barbara Kelly, Benny Lee, Pearl Carr, Nat Temple and his Orchestra

Produced by
Pat Dixon

19 January 1951–27 July 1951
Broadcast Fridays 2130–2200 (except Week 14, at 2145–2215; Week 15, 1900–1930 owing to Festival of Britain coverage; Weeks 17, 24, at 2200–2230; Week 18 on a Friday from 2200–2230; Week 19, at 2030–2100)
Broadcast on the Home Service

Series 3 – (35 Weeks)

Featuring
Cast as previous series, but with Ronald Fletcher from Week 15 on 7 March 1952

16 November 1951–25 July 1952
Broadcast Fridays 2130–2200
No show 15 February 1952 owing to the death of King George VI
No show 11 April 1952
Broadcast on the Home Service

Series 4 – (37 Weeks)

Featuring
The Bradens with Benny Lee, Pearl Carr, Ronald Fletcher, Nat Temple and his Orchestra

Produced by
Pat Dixon

7 November 1952–24 July 1953
Broadcast Fridays 2130–2200 (no show 5 May 1953)
Broadcast on the Home Service

Back With Braden

16 Weeks

Written by
Galton and Simpson

Featuring
Bernard Braden, Annie Ross, Benny Lee, Franklyn Boyd, Nat Temple and his Orchestra (Barbara Kelly in Week 2)

Produced by
Pat Dixon

24 April 1956–7 August 1956
Broadcast Tuesdays 2030–2100
Broadcast on the Home Service

Educating Archie

1950–1959

Transmission Details

Archie Takes The Helm
(This was a segment of *Navy Mixture*)

4 May 1944–8 February 1945
Broadcast on the Light Programme

Two's A Crowd

8 Weeks

Written by
Gene Crowley

Featuring
Peter Brough and Peter Cavanagh, aided, abetted and annoyed by Archie Andrews (first regular series to star a ventriloquist's dummy; all voices other than Archie and Brough supplied by Cavanagh)

Produced by
Charles Maxwell

19 February 1948–8 April 1948

Educating Archie

Series 1 – (29 Weeks)

Written by
Eric Sykes and Sid Colin

Featuring
Robert Moreton, Hattie Jacques, Max Bygraves (not in last show), Julie Andrews,

This was the only major British radio comedy series to star a ventriloquist's dummy. ***Educating Archie*** is significant in that it made many relatively unknown performers into star names, among them Julie Andrews, Robert Moreton, Tony Hancock, Hattie Jacques and Beryl Reid.

Peter Brough was the ventriloquist in question. His father and grandfather had also been ventriloquists. His father Arthur Brough's skills were featured in the Ealing film *Dead of Night*. It was his final professional performance.

Archie and Brough made their radio debut in an edition of *Music Hall*. A year later they were offered a spot in the service show *Navy Mixture*. This was a great success and led to a regular spot in the show called *Archie Takes the Helm*, written by Sid Colin and Ted Kavanagh, which ran for 46 weeks.

Archie was featured each week with a guest star. Other early broadcasts included *Variety Bandbox*, *Workers' Playtime* and *Henry Hall's Guest Night* (Archie sang 'It's Time to Say Goodnight' while Henry Hall played the piano).

Inspired by the success in America of the ventriloquist Edgar Bergan and his dummy Charlie McCarthy, Brough kept trying for a series on the BBC. An unsuccessful pilot show, *The Archie Andrews Radio Show* (written by Sid Colin), was recorded in 1947 with Bonar Colleano and Jon Pertwee.

An ***Educating Archie*** pilot was recorded two years later and was accepted for a run of six weeks with the option of a further six. The cast had Robert ('Bumper Fun Book') Moreton ('Oh, get in there, Moreton') as Archie's tutor (a private tutor was cheaper than a class full of scholars). Max Bygraves ('I've arrived and to prove it I'm here', and 'A good idea – son!') played an odd-job man, while Hattie Jacques was Moreton's girlfriend Agatha Dinglebody.

Julie Andrews, then just thirteen, sang, and Peter Madden played character parts. Musical interludes were provided by the Tanner Sisters and the Hedley Ward Trio. The script was by Sid Colin and Eric Sykes (who had been introduced to Brough by Frankie Howerd).

> I'm not exaggerating when I declare that the timely arrival on the scene of Eric Sykes was to prove the key to the entire situation. Without him there might have never been an ***Educating Archie*** series at all – Peter Brough.
>
> You can always spot a Sykes script. It shows imaginative writing of the highest order – Peter Brough.

Educating Archie was an immediate success and the series was extended to 30 weeks. Listeners were soon estimated at twelve million. The show won the Top Variety series award in the *Daily Mail* National Radio and Television Awards for 1950.

The programme became very popular with children, and with success came merchandising. There were ventriloquist dolls, key rings, masks, mechanical dolls, Archies made of soap,

Peter Madden, Ronald Chesney, the Tanner Sisters, the Hedley Ward Trio, the Music Teachers conducted by Peter York, the BBC Revue Orchestra conducted by Anton (Week 12), conducted by Owen Walters (Week 13), conducted by Robert Busby (Week 14)

Produced by
Roy Speer, with Weeks 26, 27 and 28 produced by Charles Chilton

6 June 1950–19 December 1950
Broadcast Tuesdays 2000–2030 (last few weeks at 1930–2000)
Broadcast on the Light Programme

Archie Andrews' Christmas Party

(From St Andrew's Youth Club, Vauxhall, London)

Written by
Eric Sykes and Sid Colin

Featuring
Robert Moreton, Hattie Jacques, Peter Madden, the Tanner Sisters, the Hedley Ward Trio and Dan Loruso

Produced by
Charles Chilton

Boxing Day 1950
Broadcast 1830–1900
Broadcast on the Light Programme

Archie Andrews' Easter Party

Featuring
Max Bygraves, Gilbert Harding, Hattie Jacques, Julie Andrews, Peter Madden, the BBC Revue Orchestra conducted by Robert Busby
Produced by
Roy Speer

26 March 1951 (Easter Monday)
Broadcast on the Light Programme

Educating Archie
Series 2 – (26 Weeks)
Written by
Eric Sykes and Sid Colin
Featuring
Max Bygraves, Tony Hancock, Julie Andrews, Peter Madden, the Tanner Sisters, the Hedley Ward Trio, Ronald Chesney, Anton and his Orchestra; Bygraves replaced by Alfred Marks in Weeks 11 and 12; Gilbert Harding in Weeks 13, 14 and 21; John Sharp in Weeks 15–18; Robert Moreton in Week 19; Jack Train in Week 22; Albert Modley in Week 23; Bernard Miles in Week 24; Herbert Lom in Week 25. Bygraves returned for the last show in the series on 25 January
Produced by
Roy Speer

3 August 1951–25 January 1952

jigsaws, books, clothing and confectionery. The Archie Andrews Lolly Club had more than 200,000 members.

Before the second series, Brough had his tonsils removed. The result was that Archie's voice became appreciably higher. From the eleventh show Max Bygraves was in America appearing with Judy Garland and was unable to broadcast until the final show in the series. He was replaced by a series of guests: Alfred Marks, Gilbert Harding, John Sharp, Robert Moreton, Jack Train, Albert Modley, Bernard Miles and Herbert Lom.

Robert Moreton was replaced as tutor by Tony Hancock, whose pompous character and catchphrase 'Flippin' kids!' were a great success.

BROUGH: **What have you got on besides the film? You said something about a stage show. Is that right?**
HANCOCK: **Oh yes, a smashing stage show. We've got a comedian here this week. Laugh? Oh dear! He's terrific, really worth seeing, he is.**
ARCHIE: **And when does he go on?**
HANCOCK: **Just as soon as I can get round the back and change into me funny hat.**

Max Bygraves returned for the third series. The new tutor was Harry Secombe. Beryl Reid scored a big hit as Monica the schoolgirl – 'Aren't I the absolute terminus!'

She always wore gymslips and pigtails during the broadcast. Also making his debut was Ronald Chesney with his magic talking harmonica. The show won the *Daily Mail* award again for 1952–53.

In the final show of the series, Archie actually broadcast with Charlie McCarthy (thanks to pre-recording).

Max Bygraves left and was replaced in the fourth series by the film actor Ronald Shiner, who was in turn replaced by Bernard Miles, who played a tinker with a donkey called Knocker.

After the fifth series, there was a misguided attempt to break free of the ***Educating Archie*** format in November 1954, with *Archie's The Boy*. In this series, Archie's education was complete. The series was not a success and ***Educating Archie*** returned in September the following year.

Another oddity from 1954 was the first writing collaboration between Eric Sykes and Spike Milligan. ***Educating Archie*** and *The Goon Show* were merged to produce a one-off 'experimental frolic', in which Brough and Archie entered Goonland via a mousehole and encountered a fantastic adventure involving the destruction of London – and mice! This was called *Archie in Goonland* and went out in June of that year.

Another popular comedian – who went on to do great things in TV – was Dick Emery, who arrived in the seventh series of ***Educating Archie***, often playing as many as six character parts in each show. His most famous creation was Grimble, and his catchphrases were 'I hate you!' and 'Livid I was!' Other regulars were Ken Platt, Graham Stark, Warren Mitchell, Gladys Morgan and Bernard Bresslaw, and in the tenth series Archie's final tutors were Bruce Forsyth followed by Sidney James.

Archie and Brough were castaways on *Desert Island Discs*, on 5 February 1952.

Broadcast Fridays 2045–2115
Broadcast on the Light Programme

Archie Andrews' Party
(From the NAAFI Club, Colchester)
Written by
Eric Sykes and Sid Colin
Featuring
Tony Hancock, Julie Andrews, Hattie Jacques, Peter Madden, the Ilford Girls' Choir

(The team also broadcast on the National Radio Awards of 1952, on Sunday 2 March, from 2100–2200 on the Light)

Educating Archie
Series 3 – (27 Weeks)
(This series was interrupted after Week 21 to give everyone a rest. Archie had a new head built and the new model had a bright red tongue, which he could actually put out!)
Written by
Eric Sykes and Sid Colin (Sykes alone from Week 3)
Featuring
Max Bygraves, Harry Secombe, Beryl Reid, Ronald Chesney, Hattie Jacques, Peter Madden (Week 11 featured the Kirkintilloch Junior Choir conducted by the Rev. J. R.

MacPherson), BBC Revue Orchestra conducted by Robert Busby (Weeks 4–6, conducted by Guy Daines; thereafter no conductor credited until Week 12: Peter Yorke and his Orchestra)

18 September 1952–12 February 1953 and 21 May 1953–26 June 1953
Broadcast Thursdays 1930–2000
Broadcast on the Light Programme

Archie Andrews' Christmas Party
Christmas Day – from the NAAFI Club, Colchester

Written by
Eric Sykes

Featuring
Usual cast but with Eric James instead of Harry Secombe, and including the Ilford Girls' Choir

Produced by
Roy Speer
(Brough and Archie broadcast from the *Daily Mail* Radio Awards at the Scala Theatre on Sunday 1 February 1953 on the Light. Featuring Max Bygraves, Harry Secombe, Beryl Reid, Ronald Chesney, Peter Madden, Hattie Jacques)

Much has been made of the irony of ventriloquism on the radio, but throughout the series the illusion of the two voices, and their contrasting personalities (the often badtempered Brough and the calm but impudent Archie) was always totally convincing.

Educating Archie

Series 4 – (25 Weeks)

Featuring
Ronald Shiner, Harry Secombe, Beryl Reid, Hattie Jacques, Ronald Chesney, Peter Madden, Bernard Miles, Max Bygraves (guest artist on the Christmas edition), BBC Revue Orchestra conducted by Harry Rabinowitz

Produced by
Roy Speer

15 October 1953–1 April 1954
Broadcast Thursdays 1930–2000
Broadcast on the Light Programme

Series 5
Ronald Shiner was replaced by Bernard Miles

Broadcast details not available

Here's Archie

(1st TV show – one-off)

Written by
Ronnie Wolfe and John Waterhouse

Featuring
Irene Handle, Francis de Wolff, Ronald Chesney and Sylvia Campbell

30 May 1956
Broadcast Wednesday 2115–2200
Broadcast on the BBC

Series 6 – (20 Weeks)

Featuring
James Robertson Justice, Beryl Reid, Ken Platt, Graham Starke, Ronald Chesney, the Coronets, the Dennis Wilson Quartet

Written by
Ronald Wolfe and George Wadmore

Produced by
Roy Speer

Broadcast 30 September 1955–10 February 1956 on the Home Service 1930–2000

Educating Archie

Series 7 – (26 Weeks)

Written by
Wolfe, Wadmore and Dunlop

Featuring
Beryl Reid, Ken Platt, Dick Emery, Alexander Gauge, Ronald Chesney and the BBC Revue Orchestra conducted by Harry Rabinovitz (Dora Bryan in Week 2, Beryl Reid in Weeks 3, 5, 7–11, 15, 17, 21, 23, 25, Max Bygraves in Weeks 13 and 14)

Produced by
Roy Speer

19 September 1956–13 March 1957
Broadcast Wednesdays 1930–2000
Broadcast on the Light Programme

Archie in Australia

(One-off)

Written by
Ronald Wolfe and Hugh Stuckey

Featuring
Ronald Chesney, June Salter, Wendy Blacklock, Reg

Quarterly, Reg Goldsworthy, Ray Barrett, Sir Donald Bradman

Produced in Australia by
Harry Pringle

18 September 1957
Broadcast Wednesday 1930–2000
Broadcast on the Light Programme

Educating Archie

Series 8 – (26 Weeks)

Written by
Ronald Wolfe, George Wadmore and David Climie

Featuring
Dick Emery, Warren Mitchell, Pearl Carr, Ronald Chesney, Jerry Desmonde (first show only), BBC Variety Orchestra conducted by Paul Fenoulhet (also Stanley Unwin in Weeks 3 and 4, Hilda Braid in Week 8, Beryl Reid in Weeks 10 and 12, Max Bygraves in Week 14, Ken Platt in Weeks 16 and 25, Eamonn Andrews in Week 23, Freddie Mills in Week 26)

Produced by
Roy Speer (Jacques Brown from Week 17 onwards)
25 September 1957–19 March 1958
Broadcast Wednesdays 1930–2000 (except Week 14, broadcast at 2000–2030)
Broadcast on the Light Programme

Series 9

Broadcast details not available

Educating Archie

Series 10 – (20 Weeks)
(Week 1 was the 200th episode)

Written by
Ronald Wolfe, Ronald Chesney and Marty Feldman

Featuring
Peter Brough, Bruce Forsyth (replaced by Sid James from Week 13 onwards), Marty Feldman, Hattie Jacques (Weeks 6 and 8), Max Bygraves (Week 10), Warren Mitchell (Week 11), BBC Variety Orchestra conducted by Paul Fenoulhet

Produced by
Geoffrey Owen

7 October 1959–17 February 1960
Broadcast Wednesdays 1930–2000 (repeated Sundays 1345)
Broadcast on the Light Programme

Paradise Street

(13 Weeks)
Max Bygraves takes a stroll down Paradise Street (spin-off)

Written by
Eric Sykes

Featuring
Adele Dixon (first six shows), Spike Milligan (first six shows), Hattie Jacques, the Paradise Street Kids, the Tanner Sisters, David Jacobs, Peter Sellers (from Week 7), Augmented Revue Orchestra conducted by Harry Rabinowitz

Produced by
Eric Speer

20 April 1954–13 July 1954
Broadcast Tuesdays 2130–2200
Broadcast on the Light Programme

Archie in Goonland

Written by
Eric Sykes and Spike Milligan

Featuring
Peter Sellers, Harry Secombe, Spike Milligan, Hattie Jacques, the BBC Variety Orchestra conducted by Paul Fenoulhet

Produced by
Roy Speer

11 June 1954
Broadcast 2145–2215
Broadcast on the Home Service
(Archie introduced *Children's Favourites* with Brough's assistance, from 10 July to 4 September 1954, Saturdays 0910–0955 on the Light. Joined by Max Bygraves later in series, and he eventually took over the programme)

Archie's the Boy

(20 Weeks)

Featuring
Beryl Reid, Benny Hill and Graham Starke with Shirley Eaton, Peter Madden, The Coronets, Augmented Revue Orchestra conducted by Harry Rabinowitz

Written by
Eddie Maguire, Ronald Wolfe and Rex Dawe

Produced by
Roy Speer

11 November–24 March 1955
Broadcast Thursdays 1930–2000
Broadcast on the Light Programme

The Great Gilhooly

October–December 1950

Transmission Details

The Great Gilhooly
13 Weeks
Written by
Ted Kavanagh
Featuring
Hugh Morton, Jean Capra, Joe Linnane, the Four Ramblers, the Dance Orchestra conducted by Stanley Black (the BBC Revue Orchestra conducted by Robert Busby in Week 12)
Produced by
Gordon Crier (show 10 by John Watt)

2 October 1950–25 December 1950
Broadcast Mondays 2015–2045 (except Week 13, at 1900–1930)
Broadcast on the Home Service

This was scripted by *ITMA*'s Ted Kavanagh, and was set in the world of sport. It chronicled the adventures of 'a fantastic funster', who became an amazing 'colossus of sport' when pitted against the best athletes in the land.

It starred the Irish character actor Noel Purcell in the title role, and co-starred Jack Train in several new character parts, as well as that of *ITMA*'s Colonel Chinstrap.

Each week Gilhooly was challenged by a celebrated sportsman; the resulting contest was described by a BBC sports commentator.

Boxing was featured in the first show, followed by hockey, cricket, speedway, the Grand National, swimming the Channel – and marbles.

Celebrity guests included Jimmy Wilde, Richard George and John Glyn-Jones.

Life With The Lyons

1950–1961

Described as Hollywood's happiest married couple, Ben Lyon and Bebe Daniels provided us with a long-running series of cheerful domestic comedies, along with their children Barbara and Richard Lyon. Their radio personalities were only a slightly exaggerated version of the real thing.

The supporting cast included Molly Weir as the housekeeper Aggie MacDonald, Doris Rogers as the next-door neighbour Florrie Wainwright and Horace Percival as Mr Wimple.

It was one of the first half-hour comedy shows to dispense with musical interludes.

BEN: **Am I wrong or do I feel some tension in this room?**
BEBE: **What makes you think that?**
BEN: **I was under the impression you all gave me a dirty look but perhaps it's just my imagination.**
FLORRIE: **Our looks weren't dirty, but I don't know about your imagination.**

The show ran for ten series, right up to 1960, and spawned a film that took its title from the radio series ***Life With The Lyons*** (1953). It featured Hugh Morton, Horace Percival, Doris Rogers, Molly Weir, Gwen Lewis, Arthur Hill and Belinda Lee and was directed by Val Guest. Guest shared the scripting with the producer, Robert Dunbar, and the studio was

Transmission Details

Life With The Lyons

Series 1 – (25 Weeks)

Written by
Bebe Daniels, Robert Block and William Harding

Featuring
Bebe Daniels, Ben Lyon, Barbara Lyon, Richard Lyon, Horace Percival, Mollie Weir, David Enders, Deryck Guyler, Ian Sadler, Doris Rogers

Music by
The Dance Orchestra conducted by Stanley Black; incidental music by Arthur Wilkinson

Produced by
Tom Ronald

Episode List includes
Thirteen for Dinner; Ben Bluebeard; Ben Does It Again; Time Marches Back; The Green Eyed Monster

5 November 1950–29 April 1951
Broadcast Sundays 1500–1530
Broadcast on the Light Programme

Series 2 – (29 Weeks)

Written by
Bebe Daniels, Robert

Block and William Harding

Featuring
The Lyons with Doris Rogers, Molly Weir, Horace Percival, David Enders, Philip Ray

Music by
The Dance Orchestra conducted by Stanley Black; incidental music by Arthur Wilkinson (the BBC Variety Orchestra conducted by Paul Fenoulhet took over from Week 14)

Produced by
Tom Ronald

Episode List includes
Sorry, Right Number; Trouble in the Waxworks; This Won't Hurt; Family Secrets

27 September 1951–10 April 1952
Broadcast Thursdays 2130–2200 (Week 21 rescheduled because of King's death to Sunday 17 February 1952, 1700–1730)
Broadcast on the Light Programme
(The Lyons broadcast on the National Radio Awards of 1951, Sunday 2 March 1952, Light Programme. Also the Lyons' offspring had a programme of gramophone records called *The Young Lyons*, presented by Barbara and Richard Lyon – Sundays on the Light, July 1952)

Hammer – associated in many minds with horror of the Christopher Lee and Peter Cushing variety.

A second film was called *The Lyons in Paris* (1954), and featured Martine Alexis, Reginald Beckwith, Pierre Dudan, Dino Galvani, Horace Percival, Molly Weir, Doris Rogers, Gwen Lewis and Hugh Morton. Again, it was directed by Val Guest, who wrote the screenplay, and was produced by Robert Dunbar, for Hammer.

There were also three television versions, one made by Associated Rediffusion in 1957 and two by the BBC in 1955 and 1961.

Series 3 – (33 Weeks)

Written by
Bebe Daniels, Robert Block and Bill Harding

Featuring
Hugh Morton, Horace Percival, Doris Rogers, Molly Weir, Clive Baxter, David Enders

Music by
BBC Variety Orchestra conducted by Paul Fenoulhet; incidental music by Arthur Wilkinson

Produced by
Tom Ronald

Episode List includes
Sauce for the Gander; Muscles; Stupid Cupid; You Can't Get Blood Out of a Stone; Once a Ham; Back in the Autumn (first in series)

14 November 1952–26 June 1953
Broadcast Fridays 2145–2215 (Week 7 was Boxing Day – broadcast 2000–2030)
Broadcast on the Light Programme

Series 4 – (26 Weeks)

Written by
Bebe Daniels, Robert Block and Ray Sonin (from Week 4, Ronnie Hanbury instead of Ray Sonin)

Featuring
The Lyons with Horace Percival, Doris Rogers, Molly Weir, Hugh Morton, David Enders

Music by
BBC Variety Orchestra conducted by Paul Fenoulhet; incidental music by Arthur Wilkinson

Episode List includes
No Rest for Ben; 'Twas the Night Before; Once Upon a Mime; Love Sneaks Up On **Richard**; *I Did It With My Little Hatchet; You Can Keep Your Blinking Lawnmower*

12 November 1953–6 May 1954
Broadcast Thursdays 2130–2200
Broadcast on the Light Programme

Series 5 – (27 Weeks)

Written by
Robert Block, Ronnie Hanbuty and Bebe Daniels

2 November 1954–2 June 1955
Broadcast Thursdays 2100–2130

Series 6

Written by
Robert Block, Ronnie Manbury and Bebe Daniels

Featuring
Horace Percival, Doris Rogers, Molly Weir and Richard Bellaers

Music by
BBC Variety Orchestra conducted by Paul Fenoulhet

Produced by
Tom Ronald

Episode List includes
It's Good to be Home; Who Knows?; Happy New Year; Curtain Up; For Men Only; The Intruder; Double Trouble; The Garden Fete; It's Not Goodbye

3 November 1955–26 April 1956
Broadcast Thursdays 1930–2000
Broadcast on the Light Programme

Series 7

Written by
Robert Block, Ronnie Hanbury and Bebe Daniels

Featuring
As before

Produced by
Tom Ronald

Episode List includes
Here Comes the Bride; Barbara Buys a Bargain; A Star is Born; A House Divided; The Separation; The Birds and the Bees; A Table for Three; Richard Opens Shop; Back in the Winter

11 November 1956–5 May 1957
Broadcast Sundays 1515–1545 until Week 8, then 1415–1445 (except Weeks 20 and 21, broadcast at 1345–1415)
Broadcast on the Light Programme

Series 8

Broadcast details not available

Let's Drop in for Christmas

One-off Christmas edition

Written by
Robert Block, Ronnie Hanbury and Bebe Daniels

Featuring
As before plus Doris Rogers, Molly Weir, Carl Bernard and Peter Morris

Produced by
Tom Ronald

25 December 1957
Wednesday 1600–1630
Broadcast on the Light Programme

Series 9

Broadcast details not available

Series 10

Broadcast details not available

Series 11

Broadcast details not available

Fine Goings On – and more (Frankie Howerd)

1951–1966

Despite his four years as host of *Variety Bandbox*, immediate solo success eluded the young Frankie Howerd and his natural nervousness became a trademark, as did his other catchphrases, notably 'Titter ye not!' It was a well-worked, contrived feud with the veteran comic Derek Roy, inspired by the famous on-stage relationship of the American comedians Jack Benny and Fred Allen, that consolidated Howerd's stature as a performer. This in turn led to his first solo

Transmission Details

Fine Goings On

Series 1 – (14 Weeks)

Written by
Eric Sykes and Sid Colin

The Cast
Frankie Howerd, Marjorie Holmes, Bill

Fraser, Norman Wisdom, Janet Hamilton-Smith and John Hargreaves
Music by
The BBC Revue Orchestra conducted by Robert Busby
Produced by
Bryan Sears

Every other week from Thursday 4 January 1951–Thursday 5 July 1951
Weeks 1–14 broadcast at 1930
Broadcast on the Light Programme

Frankie Howerd Goes East
Series 1 – (8 Weeks)
Written by
Eric Sykes
The Cast
Frankie Howerd, Marcia Owen, Eric James (pianist), Blanche Moore – the 'mascot'.
Produced by
Roy Speer

Wednesday 23 April 1952–Wednesday 11 June 1952
Weeks 1–8 broadcast at 2130
Broadcast on the Light Programme
Broadcast from
1. Nicosia; 2. The Canal Zone; 3. The Canal Zone; 4. Fayid; 5. Benghazi; 6. Tripoli; 7. Malta; 8. Malta

series called ***Fine Goings On*** in 1951. Famous catchphrases from this show were 'and the best of luck!' and 'I was *amazed*'.

Support for this show came from Bill Fraser and Norman Wisdom and the part of Miss Medworthy was played by Marjorie Holmes. Another well-known performer to appear alongside Howerd was Hattie Jacques. The recurring romantic duets were provided by Janet Hamilton-Smith and John Hargreaves. Interestingly, these shows were co-written by Eric Sykes – who was beginning to make a name for himself as a comedy writer and was later to become a co-writer on *The Goon Show* – and Sid Colin. The series was produced by Bryan Sears and broadcast from 4 January 1951. However, ***Fine Goings On*** failed to make any real impact on the listeners, largely due to the size of the Paris Studio, where it was recorded.

As Howerd himself remarked in his autobiography *On The Way I Lost It*, 'I still needed a large, music-hall type auditorium in which to project myself, even for radio, and I found the Paris claustrophobic and intimidating . . . and maybe the format for the show wasn't right.'

After the relative failure of ***Fine Goings On***, Howerd went back to working a live audience and, remembering the success he'd had in the army concert party, recorded a brief series in which he entertained the troops abroad in Egypt, Jordan and Cyprus, among others. The show was called *Howerd Goes East* and a huge risk was taken by recording shows with real amateurs. However, they had once more been scripted by Eric Sykes and, according to Howerd, were 'written against time and were hardly award-winners.'

But this was an experiment that paid off, despite not being critically well received. But the amateurism, combined with young men abroad for King and Country, went down very well with the listeners.

Howerd's first real 'name' series, *The Frankie Howerd Show*, was commissioned in 1953 and broadcast on 23 November of that year with big-star support, including Tony Hancock and Richard Burton. The show was written once again by Eric Sykes with the Hancock faithfuls Galton and Simpson. Alastair Scott-Johnson produced with Billy Ternent and his Orchestra providing the music.

The Radio Times lists the first show of the second series on 22 February 1954 as one 'in which Frankie introduces the vitality of the Tanner Sisters, the versatility of the Hedley Ward Trio, the voice of Lee Young, the nimble fingers of Delores Ventura, and apologises for Gladys Morgan and Billy Ternent.'

The second series of ***Fine Goings On*** didn't reach the ears of the nation until 2 April 1958 when it ran for 20 weeks. This series was written by John Junkin along with Terry Nation, who went on to be a writer of *Dr Who* (he also created the Daleks) and creator of *Blake's 7* on BBC TV. The supporting cast was extended and incorporated Dora Bryan, Freddie Mills, Lee Young, John Ford, Ronnie Barker and Hugh Paddick. The producer was Bill Worsley.

The Frankie Howerd Show

Series 1 – (16 Weeks)

Written by
Galton and Simpson with Eric Sykes

The Cast
Howerd and assorted guests from 'Show-biz' Week 1 guests were Tony Hancock, Eve Boswell, Semprini and Richard Burton

Music by
Billy Ternent and his Orchestra

Produced by
Alastair Scott-Johnson

Monday 23 November 1953–Monday 8 March 1954
Weeks 1–16 broadcast at 2115
Broadcast on the Light Programme

Fine Goings On

Series 2 – (20 Weeks)

Written by
Terry Nation and John Junkin

The Cast
Frankie Howerd, Dora Bryan, Freddie Mills, Lee Young, John Ford, Ronnie Barker and Vivienne Chatterton

Produced by
Bill Worsley

Wednesday 2 April 1958–Wednesday 13 August 1958
Weeks 1–12 broadcast at 2000; Weeks 13–20 broadcast at 1930
Broadcast on the Light Programme

Frankie's Bandbox

Series 1 – (13 Weeks)

Written by
Barry Took and Marty Feldman

The Cast
Frankie Howerd, and assorted guests

Music by
The BBC Revue Orchestra with Billy Ternent

Produced by
Bill Worsley

Tuesday 5 April 1960–28 June 1960
Weeks 1–13 broadcast at 2000
Broadcast on the Light Programme

Now Listen!

Series 1 – (6 Weeks)

Written by
Charles Hart and Peter Bishop

The Cast
Frankie Howerd, Robertson Hare, Kenneth Connor, Carole Allen

Music by
The BBC Revue Orchestra with Billy Ternent

Produced by
Bill Worsley

Thursday 27 August 1964–Thursday 8 October 1964
Weeks 1–6 broadcast at 2000
Repeated from 15 April 1965
Broadcast on the Light Programme

Fine Goings On was a departure from the variety-based shows that Howerd was used to doing. With a fine supporting cast he could play himself in a variety of situations, which became familiar territory to him later in his career when he starred in the hugely popular *Up Pompeii.*

In 1960 Howerd returned to the variety format and borrowed half the title from the show that made him a household name. *Frankie's Bandbox* started a thirteen-week run on 5 April 1960. Its producer, Bill Worsley, wrote in *The Radio Times*:

> In his new series beginning tonight in the Light Programme, Frankie is getting away from the 'story-line' shows which he has recently been doing and concentrating more on his single act with its own fantastic style of humour, expressed in that rich, flexible voice which can convulse some of his fans with the most trivial remark. 'But in this show,' he says, 'my humour's going to have a modern slant.'

The scriptwriters Barry Took and Marty Feldman, who had written spots for Howerd in *London Lights* and *Variety Playhouse*, wrote this series, which incorporated such guests as Alma Cogan, Peter Jones, Terry Scott, Dick Emery, Petula Clarke and in the first show Max Jaffa, Rosemary Squires and Peter Cavanagh. Once again Bill Ternent and the BBC Revue Orchestra were the musical back-up to Howerd.

Howerd's catchphrases had become so well known that it was inevitable that a series should be named after one of them. *Now Listen* was a sketch format that ran for only six shows. The supporting cast were first-rate performers: Robertson Hare – the veteran farceur – Kenneth Connor and Carole Allen.

Each week a guest act would perform and the line-up is of interest with Harry H. Corbett making his radio debut. Andy Stewart, Clive Dunn, Arthur Askey, Richard Murdoch and Kenneth Horne all made appearances. The last of them is listed as appearing 'under the strange banner of Down With Women.'

Howerd played three different roles in the first show alone, including a dithering disc-jockey and a student in an art class. The writers, Charles Hart and Peter Bishop, were keen to stretch the star's talents and he proved himself to be more than able in a show that returned under the name *Frankie Howerd* in July 1966. The second series had a changed cast with June Whitfield and Wallas Eaton supporting Hare and Howerd. Charles Hart teamed up with his old writing partner Bernard Botting to write this series.

Frankie Howerd was often to be heard on radio in the late 1960s, 1970s and 1980s in both variety and game shows. He was a natural performer with an immeasurable talent who entertained generations of listeners.

Frankie Howerd!

Series 1 – (6 Weeks)

Written by
Charles Hart and Bernard Botting

The Cast
Frankie Howerd, Robertson Hare, June Whitfield and Wallas Eaton

Music by
The BBC Revue Orchestra with Billy Ternent

Produced by
Bill Worsley

24 July 1966–28 August 1966
Weeks 1–6 broadcast at 2000
Broadcast on the Light Programme

The Frankie Howerd Show

(Special Show)
From the National Radio Show – Earls Court

Written by
Galton and Simpson

The Cast
Frankie Howerd, Lee Young, Frank Weir, Joy Nichols, Dick Bentley

Music by
Billy Ternent and his Orchestra

Produced by
Alastair Scott-Johnson

Monday 30 August 1954
Broadcast at 2115–2200
Broadcast on the Light Programme

The Frankie Howerd Show

Series 2 – (8 Weeks)

Written by
Galton and Simpson with Eric Sykes and Spike Milligan

The Cast
Frankie Howerd with regular guests including Gladys Morgan, Donald Wolfit, Donald Sinden, Denholm Elliot and Richard Attenborough

Music by
Billy Ternent and his Orchestra

Produced by
Alastair Scott-Johnson

22 March 1955–12 April 1955
Tuesdays 2115–2200
Broadcast on the Light Programme

The Frankie Howerd Show

Series 3 – (14 Weeks)

Written by
Johnny Speight, John Antrobus, Terry Nation and Dick Barry

The Cast
Frankie Howerd with Gladys Morgan, Shani Wallis, Ken Morris, Joan Savage and Robin Boyle. Regular guests included Stanley Holloway, Charlie Chester, Gilbert Harding, Max Wall, Freddie Mills and Ralph Reader

Music by
The Tanner Sisters and Billy Ternent and his Orchestra

Produced by
Alastair Scott-Johnson

2 October 1955–22 January 1956
Sundays 1930–2015
Broadcast on the Light Programme

Just Fancy

1951–1957

Transmission Details

Just Fancy

Series 1 – (15 Weeks)

Written by
Eric Barker

Featuring
Eric Barker, Pearl Hackney, Desmond Walter-Ellis, Patricia Gilbert, Deryck Guyler, John Warrington

Music by
The Malcolm Mitchell Trio

Produced by
Charles Maxwell

11 January 1951–27 July 1951
Broadcast Thursdays 1930–2000 (except Weeks 10 and 11, broadcast on Fridays, 2100–2130)
Broadcast on the Light Programme

Series 2 – (12 Weeks)

Written by
Eric Barker assisted by David Climie

Featuring
Eric Barker, Pearl Hackney, Freda Bamford, Deryck Guyler, John Stevens and Elton Hayes (who sang to a small guitar)

'Ladies and gentlemen who like your radio bright and breezy, with plenty of broad down-to-earth punch – don't be selfish, because the next half-hour is for those of you who prefer the sober sort of trifle that the author Eric Barker describes as *Just Fancy*'

This was Eric Barker's favourite and happiest series – an understated antidote to the craziness of his previous *Waterlogged Spa*. There was no studio audience (until the third series), and the show contained elements of intimate revue and was designed to make the listener chuckle rather than laugh.

A series of vignettes was introduced by Barker, often with regular characters and situations, including two unnamed 'old friends' (Eric Barker and Deryck Guyler). Resident at the Cranbourne Towers Hotel, Westbourne-on-Sea, they were waited on by the slightly less elderly Stanley Muspratt (Kenneth Connor). Although continually talking at cross purposes, they both held the view that 'it is only by listening to the other feller that you get the other feller's point of view.'

In the early programmes listeners eavesdropped on their conversations with the help of a concealed microphone.

The programmes also went behind the scenes at the Tudor Restaurant, Westbourne-on-Sea, where the Lillian Fosdyke Quartet were in residence, and visited the telephone exchange at Little Tessingly, where Mrs Tombs and Mr Thorpe listened in.

The music was specifically tailored to suit the whimsical mood of the show. A small group played the signature tune, incidental music and links.

Music by
A section of the BBC Variety Orchestra conducted by Paul Fenoulhet

Produced by
Charles Maxwell

17 April 1952–3 July 1952
Broadcast Thursdays 2130–2200
Broadcast on the Light Programme

Series 3 – (11 Weeks)

Featuring
Eric Barker, Pearl Hackney, Deryck Guyler, Daphne Anderson (Marjorie Westbury from Week 9) and Peter Hawkins

Music by
BBC Revue Orchestra conducted by Harry Rabinowitz

Produced by
Charles Maxwell

29 April 1953–15 July 1953
Broadcast Wednesdays 2000–2030
Broadcast on the Light Programme

Series 4 – (8 Weeks)

Written by
Eric Barker

Featuring
Eric Barker, Pearl Hackney, Deryck Guyler, Charlotte Mitchell and Kenneth Connor

Music by
Peter Akister

Produced by
Charles Maxwell

18 June 1954–6 August 1954
Broadcast Fridays 2145–2215
Broadcast on the Light Programme

Special Christmas Edition

Written by
Eric Barker and Pearl Hackney

Featuring
Deryck Guyler, Kenneth Connor and Charlotte Mitchell

Music by
Peter Akister

Produced by
Charles Maxwell

21 December 1954
Broadcast Tuesday 2145–2215
Broadcast on the Home Service

Series 5 – (12 Weeks)

Written by
Eric Barker

Featuring
Pearl Hackney, Deryck Guyler, Charlotte Mitchell and Kenneth Connor

Music by
Peter Akister

Produced by
Charles Maxwell

26 September 1955–19 December 1955 (no show 21 November 1955)
Broadcast Mondays 2030–2100
Broadcast on the Home Service

Series 6 – (12 Weeks)

Written by
Eric Barker

Featuring
Eric Barker, Pearl Hackney, Deryck Guyler, Charlotte Mitchell and Kenneth Connor

Music by
Peter Akister

Produced by
Charles Maxwell

5 October 1956–21 December 1956
Broadcast Fridays 2145–2215 (except Week 6, broadcast Wednesday 2215–2245)
Broadcast on the Home Service

Series 7 – (9 Weeks)

Written by
Eric Barker

Featuring
Pearl Hackney, Deryck Guyler and Kenneth Connor (and Ruth Porcher from Week 2 to Week 7)

Music by
Peter Akister

Produced by
Charles Maxwell

1 November 1957–27 December 1957
Broadcast Fridays 2145–2215 (except Week 1, broadcast 2200–2230)
Broadcast on the Home Service

The Goon Show

1951–1960

Transmission Details

The Goon Show

Series 1 – (17 Weeks)
(Billed as *The Crazy People*)

Written by
Spike Milligan and Larry Stephens

Edited by
Jimmy Grafton

The Cast
Peter Sellers, Harry Secombe, Spike Milligan, Michael Bentine

Music by
The Ray Ellington Quartet, The Stargazers, Max Geldray, BBC Dance Orchestra conducted by Stanley Black (except for Weeks 6, 7 and 16 when it was the BBC Revue Orchestra conducted by Robert Busby)

Produced by
Dennis Main Wilson (Weeks 1–10 and 15–17)
Leslie Bridgmont (Weeks 11–14)

Weeks 1–9
Monday 28 May 1951–Monday 23 July 1951
Weeks 10–17
Thursday 2 August

'It is critical comedy. It is against bureaucracy and on the side of human beings. Its starting point is one man shouting gibberish in the face of authority and proving by fabricated insanity that nothing could be as mad as what passes for ordinary living' – Spike Milligan

'The public identified themselves with these characters and situations because to many of them they were more than just funny voices. They were caricatures of real people' – Peter Sellers

The Goon Show is the most famous radio show of all time. Even though at its height it still didn't attain the same kind of listening figures as *ITMA* or *Take It From Here*, it nevertheless stands out as the most innovative and influential show ever to have been heard on the radio. It launched the careers of Spike Milligan, Peter Sellers and Harry Secombe and made them all household names. But, like so many other radio programmes before and since, it took several series to metamorphose into the classic that we remember. ***The Goon Show*** wasn't even billed as such for its first series. It was known instead as *The Crazy People*.

The use of sound effects was to make ***The Goon Show*** stand out from any other radio programme of its age. Milligan was to show an amazing ability to describe sound effects in the most minute detail, which then came alive on-air with hilarious effect. Milligan was the most natural actor of the group and, ironically, the one with the least acting experience. His portrayal of characters like Eccles, Minnie and Moriarty was as strong as the performances of Sellers and Secombe, who had vast performance experience prior to ***The Goon Show***.

Sellers' ability to mimic was legendary and by the early 1950s he was a well-known impressionist. Each of his Goon characters has a unique vocal tone and his ability to switch from one to the other seamlessly is awe-inspiring. He was in direct contrast to Secombe, who spends most of ***The Goon Show*** in the guise of Neddie Seagoon, an extension of his own larger-than-life personality.

One man who can be credited for bringing about ***The Goon Show*** was Jimmy Grafton. It was due to the enthusiasm and contacts of this publican and scriptwriter that ***The Goon Show*** came to fruition. His pub, the Grafton Arms in Victoria, was used as a meeting-place after the war by actors, producers, comics and writers. Spike Milligan, a former army gunner, was renting a room above the pub and had forged a strong link with Jimmy Grafton. (It is important to stress that ***The Goon Show*** was not the result of Spike Milligan's vision alone, but came from the collective consciousness of five men: Milligan, Sellers, Secombe, Michael Bentine and Grafton.)

Milligan and Secombe had first met during the war when they were serving in the Western Desert, and their common bond was a unique brand of humour that saw them continue their friendship long after the war. Peter Sellers and Michael Bentine were also friends from wartime, when they had both appeared in the RAF Gangshow.

1951–Thursday 20 September 1951
Broadcast on the Home Service

Special Christmas Show
Cinderella
With Lizbeth Webb and Graham Stark
Broadcast on 26 December 1951

Series 2 – (25 Weeks)
(Billed as ***The Goon Show***)
Written by
Spike Milligan and Larry Stephens
Edited by
Jimmy Grafton
The Cast
Peter Sellers, Harry Secombe, Spike Milligan (except Week 11), Michael Bentine (except Week 21)
Music by
The Ray Ellington Quartet, The Stargazers (Weeks 1–6), Max Geldray
Produced by
Dennis Main Wilson

Tuesday 22 January 1952–Tuesday 15 July 1952
(No broadcast on Tuesday 12 February 1952)
Broadcast on the Home Service

Series 3 – (25 Weeks)
Written by
Spike Milligan and Larry Stephens
Edited by
Jimmy Grafton

The Cast
Peter Sellers, Harry Secombe, Spike Milligan (absent from Weeks 5–16), Dick Emery (Weeks 7, 9, 11, 13, 15, 17), Graham Stark (Weeks 10, 12, 14, 16); Announcer: Andrew Timothy

Music by
The Ray Ellington Quartet, Max Geldray

Produced by
Dennis Main Wilson

Tuesday 11 November 1952–Tuesday 5 May 1953
Week 7 (26 December 1952) was the Christmas Pantomime and lasted 45 minutes
Broadcast on the Home Service

Special Coronation Edition
Broadcast on 3 June 1953 – lasting 40 minutes, with Graham Stark

Series 4 – (30 Weeks)

Written by
Spike Milligan (Weeks 21–30); Spike Milligan and Larry Stephens (Weeks 1–9 and 11–20); Larry Stephens (Week 10)

Edited by
Jimmy Grafton

The Cast
Peter Sellers, Harry Secombe, Spike Milligan, Michael Bentine (Week 13); Announcers: Andrew

Harry Secombe bridged the gap and introduced them to Milligan, knowing that they would gel as performers. The Grafton Arms became a regular meeting-place for this group of four comics, who performed in a smoke-filled room under the watchful eye of Jimmy Grafton, who became known as KOGVOS – 'King of the Goon and Voice Of Sanity.'

These performances were becoming a regular attraction and Grafton tried to persuade the group to record a couple of the shows. Bill Boorne, a showbiz writer, announced, to virtually no notice, the formation of *The Goon Club*. But, like so many original concepts, it took several years for the powers that be to take notice and the BBC turned down the idea for three years. Eventually a young producer called Pat Dixon gave it a go, albeit with some trepidation.

As the first programmes went to air on 28 May 1951 under the name *The Crazy People*, the group continued to rehearse and perform at the Grafton Arms. James Thomas, writing in the *News Chronicle* in 1951, reported that 'Goon humour is obviously crazy and clever. It will either be loved or detested.'

If early reactions were anything to go by, it seemed as though the latter might have been more applicable. It seemed too fast for an audience more in tune with domestic situation comedies or short turns by comics. There was also a danger that the antics on stage at the Aeolian Hall (where *The Crazy People* was recorded) wouldn't translate well into the home of the listener. Milligan wholeheartedly rejected these criticisms and insisted that the audience learn to keep up or not listen at all.

By the end of the first series it seemed as though the audience took heed of Milligan's order, and listening figures rose from 370,000 for the early shows to a quite respectable 1.8 million. The series ran for seventeen episodes and is erratic to say the least.

Some of the familiar characters crop up, like Eccles and Bloodnok, but they are mere skeletons compared with the fleshed-out, rounded characters that became so familiar to the nation. There was a special one-off show to coincide with Christmas, which was broadcast after the series finished on 26 December 1951. *Cinderella* was based on the popular pantomime and starred Lizbeth Webb in the title role with Graham Stark as Prince Charming and the Goons as everyone else. This was one of the few times a woman appeared with the Goons.

The Crazy People was essentially a series of unrelated sketches interspersed with music, courtesy of the Stargazers. The producer of this series was a very young Dennis Main Wilson who went on to become one of the great comedy producers of the 1950s, 1960s and 1970s.

The BBC allowed the name of the show to be changed for the second series to ***The Goon Show***. It began on 22 January 1952 and ran for 25 episodes, one having had to be cancelled after the death of George VI. Immediately the changes in format were noticeable with the number of sketches honed down to four and no Stargazers by episode seven. Secombe emerged as a leading man with his alter-ego Neddie Seagoon beginning to take shape. Secombe, a well-known baritone, also sang in these episodes. In episode eight the four sketches were dropped in favour of the single plot, which became the norm for all Goon shows.

While Milligan was finding his own unique writing style with help from Jimmy Grafton and Larry Stephens, a professional scriptwriter, he was also

Timothy (Weeks 1–5), Wallace Greenslade (Weeks 6–30)

Music by
Max Geldray, Ray Ellington (Weeks 28–30)

Produced by
Peter Eton, Jacques Brown (Week 15)

Friday 2 October 1953–Monday 19 April 1954
Weeks 1–20 broadcast on Fridays
Weeks 21–30 broadcast on Mondays
Broadcast on the Home Service

Episode List
(This is the first series when the single plot lines were introduced and names of episodes are more definite)

1. *The Dreaded Piano Clubber*; 2. *The Man Who Tried To Destroy London's Monuments*; 3. *The Ghastly Experiments of Dr Hans Eidelburger*; 4. *The Building of Britain's First Atomic Cannon*; 5. *The Gibraltar Story*; 6. *Through the Sound Barrier in an Airing Cupboard*; 7. *The First Albert Memorial to the Moon*; 8. *The Missing Bureaucrat*; 9. *Operation Bagpipes*; 10. *The Flying Saucer Mystery*; 11. *The Spanish Armada*; 12. *The British Way*; 13. *The Giant Bombardon*; 14. *Ten Thousand Fathoms Down in a Wardrobe*; 15. *The Missing Prime Minister*;

16. *Dr Jekyll and Mr Crun*; 17. *The Mummified Priest*; 18. *The History of Communications*; 19. *The Kippered Herring Gang*; 20. *The Toothpaste Expedition*; 21. *The Case of the Vanishing Room*; 22. *The Great Ink Drought of 1902*; 23. *The Greatest Mountain in the World*; 24. *The Collapse of the British Railway Sandwich System*; 25. *The Silent Bugler*; 26. *Western Story*; 27. *The Saga of the Internal Mountain*; 28. *The Invisible Acrobat*; 29. *The Great Bank of England Robbery*; 30. *The Siege of Fort Knight*

Special programmes

Archie in Goonland

Written by
Spike Milligan and Eric Sykes

The Cast
Peter Brough and Archie Andrews, Spike Milligan, Peter Sellers, Harry Secombe and Hattie Jacques

Music by
BBC Variety Orchestra with Paul Fenhoulet

Produced by
Roy Speer

Broadcast on 11 June 1954
Broadcast on the Home Service

gaining a reputation for being difficult to work with. This was frustrating to him, as he was attempting to break new ground with sound effects, which demanded the cooperation of the BBC studio managers.

Throughout the second series Michael Bentine was showing signs that he might leave. Bentine's relentless desire to achieve absolute perfection was a long way off Milligan's wavelength. Milligan was still emerging as the writer of the group and was also beginning to have his own fixed ideas about the direction of the show.

Parting was inevitable and critics of the Goons were fast to spread rumours about an acrimonious split when in reality Bentine left to work on his own, with much success. This was in retrospect the best thing that could have happened to ***The Goon Show*** as Bentine and Milligan could not continue a professional relationship. The other change to ***The Goon Show*** was the loss of Dennis Main Wilson, who didn't have the kind of control over the cast that they needed.

The appointment of Peter Eton as replacement producer marked a milestone in the career of ***The Goon Show***. He was to bring about a change for the better, being quite stern when it came to self-indulgence by the cast. As a radio drama producer he had been experimenting with certain radio techniques which he wanted to continue with. He knew how to use the static microphones to give depth to a scene and he experimented with new and very different techniques, like artificial reverberation, which could create the impression that an actor was in a small room or a huge cathedral. This desire to explore production techniques married perfectly Milligan's increasingly adventurous use of sound effects.

Series three started on 11 November 1952 and ran

for 25 weeks, one week fewer than planned, owing to the death of Queen Mary. The format underwent yet another change, with three sketches being separated by two musical items, one by Ray Ellington and the other by Max Geldray. Eton was trying to persuade Milligan to writer longer stories rather than the sketch ideas, which did feature recurring characters – but in no way did the show's format differ in any real way from other shows on the BBC. There was even the resident BBC Dance Orchestra, not an immediate coupling, one might think, but necessary when there were two musical items in each show to break up the sketches. The BBC Dance Orchestra left after the first two series, to be replaced by a group of session players under the baton of Wally Stott, the Goons' resident musical arranger.

Milligan's health was showing signs of rapid deterioration throughout the second series and, by the fourth show of series three, he was in the throes of a nervous breakdown and was admitted to hospital. Milligan's collaborators on the scripts now took over and the next twelve episodes were largely written by Larry Stephens and Jimmy Grafton with Milligan increasingly adding material from his hospital bed. The vocally dexterous Peter Sellers took over Milligan's voices with Dick Emery and Graham Stark stepping in to help flesh out the cast.

Milligan returned for show number seventeen and he brought with him a change in format. From that show on, with the odd exception, ***The Goon Show*** started with a brief introductory sketch followed by a complete story, just the kind of change that Peter Eton had been hoping for. Series four saw ***The Goon Show*** become the show that was so influential. Two changes that happened at the start of this series, which

The Starlings

Written by
Spike Milligan

The Cast
Spike Milligan, Peter Sellers, Harry Secombe and Andrew Timothy

Produced by
Peter Eton

Broadcast on 31 August 1954
Broadcast on the Home Service

Series 5 – (26 Weeks)

Written by
Spike Milligan (Weeks 1–6); Spike Milligan and Eric Sykes (Weeks 7–26)

The Cast
Peter Sellers, Harry Secombe, Spike Milligan, John Snagge (Week 20), Valentine Dyall (Week 6), Charlotte Mitchell (Week 14); Announcer: Wallace Greenslade

Music by
Max Geldray

Produced by
Peter Eton

Tuesday 28 September 1954–Tuesday 22 March 1955
Broadcast on Tuesdays
Broadcast on the Home Service

Episode List
1. *The Whistling Spy Enigma*; 2. *The Lost Gold Mine*; 3. *The Dreaded Batter-Pudding Hurler of Bexhill-On-Sea*; 4. *The Phantom Head*

Shaver of Brighton; 5. *The Affair of the Lone Banana*; 6. *The Canal*; 7. *The Lurgi Strikes Britain*; 8. *The Mystery of the Marie Celeste*; 9. *The Tram from Clapham*; 10. *The Booted Gorilla*; 11. *The Spanish Suitcase*; 12. *Dishonoured or The Fall of Neddie Seagoon*; 13. *Forog*; 14. *Ye Bandit of Sherwood Forest*; 15. *Nineteen Eighty-Five*; 16. *The Case of the Missing Heir*; 17. *China Story*; 18. *Under Two Floorboards*; 19. *The Missing Scroll*; 20. *Nineteen Eighty-Five* (re-recorded episode 15); 21. *The Sinking of Westminster Pier*; 22. *The Fireball of Milton St*; 23. *The Six Ingots of Leadenhall St*; 24. *Yehti*; 25. *The White Box of Great Bardfield*; 26. *The End*

Series 6 – (27 Weeks)

Written by
Spike Milligan (Weeks 3–17, 19–24); Spike Milligan and Eric Sykes (Weeks 1, 2, 18); Spike Milligan and Larry Stephens (Weeks 25–27)

The Cast
Peter Sellers, Harry Secombe, Spike Milligan, John Snagge (Weeks 14, 23, 26), Valentine Dyall (Week 20), Charlotte Mitchell (Week 18); Announcer: Wallace Greenslade

began on 2 October 1953, were hugely significant. First was the indication of *character* names in the script (as opposed to the actors' names) and the second was that all the shows were now being recorded on magnetic tape, which made editing possible.

The changing of the names in the script from the actors' to the characters' indicated that the characters were beginning to take on a life of their own, and this came to be reflected when the characters started to play other characters. A comedy working on three levels, as ***The Goon Show*** did, was certainly a first in radio. A revolution in recording techniques meant shows were now being recorded on tape, opening up limitless creative possibilities to Milligan. Previously, he'd had to rely solely on the cooperation of studio managers and sound-effects technicians to achieve the kind of results he wanted. Now there was no excuse: it could be achieved in the editing.

The one personnel change to this new series – which at 30 shows made this the longest series of all – was the replacement announcer of Wallace ('Bill') Greenslade, who stepped into Andrew Timothy's shoes. Greenslade was more than just an announcer: he was often the voice of sanity, passing comments and remarks about the proceedings.

After the first three shows there was a continuous plot and characters were being fully fleshed out. This new-found format marked a change in Milligan, who finally seemed to achieve what he had envisaged when *The Crazy People* would rehearse in Grafton's pub. Grafton, by leaving as script editor, acknowledged that Milligan had at last developed his own unique style and seemed to be able to stand on his own feet. Larry Stephens left after show 20 and for the first time Milligan was the sole scriptwriter. Still, the audience

The Goon Show 1951 featuring (from left to right) Michael Bentine, Harry Secombe, Peter Sellers and Spike Milligan. Producer Dennis Main Wilson on the floor. *(BBC Photograph Library and Archives)*

Eric Barker 1953.
(BBC Photograph Library and Archives)

Just Fancy 1952 featuring Eric Barker and Pearl Hackney.
(Lew Lane Collection)

Ray's a Laugh 1953 featuring Ted Ray. *(BBC Photograph Library and Archives)*

Come to Charlee 1953 featuring Charlie Chester, Michael Bentine and Cardew Robinson. *(BBC Photograph Library and Archives)*

In All Directions 1953 featuring Peter Ustinov and Peter Jones. *(BBC Photograph Library and Archives)*

Life with the Lyons 1953 featuring the family in a shot for the feature film of the same title. *(Lew Lane Collection)*

Take it From Here 1953 featuring (seated left to right) Dennis Norden, Charles Maxwell and Frank Muir, (standing) Jimmy Edwards, June Whitfield, Alma Cogan and Dick Bentley. *(BBC Photograph Library and Archives)*

Hancock's Half Hour 1956 featuring (left to right) Kenneth Williams, Tony Hancock, Bill Kerr and Sid James. *(BBC Photograph Library and Archives)*

The Al Read Show 1954 featuring Al Read. *(BBC Photograph Library and Archives)*

Round the Bend 1957 featuring (left) Nat Temple, David Nettheim and Benny Lea;(right) Ronald Fletcher, Michael Bentine and Marie Benson. *(BBC Photograph Library and Archives)*

Educating Archie 1959 featuring Bruce Forsyth, Archie and Peter Brough. *(Lew Lane Collection)*

The Clitheroe Kid 1960 featuring Jimmy Clitheroe. *(BBC Photograph Library and Archives)*

The Navy Lark 1961 featuring Leslie Phillips. *(BBC Photograph Library and Archives)*

was slow to pick up and the figures increased only marginally over the whole of the fourth series compared with the third series.

Between the fourth and fifth series were two programmes that were a departure from the usual Goon shows. The first, called *Archie in Goonland*, was not so successful but was interesting as it combined Milligan's writing with another great comedy mind, Eric Sykes. They merged ***The Goons*** with the perennial favourite radio classic, *Educating Archie*, which at one time had Harry Secombe as the tutor to Archie Andrews. *The Radio Times* on 11 June trailed the show with these words: 'Peter Brough and Archie Andrews enter Goonland via a mousehole and are immediately involved in a fantastic adventure involving the destruction of London – and mice!' No recordings survive of this, although it seems that this was not such a popular experiment. It did mean that Eric Sykes joined Milligan in writing most of series five.

The second one-off show turned out to be one of the best known of all ***Goon Shows***, even though it was not really a *Goon* show. *The Starlings* was broadcast on 31 August 1954 on the Home Service and was an attempt by Milligan to make sure that real life did not outdo the Goons. The story came about when an article appeared in the *Manchester Guardian* about an attempt by the local councils to rid public buildings of infestations of starlings.

In Milligan's story, Bluebottle suggests that explodable bird-lime is applied to all the buildings and then on detonation the starlings will be so frightened they will leave and not return. An official ceremony is presided over by the Duchess Boil de Spudswell (Sellers giving a very good impression of the Queen, much to the disgust of BBC officials), and all goes well

Music by
Max Geldray

Produced by
Peter Eton (Weeks 1–21), Pat Dixon (Weeks 22–27)

Tuesday 20 September 1955–Tuesday 3 April 1956
Week 10 broadcast on 3 April (due to a train crash on 22 November 1955, and was replaced by a repeat of *The China Story*)
Broadcast on Tuesdays
Broadcast on the Home Service

Episode List
1. *The Man Who Won The War*; 2. *The Secret Escritoire*; 3. *The Lost Emperor*; 4. *Napoleon's Piano*; 5. *The Case of the Missing CD Plates*; 6. *Rommel's Treasure*; 7. *Foiled by President Fred*; 8. *Shangri-la Again*; 9. *The International Christmas Pudding*; 10. *The Pevensey Bay Disaster*; 11. *The Sale of Manhattan*; 12. *The Terrible Revenge of Fred Fu-Manchu*; 13. *The Lost Year*; 14. *The Greenslade Story*; 15. *The Hastings Flyer – Robbed*; 16. *The Mighty Wurlitzer*; 17. *The Raid of the International Christmas Pudding*; 18. *Tales of Montmartre*; 19. *The Jet-Propelled Guide NAAFI*; 20. *The House of Teeth*; 21. *Tales of Old Dartmoor*; 22. *The Choking Horror*; 23. *The Great Tuscan Salami Scandal*; 24. *The*

Treasure in the Lake; 25. *Scradje*; 26. *The Man Who Never Was*

Special Programmes

The Missing Christmas Parcel – Post Early For Christmas

Written by
Eric Sykes

The Cast
Peter Sellers, Harry Secombe, Spike Milligan

Devised and produced by
Peter Eton and John Lane

Broadcast on 8 December 1955

China Story

Written by
Spike Milligan and Eric Sykes

The Cast
Peter Sellers, Harry Secombe, Spike Milligan

Devised and produced by
Dennis Main Wilson

Broadcast on 29 August 1956 from the National Radio Show

Series 7 – (27 Weeks)

Written by
Spike Milligan (Weeks 2 and 23); Spike Milligan and Larry Stephens (Weeks 1, 3–22, 24–27)

The Cast
Peter Sellers, Harry Secombe, Spike Milligan, Valentine

despite the huge amount of damage to St Martin-in-the-Fields and the fact that the starlings do reappear. The new invention of rice puddings hurled by catapults is used to deal with the pests and peace is restored.

The BBC Transcription Services, the body of people who recorded shows for broadcast overseas, selected ***The Goon Show*** as one of the best BBC programmes and worthy of being taped for worldwide broadcast. From series five onwards ***The Goon Show*** could be heard in New Zealand, South Africa, Australia and a host of other countries. Listeners in Britain rose to a very respectable 4.5 million, which might have been due to better billing in *The Radio Times*, which now listed full cast lists and plot outlines.

The first six scripts of series five were penned by Milligan alone, with the remainder by both Milligan and Eric Sykes, following their collaboration on *Archie In Goonland*. The first show to be released on the BBC Radio Collection of ***Goon Show*** *Classics* is *The Dreaded Batter Pudding Hurler of Bexhill-on-Sea*, the third show from this series. It has come to be regarded as one of the first 'classic' episodes. Minnie Bannister is struck by batter puddings while out on the cliff with Henry Crun; then an epidemic of 38 hurled batter puddings besieges the town of Bexhill-on-Sea. Scotland Yard is called in to solve the mystery:

GRYTPYPE-THYNNE: **Inspector Seagoon?**

SEAGOON: **Yes.**

GRYTPYPE-THYNNE: **My name is Hercules Grytpype-Thynne, Special Investigation. This batter pudding hurler.**

SEAGOON: **Yes?**
GRYTPYPE-THYNNE: **He's made a fool of the police.**
SEAGOON: **I disagree. We were fools long before he came along.**
GRYTPYPE-THYNNE: **You silly twisted boy. Nevertheless he's got to be stopped. Now Seagoon.**
SEAGOON: **Yes, yes, yes, yes, yes, yes, yes, yes.**
GRYTPYPE-THYNNE: **Please. Don't do that.**

Deviation from the plot was a regular feature, and when Seagoon hails a cab to go to the Bexhill Gas Works the sound of a bagpipe record slows down to a halt, and when he gives the order to drive the record speeds up to normal speed. Wallace Greenslade interjects:

> Listeners may be puzzled by a taxi sounding like bagpipes. The truth is, it is all part of the BBC's new economy campaign. They have discovered that it is cheaper to travel by bagpipes. Not only are they more musical but they come in a wide variety of colours. See your local bagpipe officer and ask for particulars. You won't be disappointed. It's all rather confusing really.

The action switches to Africa, when Minnie receives a letter from the hurler postmarked 'Africa'. Seagoon calls for his 'power-packed giant assistant' Bluebottle:

BLUEBOTTLE: **I heard you call me captain. I heard my captain call me. Waits for audience applause, not a sausage.**

Dyall (Weeks 2, 5), Jack Train (Week 17), Bernard Miles (Week 16); Announcer: Wallace Greenslade

Music by
Max Geldray

Produced by
Peter Eton (Weeks 1 and 2), Pat Dixon (Weeks 3–25)

Thursday 4 October 1956–Thursday 28 March 1957
Week 6 postponed to 14 February (due to the Hungarian Revolution, and was replaced by a repeat of *The Greenslade Story*)
Broadcast on Thursdays except Weeks 10 and 13, which were broadcast Wednesdays
Broadcast on the Home Service

Episode List
1. *The Nasty Affair at the Burami Oasis*; 2. *Drums Along the Mersey*; 3. *The Nadger Plague*; 4. *The MacReekie Rising of '74*; 5. *The Spectre of Tintagel*; 6. *The Sleeping Prince*; 7. *The Great Bank Robbery*; 8. *Personal Narrative*; 9. *The Mystery of the Fake Neddy Seagoons*; 10. *What's My Line?*; 11. *The Telephone*; 12. *The Flea*; 13. *Six Charlies in Search of an Author*; 14. *Emperor of the Universe*; 15. *Wings Over Dagenham*; 16. *The Rent Collectors*; 17. *Shifting Sands*; 18. *The*

Moon Show; 19. *The Mysterious Punch-up-the-Conker*; 20. *Round The World in Eighty Days*; 21. *Insurance, the White Man's Burden*; 22. *The Africa Ship Canal*; 23. *Ill Met by Goonlight*; 24. *The Missing Boa Constrictor*; 25. *The Histories of Pliny the Elder*

Special Programmes

Robin Hood

The Cast
Peter Sellers, Harry Secombe, Spike Milligan, with Valentine Dyall and Dennis Price

Produced by
Pat Dixon

Recorded on 2 December 1956 for broadcast overseas
Recorded for the Transmission Service

Operation Christmas Duff

The Cast
Peter Sellers, Harry Secombe, Spike Milligan

Produced by
Pat Dixon

Broadcast on 24 December 1956
Broadcast on BBC General Overseas Service

The Reason Why

The Cast
Peter Sellers, Harry Secombe, Spike Milligan and Valentine Dyall; Announcer: Wallace Greenslade

SEAGOON: **Bluebottle, you and I are going to Africa.**

BLUEBOTTLE: **Goody goody. Can we take sandwiches?**

SEAGOON: **Only for food. Any questions?**

BLUEBOTTLE: **No.**

SEAGOON: **I can't answer that. Can you?**

BLUEBOTTLE: **No.**

SEAGOON: **Ignorant swine. Got that down Sergeant Throat?**

THROAT: **Yes! Yes!**

Throat was a smaller character played by Milligan and sounding remarkably similar to a loud belch. Milligan invented this new 'voice' unannounced and Peter Eton was angry. In his introduction to *The Book of The Goons* (Robson Books, 1974) he wrote, 'I was furious. Rounding on Spike, I bawled him out in no uncertain terms for interrupting the rehearsal, and deeply offended him. He had created this marvellous new voice, and all I could do was blow my top!'

Looking at the episode lists for this series, one sees that the most unusual inclusion is *Nineteen Eighty-Five*, which is listed twice. Inspired by the television dramatisation, Milligan and Sykes wrote an accurate spoof of Orwell's novel *Nineteen Eighty-Four*. All the major scenes from the book have their radio counterpart. Big Brother becomes the Big Brother Corporation and Room 101 is 'the listening room' in which Seagoon is subjected to title music from such shows as *Life With The Lyons*. So popular was this episode that, five weeks after its broadcast, the team recorded it once more.

Other memorable shows from this series were *The White Box of Great Bardfield*, which is the tale of exporting snow to the Sudan in cardboard boxes, and *Ye Bandit of Sherwood Forest*, which is unusual for its inclusion of a woman, Charlotte Mitchell, in the cast. The Goons were to resurrect Robin Hood as a subject in series seven in a script loosely based on this episode.

Life With The Lyons was a hugely popular domestic situation comedy of the time starring Bebe Daniels and Ben Lyon. In *Ye Bandit of Sherwood Forest*, the phone rings and Sellers perfectly imitates Lyon by saying, 'I'll get it Bebe', which was a bit of a catchphrase at the time. Milligan often lampooned other shows in his scripts and the popularity of *Life With The Lyons* made it fair game.

In *The Book of the Goons*, Peter Eton wrote in the introduction that, when *The Terrible Revenge of Fu Manchu* was recorded, the audience were in such hysterics that over four minutes of laughter was on the tape. While Eton was editing it out, Ben Lyon, who was sitting at the next editing bench, asked what he was doing. Eton said, 'Throwing away laughter.' 'Don't do that,' Lyon said, 'we're short of laughter this week' – and it was edited into *Life With The Lyons*.

Series six in 1955 saw Milligan's writing take on even greater strength. Characters were now fully fleshed out and even when plot lines were sacrificed the listener gained more of an insight into them. Sykes co-wrote the first three episodes and Larry Stephens the last three with Milligan writing the remaining 21 episodes alone. There were three special shows, the first of which was recorded for *Children's Hour* and called *The Missing Christmas Parcel – Post Early For Christmas*. It was broadcast on 8 December 1955. *The Goons Hit Wales* was a five-and-a-half-minute insert in a St

Produced by
Jacques Brown

Broadcast on 22 August 1957
Broadcast on the Home Service

Series 8 – (26 Weeks)

Written by
Spike Milligan (Weeks 1, 16, 18, 20, 22, 24, 25); Larry Stephens (Week 11); Spike Milligan and Larry Stephens (Weeks 2–10, 12–14); Spike Milligan and John Antrobus (Weeks 23 and 26); Maurice Wiltshire and Larry Stephens (Weeks 15, 17, 19)

The Cast
Peter Sellers, Harry Secombe (except Week 1), Spike Milligan, Dick Emery (Week 1), A. E. Matthews (Week 25)

Produced by
Charles Chilton (Weeks 1–5 and 17–26), Roy Speer (Weeks 6–14), Tom Ronald (Weeks 15, 16)

Monday 30 September 1957–Monday 24 March 1958
Broadcast every Monday
Broadcast on the Home Service

Episode List
1. *Spon*; 2. *The Junk Affair*; 3. *The Burning Embassy*; 4. *The Great Regent's Park Swim*; 5. *The Treasure in the Tower*; 6. *The Space*

David's Day programme and *China Story* was a special episode recorded at the National Radio Show of 1956.

Episode 21, *Tales of Old Dartmoor*, was the last to be produced by Peter Eton, who was leaving to take a job at the newly founded Independent Television. *Tales of Old Dartmoor* is a typically Milliganesque plot with prisoner Grytpype-Thynne suggesting to Governor Seagoon that the rest of the prisoners need a holiday:

GRYTPYPE-THYNNE: **Now Neddy, the prisoners are getting restless.**

SEAGOON: **What, what, what, what, what? They had Sabrina for the cabaret last night.**

GRYTPYPE-THYNNE: **Yes, I know culture is all very well Neddy, but what the lads really need is a holiday.**

SEAGOON: **Holiday? Where?**

GRYTPYPE-THYNNE: **Well I've spoken to the lads and they've all got their hearts set on the South of France.**

SEAGOON: **But I can't let them out of prison.**

GRYTPYPE-THYNNE: **Of course not Neddy. We'll take the prison with us.**

SEAGOON: **You can't move the prison. People will talk.**

GRYTPYPE-THYNNE: **Neddy, we're going to leave a cardboard replica.**

While they're on holiday at the French penitentiary Chateau d'If, Dartmoor Prison goes missing and Seagoon goes to search for it aboard the Chateau, now floating at sea. Using Eccles's ball around his ankle

Age; 7. The Red Fort; 8. The Missing Battleship; 9. The Policy; 10. King Solomon's Mines; 11. The Stolen Postman; 12. The Great British Revolution; 13. The Plasticine Man; 14. African Incident; 15. The Thing on the Mountain; 16. The String Robberies; 17. The Moriarty Murder Mystery; 18. The Curse of Frankenstein; 19. The White Neddie Trade; 20. Ten Snowballs That Shook the World; 21. The Man That Never Was; 22. World War One; 23. The Spon Plague; 24. Tiddleywinks; 25. The Evils of Bushey Spon; 26. The Great Statue Debate

Series 9 – (17 Weeks)

Written by
Spike Milligan (except Week 7 – by Larry Stephens and Maurice Wiltshire)

The Cast
Peter Sellers (except Week 11), Harry Secombe (except Week 17), Spike Milligan, Andrew Timothy (Week 14), John Snagge (Week 10); cast for Week 11 included John Snagge, Kenneth Connor, Valentine Dyall, Graham Stark and Jack Train; Announcer: Wallace Greenslade

Produced by
John Browell

they load him into the cannon and fire him at the *Dartmoor*. Grytpype-Thynne aboard the *Dartmoor* fires Eccles back at them vowing, 'Let that be a lesson to them. They can't get rid of their surplus idiots on me you know.' However the damage has been done and the *Dartmoor* sinks, leaving the cardboard replica in its place.

In his time, Peter Eton had disciplined the Goons and taught them an immeasurable amount about radio techniques. It is certainly largely due to Eton that the Goons succeeded in the way they did. In his own words, 'The difficulties inherent in working with such talent and over such long periods made my life an exciting trial, though the Bumbling Bureaucrats of the BBC presented me with far more problems than the Goons themselves.'

Ironically it was someone who had given the Goons so much encouragement when they were attempting to get *The Crazy People* on the air who took over as producer. Pat Dixon would have produced the series of *The Crazy People* had it not been for other commitments. His style was less rigid than Eton's, and the team responded well to it. But on only his second show, in February 1956, the musicians walked out on strike and Dixon was faced with a script and no one to play the music. Milligan provided the links himself and piano was played by Sellers. The show was *The Great Tuscan Salami Scandal.*

The Goons used several 'special guests', some more frequently than others. Valentine Dyall, the actor best known for providing the voice behind the 'Man In Black' in the hugely successful *Appointment With Fear*, was a regular guest in ***The Goon Show***. The BBC announcer John Snagge was also often featured in the shows and proved a champion of their cause, often fighting with BBC officials on their behalf.

Monday 3 November 1958–Monday 23 February 1959
Broadcast every Monday (except Week 12 – broadcast on Tuesday)
Broadcast on the Home Service

Episode List
1. *The Sahara Desert Statue*; 2. *I Was Monty's Treble*; 3. *The £1,000,000 Penny*; 4. *The Pam's Paper Insurance Policy*; 5. *The Mountain Eaters*; 6. *The Childe Harolde Rewarde*; 7. *The Seagoon Memoirs*; 8. *Queen Anne's Rain*; 9. *The Battle of Spion Kop*; 10. *Ned's Atomic Dustbin*; 11. *Who Is Pink Oboe?*; 12. *The Call of the West*; 13. *Dishonoured – Again*; 14. *The Secret Capsule*; 15. *The Tay Bridge*; 16. *The Gold Plate Robbery*; 17. *The £50 Cure*

Series 10 – (6 Weeks)

Written by
Spike Milligan

The Cast
Peter Sellers, Harry Secombe, Spike Milligan, John Snagge (Weeks 3, 6), Valentine Dyall (Week 5); Announcer: Wallace Greenslade

Produced by
John Browell

Thursday 24 December 1959–Thursday 28 January 1960

Broadcast every Thursday
Broadcast on the Home Service

Episode List

1. A Christmas Carol; 2. *The Tale of Men's Shirts*; 3. *The Chinese Legs*; 4. *Robin's Post*; 5. *The Silver Dubloons*; 6. *The Last Smoking Seagoon*

In series seven, a very well-known comic actor who appeared in *ITMA* as Colonel Chinstrap made his ***Goon Show*** appearance. Jack Train was special guest in an episode called *Shifting Sands*. The character of Chinstrap was renowned for being a heavy drinker and this elicits a certain response from Major Bloodnok:

BLOODNOK: **The Colonel? Chain the brandy to the wall, I know his sort.**

COLONEL: **A glass of port? I don't mind if I do.**

BLOODNOK: **By the great leather putties of Jemediah Goldstein! Colonel Chinstrap, it's you sir.**

CHINSTRAP: **Yes sir, Colonel Chinstrap is always me.**

BLOODNOK: **What a fortunate coincidence for you both.**

After a prolonged drinking session with numerous pouring sound effects that last between five and ten seconds each, Bloodnok tries to get down to business:

BLOODNOK: **Well then Colonel, I suppose you're wondering why you sent for me?**

COLONEL: **Yes I . . . Just a minute. Quiet out there. Blasted goldfish!**

BLOODNOK: **They should wear slippers, you know.**

Eton returned to the BBC to produce the first two episodes of series seven, which began in October 1956. Dixon took over once more to produce the remaining 23 shows. Larry Stephens again stepped in as co-writer for this series. Two shows were recorded for transmission overseas, *Robin Hood* (the reworking of the previous episode, *Ye Bandit of Sherwood Forest*, this time with no female in the cast) and *Operation Christmas Duff*, broadcast on Christmas Eve of 1956.

Sadly, the Goons lost another producer at the end of this series when Pat Dixon left to train as a television producer. In 1958 he died of cancer and his loss was deeply felt by the Goons and the rest of the BBC.

Series eight of ***The Goon Show*** was not of the quality of the previous few years' output. The finger of blame firmly pointed to a lack of continuity of producers. With the loss of Dixon came a line of others to fill his shoes: Charles Chilton for the first five episodes, Roy Speer for the next nine, Tom Ronald the next two and Chilton for the remaining ten. Charles Chilton proved to be the most suitable of these three but found that Goon humour was not so close to his own. One of the best-known episodes was number 25, *The Evils of Bushey Spon*, a script inspired, like many other shows, by a real-life incident.

The actor and raconteur A. E. Matthews was reported to have vehemently resisted attempts by his local council to erect a concrete lamppost outside his cottage. Whereas Milligan often just took a real-life story and blew it up out of proportion, with this script he invited A. E. Matthews to take part in the episode, which was broadcast on 17 March 1958.

The hole outside the cottage is getting bigger and Minnie and Henry are worried about its size. They are minding the cottage for their master when out of the blue they get word that he is to return:

MINNIE: **We'd better get his bath full.**
HENRY: **Don't forget he likes half water and half gin.**

MINNIE: **And he likes it half full and the other half empty Henry. Ooohh the master is coming home today. I'll lay out my new frock.**
HENRY: **He won't wear it you know.**

A. E. Matthews, playing the master, is very much playing himself and seems completely bemused by the proceedings. He remarks about the audience, 'Have they paid?' Henry Crun replies, 'Not a penny, not a penny, sir', and has to be placated by Matthews saying, 'Don't cry about it.' He deviates from the script, making no apologies:

MATTHEWS: **Do you know Camden Theatre . . . ?**
HENRY: **Camden Theatre, yes.**
MATTHEWS: **It's a bit of a thrill to me because –**
HENRY: **Yes?**
MATTHEWS: **In a . . . no I've messed that up, never mind.**

Even while he's being himself the rest of the cast insist on staying in character:

MATTHEWS: **The night before last I was on the television.**
MINNIE: **Oooooh. Oh sir, we told you not to go. It was very cold that night, you shouldn't have gone out.**
HENRY: **You shouldn't have gone out sir.**
MATTHEWS: **You're over-acting, leave it be.**

When he does attempt to communicate with them he loses patience very quickly:

MATTHEWS: **I tell you, you act too much.**
HENRY: **You've given her the vapours sir.**
MATTHEWS: **What?**
HENRY: **You've given her the vapours.**
MATTHEWS: **I didn't quite get it.**
HENRY: [Slower] **Your outburst gave her the vapours.**
MATTHEWS: **Oh, we'll leave that, I can't understand it.**

When questioned about what to do with the hole, he bravely and honestly says, 'On the whole it's done me a lot of good; it's got me two or three jobs.' That was the last line in the show, but after the final credits he cannot resist the urge to complain:

MINNIE: **Go home now, Mattie.**
MATTHEWS: **But I haven't even started yet. Do you mean I've finished?**
HENRY: **But we're very worried, the cold might . . .**
MATTHEWS: **Do you realise that is the shortest appearance I've ever made in my life? Can I have a drink now?**

In conjunction with the 26 shows in this series, the BBC Transcription Services wanted another fourteen recorded at the same time, and Milligan was finding this a tremendous strain. New listeners would have been baffled as to what on earth they were listening to and too many of the shows relied on a knowledge of previous episodes and their characters.

Larry Stephens remained as a co-writer until show nineteen at the beginning of 1958 when he left because of ill health.

The situation with producers, coupled with the task of reworking fourteen extra scripts for the Transcription Services, really took its toll, and many episodes were well below previous standards. Milligan was adamant that the producer situation be resolved for the next series. He demanded the reinstatement of Bobby Jaye, who had been studio manager for the previous three series. Jaye, being underqualified, did not get the job but another ***Goon Show*** studio manager, John Browell, who worked under Peter Eton, was chosen, as he was already a junior producer.

Browell inherited some of Eton's ability to tighten the reins around the Goons and the show was speeded up considerably. But listening figures had dropped from the heights of 4.5 million to 1 million, probably because new listeners found it impossible to keep up with the pace of writing. This series was written by Milligan with the exception of only one show, *The Seagoon Memoirs*, which was penned by Larry Stephens and Maurice Wiltshire.

Although audience figures had dropped, there were some vintage episodes from this series: *The Sahara Desert Statue*, *I Was Monty's Treble* and *Dishonoured Again* (a reworking of the fifth series episode *Dishonoured or The Fall of Neddie Seagoon*). Two episodes in the series were recorded without group regulars. *Who Is Pink Oboe?* lacked Peter Sellers, who was ill with a throat infection, and *The £50 Cure*, the last in the series, went ahead without Secombe, who was in bed with the mumps.

Although series nine was intended to be the last, the die-hard fans were not prepared to let the Goons disappear without a fight. Despite being handed a petition which called for the continuation of the show 'for ever and ever', the BBC commissioned a series of only six shows. John Browell continued as producer and Milligan wrote the shows. Once again the shows were inaccessible to non-regular Goon listeners and there were definite signs of strain in the writing.

Although there were no more radio Goon shows with the exception of *The Last Goon Show Of All*, recorded in 1972, fans were treated to two series of *The Telegoons*. These were fifteen-minute puppet films based on the radio scripts and written by Maurice Wiltshire. Seagoon, Bluebottle, Eccles, Minnie, Henry and Grytpype-Thynne were all re-created as puppets for a new audience on BBC TV in 1963 and 1964. Die-hard Goon fans didn't respond well to this deviation from their beloved radio show but *The Telegoons* was successful in reaching a new audience of mainly children.

The Last Goon Show Of All was a special one-off programme as part of the BBC's Silver Jubilee celebrations in 1972. Radio 4 recorded the show in mono (even in an age when stereo was becoming the norm) and BBC TV were filming for broadcast on television on 5 October 1972. BBC Transcription Services made their own recording of the show, which was the version that ended up as the record.

Each Goon went his separate way and pursued a very successful career. Secombe continued his work on radio but became a big star of stage, notably in the Dickensian musical *Pickwick*, before taking a seemingly endless journey on the *Highway* for television.

Milligan continued to work in radio and his first solo series as a star and writer was called *The Omar Khayyam Show*. This show was adapted from *Idiot's Weekly*, which Milligan had written and performed for

Australian radio. It retained an antipodean feel with the cast being made up of both British and Australian actors – Bill Kerr, John Bluthall, Brian Wilde, a very young Barry Humphries and Bob Todd. The series began in 1963 and was produced by Charles Chilton (who had produced the eighth series of ***The Goon Show***) and music was by George Chisholm and his Jolly Jazzers.

Sellers, by the end of the 1950s, had become a household name as a film actor of repute. By the early 1960s he was spending most of his time in Hollywood before going on to become one of the most famous comedy actors ever. Sadly he died in 1980 from a massive heart attack. Ironically this happened the night before a Goon reunion.

The influence of this radio show is impossible to chart. So many people have cited Spike Milligan and the Goons as an influence, from Ben Elton to Monty Python. Peter Eton sums up the ethos of ***The Goon Show*** very well:

> Unlike any other comedy programme of its time, ***The Goon Show*** was less a criticism of any social system than a bold and melodramatic rearrangement of all life. It was obliged to create a nightmare landscape of its own and to people it with men, beasts and machines terribly at variance with the observable universe.

Regular Characters

Major Dennis Bloodnok Ghastly but lovable bounder and coward from the Rajputana Rifles inspired by a real Indian Army major Sellers had encountered. Bloodnok is one of the first regular characters to appear and is first heard in *The Crazy People.*

As the series continue, Bloodnok becomes more and more mercenary and will take on any job as long as there is cash in it. But as he becomes more greedy his health deteriorates and his entrances are accompanied by cries of pain and agony. (*Played by Sellers*)

Bluebottle A high-voiced scoutmaster provided the inspiration for this, one of the most popular Goon characters. Bluebottle came into being in the third series sporadically, and more regularly in the fourth. He is a schoolboy who can be coerced into doing the most ridiculously dangerous tasks with the meagre reward of dolly mixtures. Bluebottle is plagued with bad luck and more often than not is on the receiving end of explosions and gunshots from which he ends up 'deaded'. (*Played by Sellers*)

Henry Crun Full name: Henry Albert Sebastopol Queen Victoria Crun. One of Sellers' great characterisations. He is a Dickens-inspired Victorian relic who is forever inventing things. He is the one Seagoon regularly turns to with requests for obscure machines. He has an infuriating short-term memory loss. His stock catchphrases were 'Morning . . . morning . . .' and 'You can't get the wood, you know.' (*Played by Sellers*)

Eccles The peabrained idiot and best friend of Bluebottle, Eccles is the original Goon. He is a regular as far back as *The Crazy People* but was initially played by Sellers. By the end of the series Milligan had taken the character over and the customary idiot voice is in place. He is a lovable idiot, ready to try anything and always willing to hold up his hands and admit that he's made a mess of it. (*Played by Milligan*)

Count Jim Moriarty The master criminal and con-man who becomes fully realised at the start of the fourth series. He is inspired by the Conan Doyle master criminal of the same name, but Milligan's creation lives in France. He is to be found at the root of most evil occurrences in ***The Goon Show*** and becomes more dangerous when he teams up with Grytpype-Thynne. (*Played by Milligan*)

Hercules Grytpype-Thynne Another arch villain who appears as early as the second series but gets named only in the fifth series. His first lines are marked in the scripts as Sanders and he was closely modelled on the actor George Sanders known for his silky smooth voice. (*Played by Sellers*)

Miss Minnie Bannister The sax-playing old lady, once the toast of the Indian Army, now living with Henry Crun. She admits at first to being Henry's auntie and then Bluebottle's auntie. Minnie likes a drink and often appears worse from the effects of alcohol. (*Played by Milligan*)

Neddy Seagoon The leek-chewing Ned of Wales and reluctant hero. Secombe's portrayal is loud and over the top, and that of someone who is always willing to burst into song at the drop of a hat. He is a man of honour willing to tackle any job so that right can triumph over evil. He is a man of integrity and an inspiration to Bluebottle and Eccles who look to him as their leader. (*Played by Secombe*)

Round The Bend

1959–1960

The one and only split within the Goons saw one of the original Crazy People leave to forge his own solo career. Michael Bentine was always a lone comedy force, although he did share his off-the-wall humour with his Goonish counterparts. The split was not, as the press at the time liked to point out, an acrimonious one.

As he wrote in his autobiography, *The Long Banana Skin*, 'They smelled a story and proceeded to blow the whole simple business up into some sort of personal feud between the four of us.' Bentine felt that at that stage his solo career was taking off and that four in a team would never work as well as three.

Directly following *The Goon Show* Bentine attempted to get a series called *The Bumblies* on to BBC children's television. However, they paid him so poorly for the show that he had to foot the bill for most of the expensive production costs, leaving himself considerably out of pocket. Immediately, he left for Australia, where he was contracted to appear in various shows and stayed for two years. At this time *The Goon Show* was just hitting Australia and Bentine found himself a cult celebrity and the first of the Goons to visit the country.

An early version of ***Round the Bend*** was broadcast in 1957 on the Light Programme. Written by Bentine and David Nettheim, and produced by Pat Dixon, it ran for twelve weeks.

In 1958 Sellers and Milligan had teamed up to produce a series of shows called *Fred* and *Son of Fred*,

Transmission Details

Round The Bend

Series 1 – (12 Weeks)

Written by
Michael Bentine, Dick Lester and John Law

The Cast
Michael Bentine, Benny Lee, Peter Hawkins, Dick Lester and Jean Campbell; Announcer: Tim Gudgen

Music by
Nat Temple and his Orchestra

Produced by
Charles Chilton

Friday 2 January 1959–Friday 20 March 1959
Broadcast 1900 except Week 12 at 2000
Repeated from Monday 20 July 1959 at 2030 on the Light Programme
Broadcast on the Home Service

Series 2 – (12 Weeks)

Written by
Michael Bentine and John Law

The Cast
Michael Bentine, Ron Moody, Clive Dunn, Benny Lee, Janet

Waters, Dick Lester and Judith Chalmers; Announcer: Tim Gudgen

Music by
Nat Temple and his Orchestra

Produced by
Charles Chilton

Friday 20 May 1960–Friday 12 August 1960
Broadcast at 2145
Broadcast on the Home Service

which were produced by a young American called Dick Lester. Sellers was contracted to produce another six shows and Bentine replaced Milligan, who was working on a film. This outing was called *Yes, It's the Cathode Ray Tube Show*, which was a critical flop. The upside of this project was that Bentine was beginning to hone his writing style. He had forged a friendship, through Sellers, with Dick Lester founded on a shared enthusiasm for the same kind of comedy. The result was the series called ***Round The Bend***.

The Radio Times writes of Bentine:

> Few professional funny men have displayed a greater wealth of comic invention than Michael Bentine. Not for him a long-term strategy in dealing with an audience: shock tactics are his strong suit.

Round The Bend is certainly an apt title for a show that promised the unpredictable and lived up to its zany name. It was written by Bentine with Dick Lester and John Law. Pat Dixon produced the show initially, but, when he was tragically struck down with cancer, Charles Chilton produced the remainder of the shows, which ran initially for 12 episodes on Friday nights. The cast for this loosely based sketch-format show included Bentine, Benny Lee, Peter Hawkins, Dick Lester and Jean Campbell.

The style was Goonish and demanded that the imagination of the listener be taken to new heights. In one sketch an RAF aerobatic pilot is having his voice relayed over the PA system at the Farnborough Air Show. However, a fault on the line connects him to a public phone box where a young man is speaking to his girlfriend. At the commander's orders of 'Close up there – you're lagging behind!' the phone box takes off and joins the rest of the air display team in aerobatic manoeuvres.

This was a refreshing comedy programme which Bentine describes as 'that strange effective series.'

With the second series, Bentine dispensed with the studio audience. This was still highly irregular for light-entertainment radio programmes. His innovative techniques went against the grain and resulted, among other things, in his adapting a television show for radio, which was the opposite of the norm, whereby radio plays and shows were adapted for the small screen.

Bentine's adaptation ended up as four minutes of sound effects with no speech. ***Round The Bend*** was perhaps too far advanced for audiences who only just came to grips with the speed and sound effect techniques of *The Goon Show.*

Bentine wrote the second series with John Law and was joined by Ron Moody, Clive Dunn, Benny Lee, Janet Waters, Dick Lester and Judith Chalmers. Charles Chilton continued to produce, with music by Nat Temple and his Orchestra. The announcer for both series was Tim Gudgen.

Happy-Go-Lucky (including The Eager Beavers)

August–December 1951

Transmission Details

Happy-Go-Lucky

14 Weeks

Written by
Ralph Peterson, John Law, Bill Craig, John Vyvyan; later: Rona Ricardo, Galton and Simpson

Featuring
Derek Roy with guests throughout the series: Suzette Tarri, Benny Hill, Charlie Chester, Beryl Reid, Dick Emery, Avril Angers, Ken Platt, Terry-Thomas, Leon Cortez, Miriam Karlin, Janet Brown

Music by
Stanley Black and the Augmented Dance Orchestra, with Jack and Daphne Barker, Harry Noble and Francis King and the Sam Browne Singers

Produced by
Roy Speer (last two shows produced by Dennis Main Wilson)

This variety series was hosted by the comedian Derek Roy and included a feature called 'Wedding Anniversary', in which a couple with an anniversary coinciding with the date of the broadcast were introduced and treated to a studio rendition of their favourite song.

A song from the Naughty Nineties came from Doreen Harris and the Bar-Room Ballad Four, and 'Rhapsody at Random' was the name of a musical request feature, presented by Peggy Cochrane.

This series is now remembered chiefly for its regular scouting sketch, 'The Eager Beavers'. The boy scouts were Bill Kerr as Dilberry, Peter Butterworth as Botterill and Graham Stark as Creep, while Tony Hancock played the leader, Mr Ponsonby.

Happy-Go-Lucky is also significant in that it was one of the first shows in which Tony Hancock was associated with the writers Ray Galton and Alan Simpson.

2 August 1951–10 December 1951
Broadcast mostly Thursdays 2100–2200; fortnightly from Week 8; Mondays from Week 9
Broadcast on the Light Programme

The Al Read Show

1951–1968

Born in Salford in 1909, Al Read came to show business fairly late in life. He'd started his working life as a businessman, having inherited the family's meat-processing factory, which was, incidentally, very successful – his grandfather being the first person to pack meat in tins.

'As a brilliant observer of the domestic scene, a master reporter of life as we know it, Al Read is supreme in what one may call the "natural" school of comedy,' remarked *The Radio Times*.

By the time he was 23, he had worked his way up through the ranks of the company to become the director of the business which, as he later reflected, was a huge advantage to him as a comedian. He differed from other comedians of the time in that he was one of the first genuinely observationalist comics. Before his radio career began, he gained a considerable reputation both as an after-dinner speaker and amateur performer. His brand of comedy, which he called 'pictures from life', developed from '. . . my sales talk, telling jokes on my rounds, practising different accents and creating thumbnail sketches of the more colourful characters in our neighbourhood' – Al Read (1983).

Read initially performed at the Grocers' Society annual dinner-dance before gaining a reputation as a talented amateur. He had befriended many other performers through his golf club and began writing material for them, most notably *The Artist Sketch* for Sid Field.

Shortly after World War Two, he was improvising a routine (depicting a visit to the doctor) for his friends

Transmission Details

First Broadcast
In *Variety Fanfare*, heralding variety in the north. Resident comedian was Dave Morris.

Broadcast Friday 10 March 1950
Broadcast on the Light Programme

The Al Read Show
One-off, leading to several series of ***The Al Read Show*** throughout the 50s

Featuring
Al Read, Jimmy Edwards, Pat Kirkwood, the Kordites, Northern Variety Orchestra conducted by Vilem Tausky

18 September 1951
Broadcast 2100–2130
Broadcast on the Light Programme
(Read also contributed to the National Radio Awards show in 1951 – Sunday 2 March on the Light, 2100–2200)

***The Al Read Show* First Occasional Series – (5 Editions)**

Featuring
Jimmy Edwards, Louise Trail, the Kordites, the Augmented Northern Variety Orchestra conducted by Vilem Tausky

Produced by
Ronnie Taylor

21 September 1952–19 February 1953
Broadcast various days on various weeks, not consecutive: Week 1, Sunday 21 September, 1730–1800; Week 2, Wednesday 22 October, 2130–2200; Week 3, Thursday 4 December, 2045–2115; Week 4, Monday 29 December, 2130–2200; Week 5, Thursday 19 February, 1930–2000
Broadcast on the Light Programme
(Al Read and the Kordites broadcast from the *Daily Mail* National Radio Awards at the Scala Theatre on Sunday 1 February 1953; ***The Al Read Show*** was voted 'most promising new programme')

Second Occasional Series – (5 Editions)
(In which Al Read 'takes life as he finds it and introduces a famous guest, a highlight in music and the Lifetimers')

Featuring
The Lifetimers, the Augmented Northern Variety Orchestra (conducted by Vilem

in a Blackpool bar. He was spotted by a promoter and offered a spot in a semi-professional show at the Midland Towers holiday camp the following week. He used the same routine, about visiting the doctor, and the impresario Jack Taylor immediately gave him a Sunday spot at the Regal Theatre in Blackpool. However, an attack of nerves put his show-business career on hold for a while and he returned to his former trade saying, 'The sausages seemed like old friends.'

His full professional debut followed in due course and Read spent a week supporting Revnell and West at the Grand Theatre in Bolton. Immediately after this he was back at the sausage business and spent a short period dabbling in boxing promotion. It was not until 1950 that Read received his biggest break.

At an after-dinner speech he was giving for his best customers, he performed a sketch called *The Decorator*. The BBC producer Barker Andrews was present and Al was booked for a spot on *Variety Fanfare*. Before the show, he was introduced to Ronnie Taylor (another producer) and together they worked *The Decorator* into a proper script. The broadcast was a success. This was a fortuitous coupling which became a long professional collaboration, with Taylor involved in all Al's shows from then on.

The next step was to write a longer script built around Read. The right vehicle for his talent didn't emerge immediately and the first attempt was a show in the style of *ITMA*. A pilot was recorded and rejected by the BBC. Al even destroyed the acetate, as he was unhappy with the result. The eventual agreement with the BBC was a first in radio comedy. It was decided that Read could record a series of monthly shows in order to continue his business commitments.

In this respect, he was similar to Kenneth Horne

who managed, for several years, to hold down a job in broadcasting while continuing a career in business.

The new series of shows proved far more suitable for Read, being in the familiar 'pictures from life' style. They were recorded at the Paris Studio with regular guests that included Donald Peers and Rawicz and Landauer. These early broadcasts, the first of which was transmitted on 18 September 1951, were really one-man comedy shows. Al sang the theme 'Such is Life' and the song became his signature tune. The catchphrases 'Right Monkey!' and 'You'll be lucky – I say you'll be lucky!' (the latter originally heard at an Old Trafford turnstile) caught on with the public, and, within a few months, Al Read was a star. He did have support from Jimmy Edwards and Pat Kirkwood, but they were most certainly in the background, overshadowed by the multi-talented Read. The series won the *Daily Mail* Radio Award for the most promising new comedy show of 1951. That Christmas saw Read entertaining the Royal Family at Windsor Palace, giving a performance of *The Decorator* and *The Gardener*. Read went down so well that the King himself requested a recording of *The Gardener*.

A one-man repertory company, Al Read was a natural broadcaster. His shows were peopled by a vast gallery of Northern characters: bus conductors, teachers, irate wives ('Are you going to mow that lawn – or are we putting some sheep on it?'); shop assistants, over-inquisitive children, overbearing Johnny know-alls, nervous types who tried to assert themselves ('Ju-ju-ju-ju-ju-ju-just a minute!'); dustmen, dentists, bank-managers, dissatisfied customers, bus crews, gas men and inebriates. All were played by Al (who even produced the occasional sound-effect).

All of them involved everyday situations: a telephone

Tausky in Weeks 2–4; Alyn Ainsworth in Week 5)

Produced by
Ronnie Taylor

8 October 1953–2 September 1954
Broadcast on various days, various weeks: Week 1, Thursday 8 October 1953, 2000–2030; Week 2, Thursday 5 November 1953, 2100–2130; Week 3, Tuesday 26 January 1954, 2000–2030; Week 4, Monday 15 February 1954, 1930–2000; Week 5, Thursday 2 September 1954, 1930–2000 from the National Radio Show at Earls Court
Broadcast on the Light Programme

(Al Read featured in an excerpt from *You'll Be Lucky* on Monday 16 August 1954 on the Light – 2130–2200; from the Adelphi Theatre, London, presented by Jack Hylton and George and Alfred Black, with Shani Wallis, Lauri Lupino Lane and George Truzzi; directed by Alec Shanks and Joan Davis; introduced by Brian Johnston)

Third Occasional Series – (14 Editions)

Featuring
The Kordites, the Augmented Orchestra conducted by Alyn

Ainsworth, the Gaunt Brothers, John McHugh, the Littlewood Songshow, the Coronets
Produced by Ronnie Taylor
26 October 1954–11 August 1956
Broadcast various days, various weeks: Week 1, Tuesday 26 October 1954, 2130–2200; Week 2, Thursday 25 November 1954, 2130–2200; Week 3, Saturday 25 December 1954, 1915–1945; Week 4, Tuesday 4 January 1955, 2000–2030; Week 5, Tuesday 25 January 1955, 2000–2030; Week 6, Tuesday 22 February 1955, 2000–2030; Week 7, Friday 2 September 1955, 2100–2130; Week 8, Tuesday 25 September 1955, 1345–1415; Week 9, Tuesday 8 November 1955, 2100–2130; Week 10, Wednesday 7 December 1955, 2130–2200; Week 11, Thursday 22 December 1955, 2000–2030; Week 12, Tuesday 14 February 1956, 2130–2200; Week 13, Sunday 1 April 1956, 2130–2200; Week 14, Tuesday 11 September 1956, 1900–1930
Broadcast on the Light Programme

call, a marital row or a disgruntled wife informing her husband, at breakfast, of what he did the night before ('The next time you get one of your pals to ring up saying you're delayed at the office, tell him to ring off before he shouts, "Anyone else's missus while I'm at it?" ').

There were sketeches set in hospitals (it was nothing unusual for Al to play doctor, nurse, patient and visitor in the same routine) and doctors' waiting rooms ('All I wanted was a sick note for a day off work. He could see there was nothing wrong with me – and he made me strip right off. I wouldn't care, but I'd only washed for a stiff neck.').

Each show was a virtuoso *tour de force* with Read switching from one character to another at lightning speed. There were also songs and occasional comic monologues, in the classic Marriott Edgar style, with lines such as, 'Try it the other way round' and 'Our Joe won't be with us much longer.'

The radio shows also spawned three stage shows. In 1951, Henry Hall booked Read for a Blackpool season, which saw him successfully make the transition from radio to stage. *Right Monkey!* ran for sixteen weeks. He was later invited to fill a gap left by Frank Randle – who lasted only two weeks – in a show at the Adelphi Theatre in London. This gap-filler ended up as nearly a year-long run in 1954 entitled *You'll be Lucky*. His second London stage run, entitled *Such is Life* (1957), was equally popular. It was during the run of *Such is Life* that Read finally sold his business and joined the entertainment world full time.

A chocolate bar was marketed

called *Lucky Double*, and plans were made for *Right Monkey!* chewing gum. Two of his routines were utilised by the American comedian, Bob Newhart, who borrowed parts of Al's *The Bus Driver* and *Teaching the Wife to Drive* (which became *The Driving Instructor*).

Read's first weekly series started in 1956. ***The Al Read Show*** began on 2 December 1956 and dispensed with the supporting actors. *The Radio Times* carried the trailer: 'Al takes life as he finds it and shares the fun with some friends from the world of music.' The music came from the Kordites and the Northern Variety Orchestra, under the baton of Alyn Ainsworth.

The second weekly series began in September 1958 with music provided by The Allegros, and the run was extended to thirteen weeks finishing with *The Al Read Christmas Show* on 22 December 1958.

Compared with that of Ken Dodd and Frankie Howerd, Al Read's radio output was quite sparse. The next series wasn't broadcast until 1964 and was titled *Al Read '64*. Ronnie Taylor remained his writer and Bill Worsley produced this series of twelve shows. In December 1965 the series reverted to the original title of ***The Al Read Show*** for this, the first series to be aired on the coveted Sunday afternoon slot. Weekly guests included Rawicz and Landauer, Anita Harris, the Barron Knights, the Headliners and many others, keeping the musical content fresh for each programme.

Al Read's final series of only six shows began on 21 January 1968, and once again the musical guests were changed weekly. The only personnel change was when the Goon producer John Browell replaced Bill Worsley. Al made several television series in the 1960s but he was never really happy with the medium. He said, 'I

The Al Read Show
Series 1 – (10 Weeks)

Written by
Ronnie Taylor

Produced by
Bill Worsley

Broadcast on various days, various weeks: Week 1, Sunday 2 December 1956, 2230–2300; Week 2, Sunday 9 December 1956, 2230–2300; Week 3, 16 December 1956, 2230–2300; Week 4 (*The Al Read Christmas Show*), 1930–1955; Week 5, Saturday 2 February 1957, 1930–2000; Week 6, Sunday 3 March 1957, 1600–1630; Week 7, Sunday 24 March 1957, 1600–1630; Week 8, Monday 23 September 1957, 2100–2130; Week 9, 21 October 1957, 2100–2130; Week 10, 18 November 1957, 2100–2130
Broadcast on the Light Programme

Series 2 – (13 Weeks)

Written by
Ronnie Taylor

Produced by
Bill Worsley

Monday 29 September 1958–Monday 22 December 1958
Weeks 1, 2, 4–12 broadcast at 2100; Week 3 at 2030; Weeks 1–12, repeated following Sunday at

1830; Week 13 repeated following Monday at 1830; Week 6 repeated 7 September 1959 as part of *The Best of the Best*
Broadcast on the Light Programme

Series 3 – (12 Weeks)
Written by
Ronnie Taylor
Music by
Woolf Philips and his Orchestra
Produced by
Bill Worsley

Sunday 27 September 1964–Sunday 20 December 1964
Weeks 1–12 at 1830; Weeks 1–12 repeated following Friday at 2000
Broadcast on the Light Programme

was surrounded by a small army of people, all of whom had to justify their existence by interfering with my progress on the screen.'

Two final radio series were made in 1976 and 1983 and there was an autobiographical series of ten-minute shows called *Such is Life* in 1985. These shows gave a new generation of listeners a chance to hear this unique and influential comedian. All recordings of ***The Al Read Show*** up until 1976 were destroyed by the BBC. Lucky for us, Al kept the acetates. Al Read died in 1987 aged 78.

Series 4 – (13 Weeks)
Written by
Ronnie Taylor
Music by
Woolf Philips and his Orchestra
Produced by
Bill Worsley

Sunday 12 December 1965–Sunday 6 March 1966
Weeks 1–13 at 1330; Weeks 1–13 repeated following Thursday at 2000
Broadcast on the Light Programme

Series 5 – (6 Weeks)
Written by
Ronnie Taylor
Produced by
John Browell

Sunday 21 January 1968–Sunday 18 February 1968
Weeks 1–6 at 1400; Weeks 1–6 repeated following Wednesday at 1945
Broadcast on Radio 2 and Radio 1

Bumblethorpe

November–December 1951

Transmission Details

Bumblethorpe
8 Weeks
Written by
Spike Milligan, Larry Stephens and Peter Ling
Featuring
Avril Angers, Valentine Dyall (as Pike),

This was a weekly search by Robert Moreton, famous for his *Bumper Fun Book*, for someone who answered to the name of Bumblethorpe.

His footsteps were dogged by two crooks named Pike and Nibbs.

There were eight editions in all at the end of 1951, and some of the names that cropped up in the credits were Spike Milligan, Jack Train, Bernard Miles, Kenneth Connor and Alfred Marks.

Not only did the Goon Milligan take part but he shared the writing credits with Larry Stephens and Peter Ling.

Kenneth Connor (as Nibbs); others appearing throughout the series included Graham Stark and Spike Milligan; first and seventh Bumblethorpe was Leon Cortez; others were Alfred Marks, Jack Train, Bernard Miles, Bonar Colleano and Eric Barker

Music by
Robin Richmond at the organ, the Dance Orchestra conducted by Stanley Black

Produced by
Peter Eton

12 November 1951–31 December 1951
Broadcast Mondays 1945–2015; Week 7 Thursday 1830–1900
Broadcast on the Home Service

In All Directions

1952–1955

This ground-breaking series was written and performed by Peter Ustinov and Peter Jones (the first series was written by Ustinov only). They employed an unusual method of writing, initially improvising into a tape recorder, typing up the result, editing it, learning it, discarding it, then re-improvising it on the day of recording. Ustinov claimed that it gave 'a degree of freshness and uncertainty'.

The show had a stream-of-consciousness quality to it, with sketches and situations arising from one another. Jones and Ustinov provided an impressive range of voices and even some sound effects.

The unifying theme of the first series was a car journey, with Jones and Ustinov (as themselves) continually thwarted in their search for Copthorne Avenue. They encountered many different characters and situations in their attempt, some real, some imagined. In line with the car-journey theme, the show continually changed direction, new characters were encountered

Transmission Details

In All Directions

Series 1 – (6 Weeks)

Written by
Peter Ustinov

Edited by
Frank Muir and Dennis Norden

Featuring
Peter Ustinov, Peter Jones, the Aeolian Players and Rose Hill

Produced by
Pat Dixon

26 September 1952–31 October 1952
Broadcast Fridays 2130–2200
Broadcast on the Home Service

Special Christmas Edition
Written by
Peter Ustinov and Peter Jones
Edited by
Frank Muir and Dennis Norden
Featuring
Peter Ustinov, Peter Jones, the Aeolian Players
Produced by
Pat Dixon

24 December 1952 (Wednesday)
Broadcast on the Home Service

Series 2 – (6 Weeks)
Written by
Peter Ustinov and Peter Jones
Featuring
Peter Ustinov, Peter Jones, the Aeolian Players
Produced by
Pat Dixon
Episode titles included
Some Diversions on a Projected Transatlantic Expedition; Some Diversions in Search of Talent; Some Diversions in Search of True Love; Some Diversions in Search of Truth

(For third series, see *We're in Business*)

Jones and Ustinov were reunited in two special shows, the hour-long *In All Directions*, broadcast on the Light Programme on 26

en route, such as this aggressive pedestrian whom they met on a zebra crossing:

> It's my birthday today and I'm having a little celebration – I'm going to find a dwarf and knock the hell out of him. Goodnight!

Two characters who turned up in every show were 'those two shabby businessmen' – the wheeler-dealers Maurice and Dudley Grosvenor (catchphrase: 'Run for it!'). In one episode they were attempting to sell Frank Muir a rather dilapidated house. Ustinov played Maurice, while Jones played Dudley . . .

MAURICE: **Dry rot is only a word. Don't let yourself be frightened by a word.**

DUDLEY: **You can't possibly have dry rot *and* damp bricks as well, can you? You've got to make up your mind what you're going to complain about, sir.**

In another they were hatching a scheme whereby sick patients would be forced to build their own hospital as a form of therapy.

Rose Hill – 'the soprano with a sense of humour' – was heard in the first series; her contributions were incorporated into the storyline rather than presented as separate musical items.

The theme and frequent music links were provided by the Aeolian Players.

The quest for Copthorne Avenue was abandoned from the second series in favour of more abstract pursuits, including searches for talent, true love and truth. The third series began with a search for a 'guide, philosopher and friend' – the show's producer, Pat Dixon.

As each show ended, Ustinov and Jones were never any nearer their goal:

USTINOV: **I'll drive on.**
JONES: **Where?**
USTINOV: **Anywhere.**

December 1955, and *In Third Gear*, broadcast on the Third Programme on 29 September 1956.

We're In Business

1959–1960

Peter Jones went on to a solo twelve-week series called *Talk About Jones* in 1954, written by himself with John Jowett and featuring a cast that included Linda Joyce from *ITMA*, Mary MacKenzie and Sydney Tafler. A second series, of seven weeks, was broadcast in 1955 with largely the same personnel. Both series were broadcast on the Home Service on Friday evenings.

Peter Jones resurrected the idea of *In All Directions* but changed the characters, added a new co-writer and found a new sidekick in Harry Worth. ***We're In Business*** continued the theme of small-time businessmen out to make a fast buck. Dudley Grosvenor, played by Jones, would regularly use Harry Worth's money to attempt to make more with ridiculous schemes that were destined to fail from their instigation at their business HQ of Syd's Café.

Transmission Details

We're In Business

Series 1 – (13 Weeks)

Written by
Peter Jones and George Wadmore

The Cast
Peter Jones, Harry Worth, Paddy Edwards, Betty Marsden and Harry Locke

Produced by
Charles Maxwell

Friday 3 April 1959–Friday 26 June 1959
Broadcast 1900 (except Week 8 at

2000 and Week 10 at 2030)
Repeated on the following Monday at 2100
Broadcast on the Light Programme

Series 2 – (13 Weeks)

Written by
Peter Jones, Barry Took and Marty Feldman

The Cast
Peter Jones, Harry Worth, Irene Handl, Dick Emery and Frederick Treves

Produced by
Charles Maxwell

Friday 19 February 1960–Friday 13 May 1960
Broadcast 1945
Repeated from 24 June 1960
Broadcast on the Light Programme

The first series of ***We're In Business*** was broadcast from Friday 3 April 1959 and lasted thirteen weeks. As with its predecessor, *In All Directions*, Peter Jones was a creator and writer but had as a co-writer George Wadmore. The cast also included Paddy Edwards, Betty Marsden and Harry Locke. Charles Maxwell produced the series, which picked up an audience very quickly and ensured a second series the following year.

This second series was an example of a show much improved. The characters were now fully fleshed out and so the setting was changed. Dudley and Harry now had their business operating from a boarding-house run by the ever-lovable Irene Handl as Miss Jubilee Boot. Joining Handl in the cast was the character comic Dick Emery. The funnier scripts of this thirteen-episode series may well be attributed to the two new co-writers, Barry Took and Marty Feldman, who had already established themselves as gag-writers of the highest order.

The Guy Fawkes Show

1952

This was a one-off musical-comedy travesty of history, part of the occasional series *Sing a Song of London.*

It went out on Wednesday 5 November 1952 from 2000 to 2045 on the Light and featured Tony Hancock as Hancock the butler and his ancestor Guy Fawkes. The conspirators included Joy Nichols as Lady Fitz-Baddley and Miss Winter, Max Bygraves as Thomas Winter, her brother, and Wilbur Evans as Robert Catesby, Graham Stark as Thomas Percy and Sir Francis Tresham, and Professor Jimmy Edwards.

The George Mitchell Choir played the Citizens of London, courtiers and so forth, and music came from the Dance Orchestra conducted by Stanley Black.

The show was written by Jimmy Grafton and produced by Dennis Main Wilson.

Meet The Huggetts

1952–1961

This was a light-hearted comedy drama starring that class act Jack Warner and Kathleen Harrison.

As Joe and Ethel Huggett they were already familiar to the British public, thanks to the films *Holiday Camp* (1947), *Here Come the Huggetts* (1948), *Vote for Huggett* (1948) and *The Huggetts Abroad* (1949).

Solid dependable Joe Huggett was a former special constable. Ethel Huggett was a worrier and had a tendency to become mildly hysterical.

They had two very well-spoken children, Jane and Bobby, who lived at home, and another, Harry, who was in the forces. They also had a relentlessly cheerful neighbour called Fred Stebbins. Ethel said of him, 'He does insist on talking when other people want to interrupt.'

Some of the titles from the second series were *You Can't Please Everyone*, in which Joe 'has one of those bad patches when everything he does goes wrong'; *Emergency Call*, when Jane Huggett 'decides to take up nursing – with unexpected results'; and *Family Flitch*, when the local vicar, played by Kenneth Connor, hit upon the idea of a Family Flitch to raise funds, but

Transmission Details

Meet The Huggetts

Series 1 – (19 Weeks)

Written by
Eddie Maguire

Additional material by
Betty Davies

Featuring
Jack Warner, Kathleen Harrison, Joan Dowling, Anthony Green, Sydney Vivien, Kenneth Connor; others playing supporting roles in the first series were Graham Stark and Harry Fowler

Produced by
Peter Eton (Programme 13 by Audrey Cameron)

2 July 1953–5 November 1953
Broadcast Thursdays 2000–2030

Broadcast on the Light Programme

Series 2 – (16 Weeks)

Written by
Eddie Maguire

Featuring
Same as first series, with Vera Day as Jane Huggett; other supporting actors included Graham Stark, Dick Emery, Sam Kydd, Dorothy Summers

13 May 1954–26 August 1954
Broadcast Thursdays 2100–2130
Broadcast on the Light Programme

Series 3 – (17 Weeks)

Written by
Eddie Maguire

Featuring
Same as second series, but with Valerie Jene as Jane Huggett, Anthony Green as Bobby Huggett, Charles Leno as Fred Stebbins and Beatrice Varley as Clara Stebbins. Supporting actors included Kenneth Connor, Neal Arden, Derek Prentice and Malcolm Hayes.

Produced by
Peter Eton

9 June 1955–29 September 1955
Broadcast Thursdays 2130–2200
Broadcast on the Light Programme

scarcely realised how difficult he was making things – for a man and his wife to live in harmony is one thing, but to expect a whole family to live in complete agreement for a whole fortnight was straining human nature to its absolute limit.

Connor played as many as three supporting roles per episode.

Special Christmas Edition

Broadcast 20 December 1955 at 2030–2100 on the Light Programme

Series 4 – (20 Weeks)

Featuring
Same as third series, but with Marian Collins as Jane Huggett, Christopher Saunders as Bobby Huggett, and Molly Lumley as Clara Stebbins. Supporting actors included Kenneth Connor, Dick Emery and Martin Starkie

Produced by
Peter Eton

3 May 1956–13 September 1956
Broadcast Thursdays 1930–2000
Broadcast on the Light Programme

Series 5 – (20 Weeks)

Featuring
Same as fourth series, but with George Howell as Bobby Huggett

Produced by
Jacques Brown

12 May 1957–22 September 1957
Broadcast Sundays 1345–1415
Broadcast on the Light Programme

Series 6 – (20 Weeks)

Featuring
Same as fifth series, but with Cynthia Bizeray as Jane Huggett. Supporting actors included John Cazabon and Warren Mitchell

Produced by
Jacques Brown

11 May 1958–21 September 1958
Broadcast Sundays 1345–1425
Broadcast on the Light Programme

Series 7 – (20 Weeks)

Featuring
Same as sixth series, but with James Langley as Bobby Huggett and Alanna Boyce as Jane Huggett. Supporting actors included Charles Leno and Warren Mitchell

Produced by
Jacques Brown

22 May 1959–2 October 1959
Broadcast Fridays 1930–2000
Broadcast on the Light Programme

Series 8 – (20 Weeks)

Featuring
Same as seventh series, but with Michael Hammond as Bobby Huggett

Produced by
Jacques Brown

15 June 1960–26 October 1960
Broadcast Wednesdays 1930–2000
Broadcast on the Light Programme

Series 9 – (15 Weeks)

Featuring
Same as eighth series, but with Malcolm Ronson as Bobby Huggett

Produced by
Jacques Brown

2 June 1961–8 September 1961
Broadcast Fridays 1930–2000
Broadcast on the Light Programme

A Life Of Bliss

1953–1969

David Alexander Bliss was a shy young man and this was his story – the biography of a bachelor. Bliss was easily confused and just a little slow on the uptake.

His best friend was a female wire-haired terrier called Psyche (played by Percy Edwards).

TONY FELLOWS: **We mustn't be too hard on him – put it down to love.**
ANNE FELLOWS: **That's true – we're all the same.**
DAVID BLISS: **Same?**
TONY FELLOWS: **When we're in love.**
ANNE FELLOWS: **In a dream.**
TONY FELLOWS: **That's his natural state of course – add the two together and what do you get?**
ANNE FELLOWS: **A coma.**

For the first seven episodes David was played by David Tomlinson. Thereafter the part was taken by George Cole. Throughout the run David's girlfriends included Moira Lister (Shirley Summers), Louise Gainsborough (Jill), Lana Morris (Georgina Jay), Noelle Middleton (Joy Joel), Petula Clark (Penny Gay), Sheila Sweet (Zoe Hunter), Muriel Pavlov (Tina). There were six series of ***A Life Of Bliss***, all written by Godfrey Harrison and produced by Leslie Bridgmont.

There was a TV series in 1969.

Transmission Details

A Life of Bliss

Series 1 – (30 Weeks)

Written by
Godfrey Harrison

Featuring
David Tomlinson (replaced by George Cole from Week 7), Nora Swinburn, Esmond Knight, Gladys Henson, Moira Lister, Eileen Thorndike, Percy Edwards, Philip Ray

Music by
Louis Vass and his Orchestra, BBC Revue Orchestra conducted by Harry Rabinowitz (from Week 3), BBC Variety Orchestra conducted by Paul Fenoulhet (from Week 15)

Produced by
Leslie Bridgmont

29 July 1953–17 February 1954
Broadcast Wednesdays 1900–1930 (except Week 22, at 1845–1915)
Broadcast on the Home Service
(First 14 Weeks broadcast in London area only)

Series 2

Broadcast details not available

Series 3 – (19 Weeks)

Written by
Godfrey Harrison

Featuring
Diana Churchill, Colin Gordon, Donald Sinden, Petula Clark, Gwen Cherrill, Gladys Henson, Nicholas Parsons

Music by
BBC Variety Orchestra conducted by Paul Fenhoulet

Produced by
Leslie Bridgmont

19 October 1955–22 February 1956
Broadcast Wednesdays 1900–1930 (except Week 10, on Monday 1900–1930, and Week 15, on Wednesday 1830–1900)
Broadcast on the Home Service

Christmas Edition
One-off special

Written by
Godfrey Harrison

Featuring
Cast as Series 3, but Nora Swinburne instead of Diana Churchill

Produced by
Leslie Bridgmont

26 December 1956
Broadcast Wednesday 1900–1930
Broadcast on the Home Service

Series 4 – (16 Weeks)

Written by
Godfrey Harrison

Featuring
Cast as Series 3, plus Moira Lister and Sarah Lawson

Produced by
Leslie Bridgmont

28 May 1957–10 September 1957
Broadcast Tuesdays 2030–2100
Broadcast on the Home Service

Christmas Edition
One-off special

Written by
Godfrey Harrison

Featuring
Cast as Series 4

Produced by
Leslie Bridgmont

25 December 1957
Broadcast Wednesday 2115–2145
Broadcast on the Home Service

Series 5

Broadcast details not available

Series 6

Broadcast details not available but final episode broadcast on 3 March 1969

Just As You Please

September–November 1953

Just As You Please was a variety show from Scotland starring Jimmy Logan and Stanley Baxter, who were running their own radio station.

Also involved was Willie Joss, a Glasgow businessman for whom broadcasting was a sideline.

There were just nine editions from 29 September to 24 November, also featuring Willie Joss, Madeline Christie, Sheila Prentice, Betty Pringle and the Harlequins.

It was written by John Law and Bill Craig and produced by Eddie Fraser with music from the BBC Scottish Variety Orchestra conducted by Kemlo Stephen.

You're Only Young Once

July–August 1954

Morecambe and Wise went on to become great names in television. They were the most popular double act of the 60s and 70s, but first broadcast as long ago as 1942 in *Strike a New Note.*

They didn't broadcast regularly until 1951, when they were guests on the northern show *Variety Fanfare.*

After convincing the producer (through information leaked by a third party) that they were about to be offered a residency on the prestigious *Variety Bandbox*, they were re-booked 45 times.

You're Only Young Once (known as *YOYO*) was broadcast live from Manchester on Sunday nights. The shows consisted of sketches and music with a guest star, and were built around the framework of the Morecambe and Wise Detective Agency.

Pearl Carr played their secretary and Deryck Guyler was the office boy. Each week a guest star came to the agency for help.

Many of the sketches were derived from ideas and jokes supplied by the stars.

Transmission Details

You're Only Young Once (YOYO)

5 Weeks

Written by
Frank Roscoe

Additional material by
Morecambe and Wise

Featuring
Morecambe and Wise, Pearl Carr, Deryck Guyler (replaced by Kenneth Connor in Week 3 only), the Three Imps, the Augmented Northern Variety Orchestra conducted by Alyn Ainsworth (conducted by Vilem Tausky in Week 4); guest artists throughout the series included Robert Beatty, the Dargie Quintet, Charlie Chester, the Maple Leaf Four, John Slater, MacDonald Hobley, the Ray Ellington Quartet, the Radio Revellers and Harry Secombe

Produced by
John Ammonds

20 July 1954–17 August 1954
Broadcast Tuesdays 2000–2030
Broadcast on the Light Programme
Previously broadcast on the North of England Home Service 6 May 1954–10 June 1954

Spotlight On Laughter
2 Editions

Written by
Jack Bradley and Ray Davies

Featuring
Morecambe and Wise with Ted Lune and Brian Reece

Produced by
Roger Miller

21 March 1955 and 11 April 1955
Broadcast Mondays 1930–2000
Broadcast on the Light Programme

The Show Goes On
8 Editions
High-speed variety series introduced by Morecambe and Wise

Featuring
The Kordites, the Raymond Woodhead Choir, the Augmented Northern Variety Orchestra conducted by Alyn Ainsworth (last two shows conducted by Steve Race); guests artists included Ken Dodd, Richard Murdoch, Gladys Morgan, Robb Wilton, Betty Driver, Dennis Goodwin, Ken Platt, Peter Cavanagh, Jimmy James and Company, Stan Stennett, The Beverley Sisters, Arthur English, Ted Lune, Jimmy Young, Bill Waddington

Produced by
Geoffrey Wheeler and Ronnie Taylor

21 April 1955–9 June 1955
Broadcast Thursdays 1930–2000
Broadcast on the Light Programme

Other series were:
Laughter Incorporated (1958); *The Morecambe and Wise Show* (1966); *The Eric Morecambe and Ernie Wise Show* (1974)

Laughter Incorporated

July–September 1958

Transmission Details

Laughter Incorporated
10 Weeks

Written by
Edward Taylor

Featuring
Eric Morecambe, Ernie Wise, Peter Goodwright, Judith Chalmers, Leonard Williams, Jack Watson

This was a short-lived Morecambe and Wise series. *The Radio Times* lists this duo as 'presiding over a company of unlimited laughter-makers'.

This show was written by Edward Taylor and produced by Eric Miller. Roger Moffat was the announcer and music came from the Northern Dance Orchestra with Alyn Ainsworth, Sheila Buxton and Max Geldray.

Judith Chalmers and Peter Goodwright were listed as 'other members of the board'.

It went out for ten weeks, with scripts by Edward Taylor.

Music by
The Northern Dance Orchestra with Alyn Ainsworth, Sheila Buxton, Max Geldray

Produced by
Eric Miller

Monday 21 July 1958–Monday 22 September 1958
Broadcast 2000
Broadcast on the Light Programme

Hancock's Half Hour

1954–1959

' . . . A seemingly spontaneous stream of consciousness decorated by extraordinary inventiveness' – Barry Took.

One only has to look at the rise of Tony Hancock's career to see how powerful the medium of radio was in the 1950s. By the time the third series of ***Hancock's Half Hour*** was aired in 1955, Hancock was a national institution in demand by television, stage and film producers. His fate both professionally and personally is well documented in accounts of his life. However, here we are concerned only with an examination of the Ray Galton and Alan Simpson sitcom character, which became perhaps the greatest comic creation of the post-war years.

Many would argue that there has never been nor will be another comic character to touch Anthony Hancock. From the broadcast of the first series of ***Hancock's Half Hour*** in 1954, it was apparent that

Transmission Details

Hancock's Half Hour

Series 1 – (16 Weeks)

Written by
Ray Galton and Alan Simpson

The Cast
Tony Hancock, Bill Kerr, Moira Lister, Sidney James and Alan Simpson (except episode 6). Kenneth Williams appears in episodes 1, 2, 4, 6–12, 14, 16

Produced by
Dennis Main Wilson

Tuesday 2 November 1954–Tuesday 15 February 1955
Weeks 1–14 broadcast at 2130; Week 15 broadcast at 2000;

Week 16 broadcast at 2130
Broadcast on the Light Programme
Additional cast members
Week 1, Gerald Campion; Week 4, Paul Carpenter; Week 10, Dora Bryan and Paul Carpenter; Week 15, Peter Sellers

Series 2 – (12 Weeks)
Written by
Ray Galton and Alan Simpson
The Cast
Tony Hancock (except Weeks 1–3), Bill Kerr, Sidney James, Andree Melly, Kenneth Williams and Alan Simpson (except Week 10)
Produced by
Dennis Main Wilson

Tuesday 19 April 1955–Tuesday 5 July 1955
Week 1 broadcast at 21·30; Week 2 broadcast at 2000; Weeks 3–12 broadcast at 2130; repeated on the following Sunday at 1500
Broadcast on the Light Programme
Additional cast members
Weeks 1–3, Harry Secombe (replacing Tony Hancock); Week 4, Harry Secombe; Week 5, Dennis Wilson (piano)

this comedy differed from other domestic radio situation comedies of the 50s like *A Life of Bliss* and *Life with the Lyons*, in that the comedy was character-driven and not centred solely around domestic situations.

After meeting on a TB ward after the war (where they were both patients), Ray Galton and Alan Simpson forged a writing partnership that began with their submitting material to their hospital radio station and led to their first BBC contract, writing for Derek Roy, who was starring in *Happy Go Lucky*.

Gradually Roy used more and more of their material and Galton and Simpson were firmly on the first rung of the comedy ladder. They wrote for solo acts like Dick Emery, Peter Butterworth, Bill Kerr and Tony Hancock. Kerr and Hancock were two of the cast that made up *Forces All Star Bill*, a popular sketch show, which later shortened its name to *All Star Bill*.

After a lengthy period writing sketches and gags, Galton and Simpson concentrated on creating a sitcom that was, as Galton put it, 'non-domestic with no jokes and no funny voices, just relying on caricature and situation humour.' They were acutely aware of Tony Hancock's talent for characterisation and it was obvious to them that he should be the linchpin of this new project. It is important to stress that Tony Hancock was already a well-known radio personality, not just through *All Star Bill* but as one of the long line of tutors to the inimitable Archie Andrews in *Educating Archie*, where his catchphrase 'Flippin' kids' had become part of the national vocabulary.

The character of Hancock developed over the course of its five series, but from the outset he was a self-centred egotist, vulnerable to those he saw as potentially influential or important. His gullibility in the pursuit of a better life was the character flaw that more often than not drove the comedy. But when listening to the first show of the first series in 1954, and comparing it with one of the later classics like *The Poetry Society*, you can tell that the scripts are far more reliant on the one-liners than on character nuance. For instance, when Moira Lister is complaining about the state of Hancock's flat, or, as she puts it, 'an upholstered dustbin', she claims that 'even the mice have stopped inviting their friends round.'

With Hancock in place as the anchor of this new comedy series, the writers Galton and Simpson and producer Dennis Main Wilson were concerned to balance the comedy with the most appropriate supporting cast. Sid James, then a well-known character actor, was chosen to play the rogue element, always on hand to pull Hancock into another far-fetched scheme.

As each series progressed, the character of Sid seemed to come up with more ridiculous schemes. One such incident – which not only shows Hancock's naivety by his partaking in a criminal practice, but also shows his self-centred belief that he is the greatest comedian in the country – is highlighted when he attempts to emigrate. After being turned down by 83 countries Sid suggests that Hancock should buy a passport from him:

HANCOCK: **But I've already got a passport.**
SID: **That's no good. You've tried emigrating under your own name didn't you? Use this passport. This will get you out.**
HANCOCK: **Thanks, let's have a look. Harold Macmillan.** [PAUSE] **Harold Macmillan? Who's he?**

Series 3 – (20 Weeks)
Written by
Ray Galton and Alan Simpson
The Cast
Tony Hancock, Bill Kerr, Sidney James, Andree Melly, Kenneth Williams and Alan Simpson
Produced by
Dennis Main Wilson

Wednesday 19 September 1955–Wednesday 29 February 1956
Weeks 1–20 broadcast at 2000; repeated on the following Sunday at 1700
Broadcast on the Light Programme
Additional cast members
Week 10, Graham Stark and Ray Galton; Week 11, Dora Bryan; Week 20, John Arlott, Godfrey Evans, Colin Cowdrey and Frank Tyson

Series 4 – (20 Weeks)
Written by
Ray Galton and Alan Simpson
The Cast
Tony Hancock, Sidney James, Bill Kerr, Kenneth Williams and Hattie Jacques (after Week 5)
Produced by
Dennis Main Wilson

Sunday 14 October 1956–Sunday 24 February 1957

Weeks 1–20 broadcast at 1600; repeated on the following Tuesday at 2000 (except Week 11 – repeated at the later time of 2130 on 24 December 1956)
Broadcast on the Light Programme

Additional cast members
Weeks 1–7, Alan Simpson; Weeks 1, 2, 4, 6, 7, 9, 10, 11, Ray Galton; Week 11, Michael Anderson, Dorothy Marks; Week 20, James Robertson Justice

Series 5 – (20 Weeks)

Written by
Ray Galton and Alan Simpson

The Cast
Tony Hancock, Sidney James, Bill Kerr, Hattie Jacques and Kenneth Williams

Produced by
Tom Ronald (except Week 1 – produced by Pat Dixon)

Tuesday 21 January 1958–Tuesday 3 June 1958
Weeks 1–9, 11, 13 broadcast at 2000; Weeks 10, 12, 14 broadcast at 2031; Weeks 15–20 broadcast at 2000; repeated on the following Thursday at 2100
Broadcast on the Light Programme

The plot thickens when, on arrival at the airport, he learns that the press have got hold of the story that the Prime Minister is leaving the country on a secret visit. Sid, feeling that his ruse has gone a step too far, urges him not to talk to the press, but Hancock is deluded by self-importance:

HANCOCK: **It's obvious why they're here. They've seen through my disguise. They recognise me. Of course I must speak to them. It's not every day that England's greatest comic leaves the country for good.**

The ensuing press conference is based on double meaning. They assume that Hancock is the Prime Minister and Hancock believes they want to know why he, the greatest comic in the country, is leaving England:

REPORTER: **Sir, how long do you intend staying in America?**

HANCOCK: **For good! I'm not coming back here!**

REPORTER: **You're not coming back? Sir, do the government know about this?**

HANCOCK: **I don't suppose so. What's it got to do with them? They won't even miss me.**

REPORTER: **But if you're not coming back then who will take your place as Number One?**

HANCOCK: **Ooooh, there's plenty of good lads coming up you know. Now**

this is strictly off the record, but Jimmy Edwards is the one.

This scene works on so many levels. As we've seen, it shows up Hancock as the self-centred egotist he was. Sid is initially on hand to prey on his gullibility and when the situation looks like spiralling into disaster he is the one to try to talk Hancock out of it.

This is something that occurred only in the last series when Sid became more of a friend and confidant to Hancock. Initially Sid would have led him into an incriminating situation and not concerned himself with the outcome, as happens in the first ever episode, in which Hancock needs a flat to host a party for the BBC radio chiefs and the press. Sid suggests a house on Park Lane and assumes that a bogus telegram will leave the building vacant of its true owners. A virtual riot ensues as his guests get out of hand and leave. The owner returns, having never received Sid's telegram, forcing Hancock to make a run for it. The Stop Press the following morning says that the police are 'looking for a short fat man called Ted Ray' (the name Hancock shouts as he is running away).

Although he took part in the radio series from the start, Sid James was not regarded as a true side-kick until the television series were aired in 1956; and it was Bill Kerr (the actor who played the misery in *Wagga Wagga*) who filled this role in the early radio programmes. Kerr was the fast-talking Australian friend of Hancock who initially played a more intelligent character than Hancock, but later developed into a person of diminished intellect. He had the same kind of buddy relationship that Sid had in the television series, even down to calling Hancock by the nickname 'Tub'. Billings in *The Radio Times* listed Kerr

Additional cast members
Week 2, John Vere; Weeks 6, 10, 11, 18, 19, Alan Simpson; Week 9, Jerry Stovin; Week 12, Kathleen O'Hagan (piano); Week 18, Patricia Hayes and Christina Horniman

Series 6 – (14 Weeks)

Written by
Ray Galton and Alan Simpson

The Cast
Tony Hancock, Sidney James and Bill Kerr (except Week 13)

Produced by
Tom Ronald

Tuesday 29 September 1959–Tuesday 29 December 1959
Weeks 1–14 broadcast at 2000; repeated on the following Sunday at 1830; Week 13 also repeated on Friday 25 December 1959 on the Home Service
Broadcast on the Light Programme

Additional cast members
Week 1, Kenneth Williams, Patricia Hayes and Noel Dryden; Week 2, Kenneth Williams and Patricia Hayes; Week 3, Warren Mitchell and Hugh Morton; Week 4, Wilfred Babbage, Patricia Hayes, Anne Lancaster and Elizabeth Fraser; Week 5, Warren Mitchell, Hugh Morton

and Raymond Glendenning; Week 6, Lillian Grasson, Wilfred Babbage, Fraser Kerr and Leigh Crutchley; Week 7, Wilfred Babbage, Hugh Morton and Harry Towb; Week 8, Warren Mitchell; Week 9, Warren Mitchell, Errol McKinnon and Mavis Villers; Week 10, Wilfred Babbage, Jack Watson and Hugh Morton; Week 11, Fenella Fielding, Fraser Kerr and Warren Mitchell; Week 12, Patricia Hayes and Joan Frank; Week 13, Hugh Morton, Wilfred Babbage and Frank Partington; Week 14, Anne Lancaster, Peter Goodwright, Ronald Wilson, Jerry Stovin, Wilfred Babbage and Jack Watson

over James for the first three series, after which they were reversed owing to James's rising popularity (he was fast becoming one of the best-known character actors in film).

The third regular character was Hancock's 'girlfriend'. This was the only device that Galton and Simpson included that resembled the traditional sitcom, whereby leading male characters had girlfriends. The choice of Moira Lister was perfect as the girlfriend with a strong personality of her own who rarely gave in to Hancock's whinings and fickle-mindedness.

Lister left after the first series and was replaced in the second series by Andree Melly with a very heavy French accent which thankfully diminished with subsequent episodes.

The last main character in the series – and the one to play the voice of authority (however petty) – was a young Kenneth Williams. This was his first major radio role and was to set him up for subsequent stardom. The producer, Dennis Main Wilson, must take credit for giving the young Williams his first break after spotting him in a production of *St Joan* at London's Arts Theatre. In the original scripts Williams's characters usually appeared marked 'snide', an apt description when one takes into account the often slimy nature of those he played.

While Galton and Simpson were, from the outset of writing ***Hancock's Half Hour***, wary about using catchphrases, it was Kenneth Williams who provided the most quotable lines. Williams's ability to make even the most mundane line like 'Good evening' sound like an opportune catchphrase was enough to send the audience into paroxysms.

From what we know of Tony Hancock's vulnerability as a performer, it is little surprise that he was quick to react to this, wondering if perhaps he should have a larger quota of belly laughs. Galton and Simpson pointed out that his vulnerability of character, which the other character bounced off, was half of a winning combination. If they had created a comedy with slapstick Goonish humour, and a character who played for quick one-liners, then ***Hancock's Half Hour*** would not have had the universal appeal and longevity that made it one of the most important radio comedies of the post-war period.

The real consequence of Hancock's personal fears of not being funny enough did not reach the fore until well into his television days in the 60s, when his dismissal of Sid James, and eventually of Galton and Simpson, spelt professional, and ultimately personal, disaster.

Music was all important to the feel of the show, and the signature tune became one of the best known in radio history. Hancock's character was musically represented by the tuba. This coupling seems so perfect that it is hard to hear a tuba and not think of ***Hancock's Half Hour***. The music was scored by Wally Stott and played by the BBC Revue Orchestra conducted by Harry Rabinowitz.

The first series was broadcast in 1954 and, after thirteen weeks, ended with the promise of a second series by the BBC. Audience research showed that the modest number that tuned into ***Hancock's Half Hour*** liked the fact that there were no 'moaning crooners', 'shrieking choirs', and no 'blaring dance bands'. However the major criticism of the first few shows was that the script was thought to be too weak. By January 1955 Galton and Simpson turned their attention (albeit for only a limited time) to more popular targets. But in retrospect the first scripts were very broad in their targets and tended to display a leaning towards more gag-based comedy than the character-driven plots that made ***Hancock's Half Hour*** unique. In the first episode of series one, for instance, there is an argument between Kerr and Hancock over a wine glass that has caught the eyes of both of them:

HANCOCK: **That's mine.**
KERR: **But I saw it first.**
HANCOCK: **You're not 'aving it – my party, there's plenty of other glasses.**
KERR: **But I've taken a fancy to that one.**
HANCOCK: **So have I, let go of it.**
KERR: **Give it to me!**
HANCOCK: **Let go!**
MOIRA: **Put it down both of you. That poor goldfish has nearly fallen out three times.**

The second series was to be all important to the ongoing success of the show. More bad feedback about the script could have meant the end of ***Hancock's Half Hour***, but series two had a far better chance of success with each episode due for a repeat on the following Sunday.

Series two started in 1955 and, interestingly enough, the first three episodes, broadcast on 19 and 26 April and 3 May, have Harry Secombe in the starring role. This was due to the illness and consequent disappearance of Tony Hancock. Suffering from nervous exhaustion, he collapsed while appearing in *The Talk of The Town* at the Adelphi Theatre. An argument ensued between the producer of the show and the BBC as to whether Hancock could appear in the second series of ***Hancock's Half Hour*** at all and thankfully it was resolved in a short time. Secombe covered well in these episodes, but he was such an instantly recognisable voice that Goonish inferences were inevitable in the minds of the audience.

As thought, the Sunday afternoon repeat was crucial to the recruitment of a whole new legion of listeners, mainly families, who traditionally gathered around the wireless after Sunday lunch. By the third series, which started in October 1955, 23 Railway Cuttings had become almost as famous as 10 Downing Street. Galton and Simpson had realised their characters fully with Tony Hancock going from strength to strength with each episode.

It is interesting to note that Hancock refused to see scripts for each episode before the morning of recording. He maintained that if he held on to them for too long they would become stale and his enthusiasm for them would wane.

Series three also saw Kenneth Williams become a far more prominent character and Andree Melly losing her French accent.

The start of the fourth series of ***Hancock's Half Hour*** was fraught with difficulties. Hancock was under contract with the producer Jack Hylton to appear on stage, and Hylton extended this to cover any other appearances. Three sides then entered into a tug-of-war situation. BBC TV wanted six shows with Hancock; BBC radio wanted a new series of 20 shows and Hylton wanted Hancock to appear on the newly founded independent television channel.

The outcome of this situation was that Hancock was to do the BBC TV series of six shows, already postponed by three months owing to legal wranglings.

His commitment to Jack Hylton was to be honoured with two series of six shows for AR-TV to be made before and after the BBC series. Because of prior commitments to BBC radio, Galton and Simpson did not write these shows and the two series are credited to Eric Sykes.

A different writer meant a different style, and the twelve shows take the form of a sketch-based programme. BBC radio also got what they wanted – a fourth series of ***Hancock's Half Hour*** – and this turned out to be a landmark in the history of the programme.

Two battles were won at the outset of series four. The first was to keep Tony Hancock. The second was between the producer, Dennis Main Wilson, and the Musicians' Union over the use of the programme's special music. The BBC was cutting incidental music recorded by members of the union because of rising costs and insisting that shows use 'library records' instead. The outcome of this particular row was fortuitous for ***Hancock's Half Hour*** as the rescored music was far more in keeping with the programme, which at this stage was finding a strong foothold with the listeners of Britain.

The only major personnel change with series four was the introduction of Hattie Jacques in show five. Her role was that of an aggressive and inept secretary named Grizelda Pugh. As with many of the other characters, this changed in time and she became far softer. Sid James had become more of a confidant of Hancock's (a role he continued well into the television run of *Hancock*), and Bill Kerr was less frenetic and consequently took more of a back seat.

With the popularity of Kenneth Williams becoming greater, it was time to dispense with his nasal 'snide' character, so familiar to audiences, especially when he was using the catchphrase 'Stop messin' about'. Significantly, plots became increasingly less blatant with their targets, relying instead on the personality of Tony Hancock and the supporting cast.

Series four included *Michelangelo 'Ancock*, with Hancock entering a sculpture competition; *Last of the McHancocks*, in which Hancock has to defend his inheritance (a Scottish castle) at the Highland Games; and *The Secret Life of Anthony Hancock*, which is the most surreal of the series. In it, Hancock browses his diary for 1956 and imagines himself as a surgeon, lion-tamer and, most famously, as a test pilot. The test pilot sequence is often aired on radio and features Hancock testing a new plane. But when he becomes concerned about the mechanics, up pops Kenneth Williams, not *in* the plane, but casually introducing himself with a trademark 'Good evening' after knocking on the cockpit glass – from *outside.*

Series five was made almost a year after the previous series, during which time Dennis Main Wilson had left BBC radio to start an equally illustrious career in television. Tom Ronald became the replacement producer, after Pat Dixon produced the first show of this series. Galton and Simpson seemed to go up a gear in quality of output with each series and this one contains some of the best-known Hancock episodes: *The Sleepless Night* (with Hancock being continually distracted from a much-needed sleep by noises and the other occupants of the house); *The Male Suffragettes* (which sees Hancock attempting to reinstate male dominance into society – with a little help from Sid); and *Sunday Afternoon at Home* (show fourteen, broadcast on 22 April 1958, which was later released on gramophone record and thus became the best-known *Hancock* up to that point). There is almost no plot to speak of. The entire cast are bored on a Sunday with nothing to do – the TV and gramophone don't work and nobody can play the piano.

After this series Hattie Jacques left, returning only to record a Christmas Special to be broadcast on Christmas Day 1958.

By 1959 Hancock was a big television star and it was necessary to pre-record what was to be the final series. Radio was becoming less appealing both financially and creatively for Hancock, who feared that a new series might not live up to the previous one. This final series put to rest any doubts its star might have had and was in fact the best yet.

The end of the decade saw a rapid change in the youth movement with the emergence of teenage culture and the beatnik movement. While Galton and Simpson had stayed away from very obvious targets they did make Hancock more representative of his time. But comedy was born out of the fact that a movement based on the expression of new ideas and free thought was going to be represented by the wholly inappropriate Hancock, who forces his false intellectualism on those around him:

HANCOCK: **We are not layabouts. We are artists, mush. Writers, painters, thinkers. All men that are perturbed about the state of the world at the moment.**

Kerr asks if he can join this new band of men, whom Hancock describes as '57 throbbing intellects raring to go'. His response is a flat . . .

HANCOCK: **No you can't. This isn't a ping-pong and darts club. This is a group with lofty ideals. A cultural and discussion group dedicated to the betterment of Mankind.**

SID: **Well why can't he join then? He's Mankind.**

HANCOCK: **Well loosely, yes. Only up to a point. He's not far enough advanced for us.**

SID: **You said it was for the betterment of Mankind.**

HANCOCK: **Yes, but stone me, you've got to have something to start on!**

The departure of Kenneth Williams after two shows had no effect on the programme's popularity. The producer, Tom Ronald, had the ability to work out a balanced show order with all of them having been pre-recorded. The Christmas Special (without Bill Kerr) was slotted in as show number thirteen on 22 December 1959 and the final ***Hancock's Half Hour*** was broadcast on 29 December 1959. After five years Hancock had become a national institution and would continue to grow in popularity with more television shows and countless radio repeats.

Finkel's Cafe

July–September 1956

Transmission Details

Finkel's Cafe

9 Editions

Written by
Frank Muir and Dennis Norden (adapted from *Duffy's Tavern*, an American series by Ed Gardner)

Starring
Peter Sellers, with Sidney James, Avril Angers, Kenneth Connor and the Gypsy Tavern Ninetet

Produced by
Pat Dixon

4 July 1956–29 August 1956
Broadcast Wednesdays 2030–2100 on the Light Programme

Finkel's Cafe was 'where the elite meet to eat', and starred Peter Sellers as Eddie, the Irish manager.

This also meant a busy time for Sid James, who had just signed two contracts for the BBC. Both the first televised series of *Hancock's Half Hour* and ***Finkel's Cafe*** were due to run throughout the summer of 1956, and for James it was a rush between rehearsals, radio recordings and live TV transmissions.

But it did mean that for a while Sid James was appearing both on radio and television with two of the country's biggest stars, and this was a landmark in his career.

Finkel's Cafe also had Avril Angers, Kenneth Connor and the Gypsy Tavern Ninetet, and it came from the ever-fresh pens of Frank Muir and Dennis Norden.

The Clitheroe Kid

1958–1972

Any account of radio comedy success stories would be far from complete if it omitted James Robinson Clitheroe, known to millions as ***The Clitheroe Kid***. This diminutive comic achieved the highest worldwide ratings of any comic and yet remains sadly unknown to a post-1960s generation. In total ***The Clitheroe Kid*** ran from 1958 until 1972 and at the height of its popularity was listened to regularly by over 10 million people.

The Clitheroe Kid was built around the personality of James Clitheroe. His height, just four-foot-three, coupled with a shrill vocal range made him adopt the persona of an irrepressible schoolboy, first on stage and then on the radio.

Born in Clitheroe in 1922, Jimmy was the only child of two Lancashire weavers and spent his childhood in Blackoe on the outskirts of Nelson. George Baker, a local talent scout, launched his career in 1936. A local paper lists him as playing the accordion and doing female impersonations in revue.

He enjoyed a brief career in film as stooge to Arthur Lucan in a 1940 *Mother Riley* film, and in a 1942 film with George Formby. But it was his stage career that took off as he performed in northern variety theatres alongside the likes of Formby, Frank Randle, Al Read, Norman Evans and Jimmy James.

James Casey, a young writer, was on the lookout for a little boy with the maturity not to do an injustice to his material in the *Northern Variety Parade Show* in which his father Jimmy James was performing.

Transmission Details

Call Boy

1st Edition

Written by
Frank Roscoe and Wally Ashley

Featuring
Ted Lune, Louise Trail, Denis Goodwin, Martin Lukins, Herbert Smith and Margery Manners with a music hall memories spot

Music by
The Northern Variety Orchestra conducted by Alyn Ainsworth

Produced by
Ronnie Taylor

18 October 1955
No other broadcast details available

3 Further Editions

Written by
Cass James

The Cast
Jimmy Clitheroe, backstage at the music hall, meeting Jimmy James, Tommy Reilly, Lionel Saxon, the Three Shades, the Hindley-Taylor Singers (plus Robb Wilton in Week 2 and Ken Platt and Wyn Calvin in Week 3)

Music by
The Augmented Variety Orchestra conducted by Alyn Ainsworth
Produced by
Ronnie Taylor

27 December 1955, 24 January 1956 and 8 March 1956
Broadcast Tuesdays 1900–1930 (except Week 1, at 1830–1910)
Broadcast on the Home Service

Series 1 – (11 Weeks)
Written by
Cass James
The Cast
Tom Harrison, Herbert Smith, Frank Roscoe, Margery Manners, John Rorke, Peter Sinclair, the Hindley-Taylor Singers and the Northern Variety Orchestra conducted by Alyn Ainsworth (Billy Ternent and his Orchestra in Week 9); guests throughout the series included Ken Platt, Charlie Chester, Bernard Miles, Gladys Morgan, Jimmy Wheeler, Jimmy James, Chic Murray and Maudie and Robb Wilton assisted by Phyllis Playdell
Produced by
John Ammonds

4 April 1956–13 June 1956
Broadcast Wednesdays

Clitheroe went up to Manchester to perform a few lines and he was instantly given the job. This success led to appearances in Norman Evans's radio series *Over The Garden Wall*, followed by a series called *Call Boy*, written by Casey. Part of *Call Boy* was a recurring domestic scenario which became the most popular part of the show.

This mirrors another radio series of the 1950s, *Take It From Here*, which also had its own domestic comedy, *The Glums*. This, too, became the highlight of the programme. It was felt by Casey and the cast that a series based around this domestic set-up and starring Jimmy Clitheroe would stand up in its own right.

The pilot show was universally liked with one exception. The Head of the Light Programme objected to a midget on radio. *Call Boy* went on for another two series, by which time Casey had worked his way up to producer within the ranks of the BBC. The figures for this series were at a high and the most popular part of the show was undoubtedly Jimmy Clitheroe as the naughty boy in the seven-minute domestic sketch. The head of department eventually relented and six shows were commissioned.

To Jimmy Clitheroe the shows were a form of escape from the confines of his size. He was constantly reminded by others that he was different and became more and more an intensely private man off-air. His public persona grew by comparison and a second series was immediately commissioned.

The regular cast had minimal changes throughout the series' fourteen-year run. By the third series in 1960 the right combination had been found. The family set-up was not the traditional one. There was no father, but a grandfather with a Scottish accent, played by Peter Sinclair. Grandfather was forever down the pub, and this didn't go unnoticed by the keen eye of Jimmy:

GRANDFATHER: **I've got to go and see my pal Tommy Twig about some gardening.**

JIMMY: **Yes and guess where they're going to fill their watering cans. The Rose and Crown.**

When he's invited to a stag party in *The Evils of Tomato Juice*, Jimmy shrewdly comments, 'Grandad's always going to stag parties. That's why he looks like a red-nosed reindeer.'

Diana Day played the Kid's sister Susan, otherwise known as 'fish face', 'scraggy neck' and more. But unlike her brother she was incongruously cultivated, better-spoken.

Prior to Diana Day, a young actress called Judith Chalmers filled the role of Susan before going on to have her own radio talk-show and jet around the world collecting suntans. Alfie Hall, Susan's boyfriend, was magnificently played by the comic Danny Ross, who became part of the cast in the fourth series in 1961. Ross would often play up to the live audience at the Hulme Hippodrome in Manchester and perform his famous falls much to their delight. This must have left the listener at home wondering what they were laughing at.

Patricia Burke played Clitheroe's long-suffering mother, taking over the part from Renee Huston. Leonard Williams made up the other characters of Theodore Craythorpe and Harry Whittle, both friends of the family.

2115–2200
Broadcast on the Light Programme

One-offs

Written by
Cass James

The Cast
As before but Frank Roscoe replaced by Wally Ashby

Produced by
Ronnie Taylor

27 November 1956 and 11 December 1956
Broadcast Tuesdays 1900–1930
Broadcast on the Home Service
(There was also a BBC television broadcast occasionally from Wednesday 16 January 1957, 2000–2100)

Series 2 – (8 Weeks)

The Cast
Tony Melody, Herbert Smith, the Hindley-Taylor Singers, Frank Roscoe, Wally Ashby, Margery Manners, Peter Sinclair; guests throughout the series included Bob Monkhouse, Charlie Chester, Terry Hall, Morecambe and Wise, Harry Worth, Tessie O'Shea, Chic Murray and Maidie, Bernard Miles and Albert Modley

Music by
The BBC Northern Dance Orchestra conducted by Alyn Ainsworth (Billy Ternent and his

Orchestra from Week 6 onwards)
Produced by
John Ammonds
17 April 1957–12 June 1957
Broadcast Wednesdays 2115–2200
Broadcast on the Light Programme

Series 3 – (14 Weeks)
Written by
James Casey and Ronnie Taylor
The Cast
Jack Watson, Judith Chalmers, the Hindley-Taylor Singers, Jimmy Leach; guests throughout included Cardew Robinson, Albert Modley, Derek Roy, Ken Platt, Jewel and Warriss, Chic Murray and Maidie, Morecambe and Wise, Jimmy James, Jimmy Wheeler, Vic Oliver and Charlie Chester
Produced by
James Casey
30 December 1957–31 March 1958
Broadcast Mondays 2100–2130
Broadcast on the Light Programme

The Clitheroe Kid
One-off
The Cast
Robert Moreton, Eddie Leslie, Irene Handl, Anthea Askey, Herbert Smith, Fred Fairclough and

Alfie Hall was the Kid's partner in crime. He was a comical stooge who had the annoying habit of always blurting out the truth and landing Jimmy in trouble. As with all great situation comedies, the formula that worked initially was rarely changed. In this case the formula was messy situations tackled by Jimmy armed with ridiculously hair-brained solutions that more often than not backfired.

In *The Evils of Tomato Juice* from 1965 Alfie is chosen to be best man at his friend's wedding. Jimmy finds, as he always does, something to laugh about:

ALFIE: **Oh hello Susan, we were just trying me hat on. It's the one I'm wearing at the wedding.**
JIMMY: **Yes Susan, Alfie's the worst man.**
SUSAN: **No, he's the best man.**
JIMMY: **If he's the best, the bridegroom must be a right drip!**

After a night of drinking Alfie is woken by Jimmy to find he is £30 richer with no recollection of how he came by the money. They go to the police station and hear that the police are looking for a thief who is sure 'to get five years' for his crime. Jimmy, thinking on his feet, suggests they go back to the pub and when the landlord isn't in the bar they leave the money there. Clitheroe turns in a brilliant performance as he pretends to be a cowboy to annoy the landlord to distraction:

JIMMY: **Howdy partners. Everybody up to the bar, the drinks are on me!**
LANDLORD: **What the devil?**
JIMMY: **Damn me breeches, if the**

	saloon ain't empty. Has there been a gold strike?
ALFIE:	**Like the Lone Ranger Strikes Again.**
LANDLORD:	**What are you doing in here sonny?**
JIMMY:	**I've got me a powerful thirst. I've been three weeks in the saddle.**
ALFIE:	**Ooh no. Ta ta landlord, I think I'll be going.**
JIMMY:	**You ain't going nowhere till you have a drink with Billy the Kid. Pint of whisky for Billy the Kid and a glass of milk for the goat.**
LANDLORD:	**Now look son, clear off before I get annoyed!**
JIMMY:	[Dropping the accent] **I want a drink and if I can't have pint of whisky give me a pint of brown ale.**
LANDLORD:	**Don't be funny.**
JIMMY:	**Well half a pint then.**
LANDLORD:	**I can't serve you with beer.**
JIMMY:	**Well don't just stand there. Go and find someone who can!**

Obvious humour certainly, but this is humour steeped in a music hall tradition. The audience can often see the punchline coming but it was delivered with such a degree of panache and immaculate timing that even the most blatant of gags never failed to raise a laugh.

Norman Somers

Music by
The Jimmy Leach Organolian Quartet

Produced by
Jimmy Casey

24 April 1956
Broadcast Tuesday 1900–1930
Broadcast on the Home Service

Series 1 – (11 Weeks)

Written by
James Casey and Frank Roscoe

The Cast
Jimmy Clitheroe, Renee Houston, Peter Sinclair, Leonard Williams, Judith Daugherty, Nan Merriott-Watson and Judith Chalmers

Music by
The BBC Northern Dance Orchestra with Alyn Ainsworth; Jimmy Leach on the electronic organ

Produced by
James Casey

Monday 5 May 1958–Monday 14 July 1958
Weeks 1–11 transmitted at 2000; no repeat
Broadcast on the Light Programme

Episode List
1. *Seconds Out*; 2. *Pen Pal*; 3. *Wrong End of the Stick*; 4. *Clitheroe on the Keys*; 5. *Raising the Rent*; 6. *All By Accident*; 7. *The Kid's Last Fight*; 8. *The Mystery Trip*; 9.

Too Many Cooks; 10. No title; 11. *Wakes Week*

Series 2 – (10 Weeks)

Written by
James Casey and Frank Roscoe

The Cast
Jimmy Clitheroe, Peter Sinclair, Patricia Burke, Leonard Williams, Peter Goodwright, Betty Alberge

Music by
Alan Roper, the BBC Northern Dance Orchestra with Alyn Ainsworth

Produced by
James Casey

Monday 29 December 1958–Monday 2 March 1959
Weeks 1–10 transmitted at 2000; Weeks 1–10 repeated every Wednesday at 1930 from 1 April 1959
Broadcast on the Light Programme

Episode List
1. *What A Pantomime*; 2. *No Match For The Kid*; 3. *Mind My Bike*; 4. *I Shot an Arrow in the Air*; 5. *Cupid and the Black Hand Gang*; 6. *A Kid With a Problem*; 7. *Clitheroe and the Hound-Dog*; 8. *Message Received and Misunderstood*; 9. *Girl Trouble*; 10. *The Trouble With Higginbottom*

So popular was ***The Clitheroe Kid*** that nearly a quarter of the population would listen every Sunday lunchtime. By the mid 1960s it was breaking all records for audience figures. Jimmy Clitheroe was topping the bill in summer shows and pantos, most frequently in Blackpool, where he and his mother had settled.

In addition to his phenomenally successful radio series he was starring in a regional TV series with the independent ABC TV. In the television series, as on the stage, Jimmy's mother was played by his close friend Molly Sugden. He wanted television to be as successful a vehicle for him as radio. Sadly, TV didn't allow *viewers* to suspend disbelief in quite the way that *listeners* could. It became impossible for the viewer to regard Jimmy Clitheroe as anything other than a middle-aged midget playing a schoolboy. It was often remarked that, from a distance, he did indeed resemble a schoolboy in short trousers, but close up it was his wrinkled knees that gave him away. And television has a knack of telling the truth.

Money dominated his life, and this became a drawback in his career. Despite advice from those close to him, he often took the less good job on the basis that the money was more. He regularly paid for the substandard scriptwriters for pantos and summer seasons and consequently his performances suffered. Although he never married, he did have a female companion for many years called Sally, but chose instead to live with his mother. Much has been made of their relationship and how it affected his personal and professional life; but one thing was clear: when she died he would find it hard to carry on his life unchanged.

Nineteen seventy-two saw the final ***Clitheroe Kid***

show after a fourteen-year run. Audience figures had slumped from ten-and-a-half million to just one million. His female companion Sally had died in a car crash just before the end of the show and in the following year his mother died. Within twelve months the mainstays of his life had been taken away from him.

On the day of his mother's funeral, on 6 June 1973, Jimmy Clitheroe was found dead at their home. The newspapers at the time claimed he was 57 but he was in fact 51. The coroner's report recorded a verdict of 'accidental death due to the combined toxic effects of barbiturates and alcohol.'

Jimmy Clitheroe was an institution. Intrinsically northern, he was one in a great line of northern comics like Formby and Frank Randle. Although only a domestic situation comedy, ***The Clitheroe Kid*** touched the hearts of millions of regular listeners. Its enormous popularity with the public means that this is a programme that cannot be ignored.

Series 3 – (13 Weeks)

Written by
James Casey (unless otherwise stated – see Episode List)

The Cast
Jimmy Clitheroe, Peter Sinclair, Patricia Burke, Leonard Williams, Diana Day, Tonay Melody, Brian Trueman and Betty Alberge

Music by
Alan Roper, the BBC Northern Dance Orchestra with Alyn Ainsworth

Produced by
James Casey

Monday 4 April 1960–Monday 27 June 1960
Weeks 1–13 transmitted at 2000; Weeks 6–13 repeated the following Wednesday at 1230
Broadcast on the Light Programme
Weeks 1, 3, 4, 6, 7, 8 repeated on *Children's Hour* from Saturday 7 January 1961 at 1200 on the Home Service

Episode List
1. *The Tale of A Cat*; 2. *Clitheroe's Merry Go Round* (written by Casey and Frank Roscoe); 3. *Money, Money, Money* (written by Casey and Ronnie Taylor); 4. *All At Sea*; 5. *May The Best Man Win* (written by Casey and Ronnie Taylor); 6. *Nothing But The Truth* (written by Frank

Roscoe); 7. *Storm in a Test-Tube* (written by Casey and Ronnie Taylor); 8. *Mother's Day of Rest* (written by Casey and Ronnie Taylor); 9. *The Wheels of Mis-Fortune* (written by Casey and Ronnie Taylor); 10. *What A Picnic* (written by Frank Roscoe); 11. *Trouble With the Goggle Box* (written by Casey and Ronnie Taylor); 12. *Job For the Girl* (written by Casey and Ronnie Taylor); 13. *Almost a Holiday*

Series 4 – (13 Weeks)

Written by
James Casey and Frank Roscoe

The Cast
Jimmy Clitheroe, Patricia Burke, Leonard Williams, Danny Ross, Diana Day, Tonay Melody and Betty Alberge

Music by
Alan Roper, the BBC Northern Dance Orchestra with Alyn Ainsworth

Produced by
James Casey

Monday 20 February 1961–Monday 15 May 1961
Weeks 1–13 transmitted at 2000; Weeks 6–13 repeated the following Thursday 1000
Broadcast on the Light Programme

Episode List
1. *Pardon My English*; 2. *How Now Brown Cow*; 3. *Grandad's Back*; 4. *The Trouble With Neighbours*; 5. *My Pal Ossie – The Clot*; 6. *Goodness Gracious Me* (special guest – Tony Brent); 7. *The Girl Who Got The Message*; 8. *The Not-So-Welcome Guest*; 9. *The Keyhole Kid*; 10. *The Wreck of the Soppy Sue*; 11. *Animal Crackers*; 12. *I'm In Trouble Again*; 13. *Fishing In Troubled Waters*

Series 5 – (20 Weeks)

Written by
James Casey and Frank Roscoe

The Cast
Jimmy Clitheroe, Patricia Burke, Leonard Williams, Danny Ross and Diana Day

Music by
Alan Roper, the BBC Northern Dance Orchestra with Alyn Ainsworth

Produced by
James Casey

Monday 27 November 1961–Monday 9 April 1962
Weeks 1–20 transmitted at 2000; Weeks 1–20 repeated the following Friday at 1000
Broadcast on the Light Programme

Episode List
1. *Dig That Crazy Garden*; 2. *It's My Mother's Birthday*; 3. *After The Film Was Over*; 4. *The Kid Who Got The Bird*; 5. *Xmas Day in the Kid's House*; 6. *Breaking in the New Year*; 7. *Snake in the Grass*; 8. *Too Many Crooks*; 9. *The Old Man of the Sea*; 10. *The Crime That Never Was*; 11. *Lend Me An Ear*; 12. *The Day I Told The Truth*; 13. *I've Got Them Taped*; 14. *Collecting Trouble*; 15. *Waiting at the Church*; 16. *I Was a Stupid Cupid*; 17. *James – Mr Piano – Clitheroe*; 18. *Going to the Dogs*; 19. *Jimmy The Kid*; 20. *What A Good Boy Am I*

Series 6 – (20 Weeks)

Written by
James Casey and Frank Roscoe

The Cast
Jimmy Clitheroe, Patricia Burke, Leonard Williams, Danny Ross, Deryck Guyler and Diana Day

Music by
Alan Roper, the BBC Northern Dance Orchestra with Alyn Ainsworth

Produced by
James Casey

Monday 29 November 1962–Monday 11 March 1963
Weeks 1–20 transmitted at 1931; Weeks 1–20 repeated the following Sunday at 1430
Broadcast on the Light Programme

Episode List
1. *The House That Jim Built*; 2. *What a Guy*; 3. *Sorry You've Been Troubled*; 4. *Smile Please*; 5. *When Grandad Papered The Parlour*; 6. *We All Make Mistakes*; 7. *Accidents Will Happen*; 8. *Charity Begins At Jim's*; 9. *Just The Ticket*; 10. *Jim's Highland Fling*; 11. *Next Door To Trouble*; 12. *Love Me, Love My Dog*; 13. *Too Much To Swallow*; 14. *Dial Jim For Trouble*; 15. *Trouble From The Kick-Off*; 16. *Don't Shoot The Pianist*; 17. *The Patient's Dilemma*; 18. *One Bad Turn Deserves Another*; 19. *The Quiz Kid*; 20. *A Dream Of A Holiday*

Series 7 – (20 Weeks)

Written by
James Casey and Frank Roscoe

The Cast
Jimmy Clitheroe, Patricia Burke, Danny Ross, Deryck Guyler, Diana Day and Tonay Melody

Produced by
James Casey

Sunday 16 November 1963–Sunday 22 March 1964

Weeks 1–20 transmitted at 1430; Weeks 1–20 repeated the following Monday at 1931
Broadcast on the Light Programme

Episode List
1. *No Holds Barred*; 2. *Tramp Tramp Tramp*; 3. *Playing With Fire*; 4. *Love and Marriage*; 5. *Vote For Grandad*; 6. *Three Of A Kind*; 7. *Grandfather Christmas*; 8. *A Load of Chinese Junk*; 9. *The Gathering Of The Clan*; 10. *The Ten Pin Terror*; 11. *The Tale Of A Coat*; 12. *The Man Who Came To Lunch*; 13. *100 Not Out*; 14. *What's In A Name?*; 15. *Back To The Dressing Room*; 16. *The Kid With 9 Lives*; 17. *A Right Roman Holiday*; 18. *Nothing But The Truth*; 19. *Never Listen To A Teacher*; 20. *Gun Crazy*

Series 8 – (20 Weeks)

Written by
James Casey and Frank Roscoe (except Week 19 – written by James Casey only)

The Cast
Jimmy Clitheroe, Peter Sinclair, Danny Ross, Diana Day, Mollie Sugden, Frank Williams and John Graham

Produced by
James Casey

Sunday 18 October 1964–Sunday 28 February 1965
Weeks 1–20 transmitted at 1430; Weeks 1–20 repeated the following Monday at 1931
Broadcast on the Light Programme

Episode List
1. *Anyone For Tennis?*; 2. *An Actor's Life For Me*; 3. *Trouble Through The Looking Glass*; 4. *James The Little Gentleman*; 5. *For The Love Of Money*; 6. *One Jump Behind*; 7. *James Bond Junior*; 8. *The Kid Makes History*; 9. *Sing Something Stupid*; 10. *Jim And The Beanstalk*; 11. *Double Trouble*; 12. No title; 13. *One Quiet Day*; 14. *Help, It's A Girl*; 15. *It's A Knockout*; 16. *Swimming Against The Tide*; 17. *Up The Totem Pole*; 18. *Follow That Car*; 19. *Clitheroe's Concert Party*; 20. *It's All In The Mind*

Series 9 – (20 Weeks)

Written by
James Casey and Frank Roscoe

The Cast
Jimmy Clitheroe, Peter Sinclair, Patricia Burke, Danny Ross, Diana Day, Molly Weir and John Graham

Produced by
James Casey

Sunday 10 October 1965–Sunday 20 February 1966
Weeks 1–20 transmitted at 1400; Weeks 1–20 repeated the following Monday at 1931
Broadcast on the Light Programme

Episode List
1. *Jim And The Headless Piper*; 2. *The Mystery Of The Haggis*; 3. *For My Next Trick*; 4. *The Evils Of Tomato Juice*; 5. *Another Mother For Ossie*; 6. *Grandad's Mysterious Illness*; 7. *Weapons Of Woe*; 8. *The Unlucky Mascot*; 9. *The Case Of The Crooked Parson*; 10. *The Unfair Sex*; 11. *English As She Is Spoke*; 12. *It's The Thought That Counts*; 13. *The Sunday I Met Man Friday*; 14. *One Good Twist Deserves Another*; 15. *Give A Little Whistle*; 16. *Penny Foolish*; 17. *Watch The Birdie*; 18. *Too Many Sisters*; 19. *Sliding Into Trouble*; 20. *The Best Of Indian Luck*

Series 10 – (26 Weeks)

Written by
James Casey and Frank Roscoe

The Cast
Jimmy Clitheroe, Peter Sinclair, Patricia Burke, Danny Ross, Diana Day, Ben Trueman and Joe Gladwyn

Produced by
James Casey

Sunday 2 October 1966–Sunday 26 March 1967
Weeks 1–26 transmitted at 1400 (except Week 13 – broadcast at 1900); Weeks 1–24 repeated the following Monday at 1931; Weeks 25 and 26 repeated the following Monday at 2015
Broadcast on the Light Programme

Episode List
1. *No Room At the Digs*; 2. *Storm in a Teapot*; 3. *Forbidden Fruit*; 4. *Follow That Bride*; 5. *What You Lose On the Swings*; 6. *The Loving Neighbour*; 7. *As Advertised on the Telly*; 8. *Sales Talk*; 9. *History is a Thing of the Past*; 10. *The Scent of Trouble*; 11. *What A Welcome*; 12. *Don't Forget the Carol Singers*; 13. *Christmas Crackers*; 14. *Just A Wee Family Party*; 15. *Wet Behind the Ears*; 16. *Get Me to the Shop on Time*; 17. *The Prize Fool*; 18. *Come Into the Garden Jim*; 19. *Jim's Doggy Bank*; 20. *Nothing Like*

Music; 21. *One Day Last Summer*; 22. *No Time For Higginbottom*; 23. *What A Performance*; 24. *The Price of Silence*; 25. *The Kid from Auntie*; 26. *Beware of the Bike*

Series 11 – (20 Weeks)

Written by
James Casey and Frank Roscoe

The Cast
Jimmy Clitheroe, Peter Sinclair, Patricia Burke, Danny Ross, Diana Day and John Graham

Produced by
James Casey

Sunday 1 October 1967–Sunday 11 February 1968
Weeks 1–20 transmitted at 1431; Weeks 1–20 repeated the following Monday at 2015 (except Week 13 – broadcast at 2030) on Radio 1 and 2
Broadcast on Radio 2

Episode List
1. *Stop Crying – You're on Holiday*; 2. *Beware of the Neighbour*; 3. *Ribbin Jim and his Marrymen*; 4. *A Day on the Movie Go Round*; 5. *The Day I Met the Knight*; 6. *Keep Your Gunpowder Dry*; 7. *Is There a Doctor in the Pub?*; 8. *Why Boys Leave Home*; 9. *The Pianist and his Fiddle*; 10. *Mr Higginbottom – Me Best Enemy*; 11. *Have Snake – Must Travel*; 12. *Right in the Chicken Soup*; 13. *It's a Gift*; 14. *Long John Jim*; 15. *Two Crimes Are Better Than One*; 16. *For Love and Money*; 17. *Ours is a Nice House, Ours is*; 18. *Alfie Hall, The Smuggling Twit*; 19. *Storm in a Fire Bucket*; 20. *No Room at the Table*

Series 12
Broadcast details not available

Series 13 – (20 Weeks)

Written by
James Casey and Frank Roscoe

The Cast
Jimmy Clitheroe, Peter Sinclair, Patricia Burke, Danny Ross, Diana Day, John Graham

Produced by
James Casey

Sunday 17 August 1969–Sunday 28 December 1969
Weeks 1–20 transmitted at 1431; Weeks 1–20 repeated the following Tuesday at 2045 (Radio 1 and 2)
Broadcast on Radio 2

Episode List
1. *It's Quicker By Dream*; 2. *Take A Running Walk*; 3. *Answer That Phone*; 4. *Any More For The Beach*; 5. *Private Alfie – General Twit*; 6. *Too Many Decorators*; 7. *Never Believe What You Hear*; 8. *Final Score – I Foul Each*; 9. *It Shouldn't Happen To A Grandad*; 10. *Someone Somewhere Wants A Letter*; 11. *There's Something The Matter With Glasgow*; 12. *Clitheroe's Castle*; 13. *The Kid Who Framed Himself*; 14. *Dr Jekyll and Mr Jim*; 15. *If The Dunces Cap Fits*; 16. *Tickets For The Punch-Up*; 17. *Little Boy – Tall Story*; 18. *Heat The Test Tube and Run*; 19. *The Share Out*; 20. *Once Upon A Pantomime*

Series 14 – (20 Weeks)

Written by
James Casey and Frank Roscoe

The Cast
Jimmy Clitheroe, Peter Sinclair, Patricia Burke, Danny Ross, Diana Day, John Graham

Produced by
James Casey

Sunday 17 May 1970–Sunday 27 September 1970
Weeks 1–20 transmitted at 1430; Weeks 1–20 repeated the following Wednesday at 1815 (Radio 4)
Broadcast on Radio 2

Episode List
1. *Get Well Soon Grandad*; 2. *Grandad For President*; 3. *Good For Money*; 4. *The Not So Artful Dodger*; 5. *Not In Front Of The Parrot*; 6. *Out Of The Mouths of Puppies*; 7. *A Funny Thing Happened At The Fair*; 8. *All At Sea With A Sailor*; 9. *A Slight Cast of Whisky*; 10. *Seated One Day at the Movies*; 11. *Once More Into The Vicarage*; 12. *A Right Son Of A Gun*; 13. *There Was A Farmer – A Scottish Farmer*; 14. *Keep Jim Off The Road*; 15. *Best Of Birthday Luck*; 16. *Taken To The Cleaners*; 17. *James – The Modest Hero*; 18. *No Licence For Jim*; 19. *A Touch of Competition Fever*; 20. *For Singing Out Loud*

Series 15 – (13 Weeks)

Written by
James Casey and Frank Roscoe

The Cast
Jimmy Clitheroe, Peter Sinclair, Patricia Burke, Danny Ross, Diana Day, John Graham

Produced by
James Casey

Sunday 4 May 1971–Sunday 3 August 1971
Weeks 1–20 transmitted at 1430; Weeks 1–20 repeated the following Tuesday at 1815 (Radio 4)
Broadcast on Radio 2

Episode List
1. *All I Want Is A Room Somewhere*; 2. *Don't Shout – I'm Only Acting*; 3. *Go West Old Man*; 4. *Once Upon A Cuptie*; 5. *Jobs For The Ladies*; 6. *Tennis Just Isn't Cricket*; 7. *Whatever Happened to Grandad?*; 8. *History Is A Thing of The Past*; 9. *Is There A Boss In The House?*; 10. *In At The Deep End*; 11. *Licked By A Stamp*; 12. *Gone Fishing*; 13. *Thinking About A Holiday*

Series 16 – (13 Weeks)

Written by
James Casey and Frank Roscoe

The Cast
Jimmy Clitheroe, Peter Sinclair, Patricia Burke, Danny Ross, Diana Day, John Graham

Produced by
James Casey

Sunday 21 May 1972–Sunday 18 August 1972
Weeks 1–20 transmitted at 1402; Weeks 1–20 repeated the following Friday at 2002 (Radio 4)
Broadcast on Radio 2

Episode List
1. *My Great Aunt's Great*; 2. *Why Mothers Leave Home*; 3. *The Day The Fun Fair Hit Town*; 4. *If You Can't Keep A Secret – Sell It*; 5. *The Swiss Family Clitheroe*; 6. *The Romantic Higginbottoms*; 7. *Why Must The Show Go On*; 8. *A Letter From America For Grandad*; 9. *A Far, Far Better School To Go To . . .*; 10. *Money For Old Gold*; 11. *Enough To Make A Kitten Laugh*; 12. *Where's The Stage and What's The Play?*; 13. *What's The Welsh For Trouble?*

Beyond Our Ken

1958–1964

'It's a difficult style of humour to describe. A slightly zany sort of comedy, a taking-the-mickey-out-of-the-things-we-don't-like humour' – Kenneth Horne

Round The Horne is firmly etched on the minds of the public as one of the seminal comedies to come out of the BBC. It enjoyed four series of success in the 1960s but its predecessor, ***Beyond Our Ken***, doesn't seem to demand the same kind of recognition. There is, however, no reasonable explanation for this. ***Beyond Our Ken*** ran for twice the length of *Round The Horne*, a total of eight series covering seven years, and its cast was virtually identical to that of *Round The Horne*. To listen to an episode from each of these series, one

Transmission Details

Beyond Our Ken

Series 1 – (21 Weeks)

Written by
Eric Merriman and Barry Took

The Cast
Kenneth Horne, Kenneth Williams, Hugh Paddick, Betty Marsden, Ron Moody, Patricia Lancaster and Stanley Unwin

Music by
The Malcolm Mitchell

Trio (Weeks 1–16), the Fraser Hayes Four (Weeks 17–21)

Produced by
Jacques Brown (Weeks 1–19), Charles Maxwell (Weeks 20, 21)

Tuesday 1 July 1958–Tuesday 19 November 1958
Weeks 1–21 transmitted at 2000; no Repeats
Broadcast on the Light Programme

Series 2 – (20 Weeks)

Written by
Eric Merriman and Barry Took

The Cast
Kenneth Horne, Kenneth Williams, Hugh Paddick, Betty Marsden, Bill Pertwee and Patricia Lancaster

Music by
The Fraser Hayes Four, Edwin Braden

Produced by
Jacques Brown

Thursday 19 March 1959–Thursday 30 July 1959
Weeks 1–20 transmitted at 2000; Week 1 repeated on the following Sunday at 1900; Weeks 2–20 repeated on the following Sunday at 1415
Broadcast on the Light Programme

Special Christmas Programme
Thursday 21

would be forgiven for thinking there was no significant difference in content and little, if any, in style.

Kenneth Horne, a very well-known and respected broadcaster, had been compering the variety show *Music Hall* (formerly *Variety Playhouse*) during the 1940s and 1950s. He was the epitome of the well-educated English radio announcer and somehow managed to balance his career in show business with his highly successful career in business (see *Round The Horne*, Page 263).

Two young writers, Barry Took and Eric Merriman, saw in Horne a perfect example of sanity and respectability around which to devise a 30-minute comedy programme. They began writing in 1957 and the first series was broadcast in 1958. It's small wonder that the first series ever reached fruition after Kenneth Horne suffered a stroke in 1957, which left him in a serious condition just after a trial recording. But a speedy recovery saw his return to broadcasting in 1958 starring in ***Beyond Our Ken***.

Beyond Our Ken was described in *The Radio Times* of 1 July 1958 as 'a sort of radio show'. This is ambiguous to say the least, but it does lead the listeners to expect the unexpected, and that is what they initially heard with a wide range of characters, quick-fire delivery and first-rate ensemble interaction.

The cast of this 'sort of radio show' was Kenneth Horne as the voice of sanity, Kenneth Williams, Hugh Paddick, Betty Marsden, Ron Moody, Patricia Lancaster and Stanley Unwin. By the second series, in 1959, Bill Pertwee was added to the cast and Moody and Unwin left. It was this core of Horne, Williams, Paddick, Marsden and Pertwee that became the *Round The Horne* team in 1964.

This new show was produced by Jacques Brown, a

well-known BBC producer, who had a firm grounding in comedy, having spent some time as the producer of *Music Hall.* Music was provided initially by the Malcolm Mitchell Trio and then, from the second series onwards, by the Fraser Hayes Four, a close-harmony quartet, who stayed with the team well into its life as *Round The Horne.*

Together, Took and Merriman wrote 42 episodes of ***Beyond Our Ken***. They had created a spectrum of characters never before heard on the radio. When another well-known writing partnership, Frank Muir and Dennis Norden, stopped writing for the immensely long-running show *Take It From Here,* Took and Merriman were asked to take over. This was to be the end of a good working relationship and they wrote separate parts of the show, Merriman penning sketches alone and Took teaming up with his long-standing friend Marty Feldman. Eric Merriman stayed as sole writer for ***Beyond Our Ken*** and continued his output of excellence for another 100 shows.

The trio of Horne, Merriman and Brown had worked together previously on the show *Variety Playhouse* – which is perhaps a clue to why ***Beyond Our Ken*** seemed to gel so effortlessly from the first episode. If members of a comedy team know each other (and by 'team' we mean cast, writers and producers), then the final product is far more likely to kick off to a more natural and confident start than if a team were thrown together by chance. Kenneth Horne is quoted as saying, 'We thought the same way, and from the first, Merriman seemed to have the knack of writing the kind of things I found it easy to say. We felt it would be a pity to break up a promising partnership; and when the twenty-six *Variety Playhouse* programmes were over Jacques said we should stick together and

December 1959 at 2030
Repeated on Wednesday 23 December 1959 at 1310 on the Home Service

Series 3 – (14 Weeks)

Written by
Eric Merriman

The Cast
Kenneth Horne, Kenneth Williams, Hugh Paddick, Betty Marsden, Bill Pertwee and Patricia Lancaster

Music by
The Fraser Hayes Four, Edwin Braden, BBC Variety Orchestra conducted by Paul Fenoulhet

Produced by
Jacques Brown

Friday 15 April 1960–Friday 15 July 1960
Weeks 1–14 transmitted at 1930; Weeks 1–14 repeated on the following Sunday at 1415
Broadcast on the Light Programme

Series 4 – (20 Weeks)

Written by
Eric Merriman

The Cast
Kenneth Horne, Kenneth Williams, Hugh Paddick, Betty Marsden, Bill Pertwee, Patricia Lancaster and Janet Waters

Music by
The Fraser Hayes

Four, the Hornets, Edwin Braden, BBC Variety Orchestra conducted by Paul Fenoulhet

Produced by
Jacques Brown

Thursday 20 October 1960–Thursday 30 February 1961
Weeks 1–20 transmitted at 1930; Weeks 1–20 repeated on the following Sunday at 1830
Broadcast on the Light Programme

Series 5 – (20 Weeks)

Written by
Eric Merriman

The Cast
Kenneth Horne, Kenneth Williams, Hugh Paddick, Betty Marsden, Bill Pertwee and Jill Day (songstress)

Music by
The Fraser Hayes Four, Edwin Braden, BBC Variety Orchestra conducted by Paul Fenoulhet

Produced by
Jacques Brown

Thursday 12 October 1961–Thursday 22 February 1962
Weeks 1–20 transmitted at 2030; Weeks 1–19 repeated on the following Sunday at 1400; Week 20 repeated on the following Sunday at 1430
Broadcast on the Light Programme

try to hit upon an idea of a series for me.' That's when Barry Took was drafted in to make the trio a quartet.

The most instantly memorable part of ***Beyond Our Ken*** was the weekly slot of 'Hornerama'. This was a direct parody of BBC TV's documentary series *Panorama.* In fact, this was such a hit with the public and the BBC radio bosses that a spin-off series was planned, but the project never came to fruition. 'Hornerama' was the only fixed spot in the show. Merriman and Took were keen not to get bogged down with too many stock characters, which they felt could stifle the performers.

This section of the show was the one in which the audience knew exactly which characters would be taking part and what catchphrases would be used (see below for the list of characters). In an interview Merriman gave to *The Radio Times* in 1960, he says, 'There were to be no stock characters; and we chose the supporting cast among revue rather than radio actors. Mind you, once given a script, and scope, Kenneth Williams and Hugh Paddick soon fathered some characters on us.'

The customary signature tune was dispensed with and each show started with a short sketch, which was invariably a play on words tied in with a film title which tended to set the tone for the next half hour:

1: **Sixteen pounds ten shillings?!? That's absolutely scandalous!**

2: **Allow me. I'll check it for you sir. Oh I see that it's for, if you pardon my whimsy, for the current quarter. Yes sir, it's**

	perfectly correct: sixteen pounds ten shillings.
1:	**That's monstrous!**
2:	**Well I'm very sorry sir, but that's the price of electricity.**
ANNOUNCER:	**That was an excerpt from *The Charge of the Light Brigade* – another in our series, *A Film Worth Remembering*, which is more than can be said for the next half hour.**

The introduction of the cast was traditionally very obscure with a list of arbitrary persons or bodies of people:

> Dame Flora Eggberg, the Male section of the Luton Girls Choir, Miss Beatrice Bird Lover (she'll do anything for a lark), Elvis Douglas Home and of course Mr Kenneth Horne.

Hugh Paddick and Kenneth Williams regularly cropped up as the very camp duo of Rodney and Charles. Without doubt these slightly effeminate characters were the foundation of the later incarnations of Julian and Sandy that proved to be the favourite characters of *Round The Horne*. Like Julian and Sandy, Rodney and Charles were always constant no matter what situation they were in. In one 'Hornerama' they play the unlikely roles of two steelworkers:

ROD:	**Isn't it hot in here? Honestly, it's just like a furnace.**
CHARLES:	**It is a furnace.**
ROD:	**Well shut the door then.**

Series 6 – (13 Weeks)

Written by
Eric Merriman

The Cast
Kenneth Horne, Kenneth Williams, Hugh Paddick, Betty Marsden, Bill Pertwee and Eileen Gourlay (songstress); Announcer: Douglas Smith ('as a sort of announcer')

Music by
The Fraser Hayes Four, Edwin Braden, BBC Variety Orchestra conducted by Paul Fenoulhet

Produced by
John Simmonds

Thursday 27 December 1962–Thursday 21 March 1963
Weeks 1–13 transmitted at 2000; Weeks 1–13 repeated on the following Sunday at 1400
Broadcast on the Light Programme

Series 7 – (13 Weeks)

Written by
Eric Merriman

The Cast
Kenneth Horne, Kenneth Williams, Hugh Paddick, Betty Marsden, Bill Pertwee and Eileen Gourlay (songstress); Announcer: Douglas Smith ('as a sort of announcer')

Music by
The Fraser Hayes

Four, Edwin Braden, BBC Variety Orchestra conducted by Paul Fenoulhet
Produced by John Simmonds
Sunday 24 November 1963–Sunday 16 February 1964
Weeks 1–13 transmitted at 1400; Weeks 1–13 repeated on the following Wednesday at 1931
Broadcast on the Light Programme

CHARLES: **All right, but wait a minute, I just want to get my chestnuts out first. Is that better?**
ROD: **No, it's still boiling.**
CHARLES: **Well it's to be expected with the condition we have to work in.**
ROD: **Well all I can say is *blast* furnaces.**
CHARLES: **Roddy, what do you think of my asbestos suit?**
ROD: **Oh it's divine. Did you sew those sequins on yourself?**
CHARLES: **Well I did asbestas I could.**

The regular slot of 'Hornerama' always included a discussion of a topical issue: the state of the British film industry, the apathy of youth and so on. Joining Kenneth Horne (as ever, playing himself) were a regular panel representing the broad cross-section of the British public:

Hankie Flowered The resident comedian who bore an uncanny resemblance to a well-known comic called Frankie Howerd and was not averse to cracking the most appalling puns.

Ricky Livid 'Britain's answer to the singing nun, though he doesn't have such clean habits.' Ricky Livid was Hugh Paddick at his best playing a slightly dim pop star who never seemed to have had any success. One introduction by Horne, which shows how highly he viewed his panelist, was '... a pop singer who hasn't actually recorded this hit song but definitely must have inspired *I Who Have Nothing*.' Such jibes never prevented him from presenting his own pearls of wisdom. When asked for a reason for the declining cinema audiences he naively answers, 'I think we are all agreed that the reason a lot of the cinemas are empty these days is 'cos the people ain't there.'

Fanny Haddock This was one of the few characters to make the transition from ***Beyond Our Ken*** to *Round The Home*. Betty Marsden played Fanny Haddock, a cook with 'a well-used oven'. Again, this was a direct impersonation of a well-known celebrity, in this case the TV cook Fanny Craddock. She was usually the most sane member of the panel but often the most over-enthusiastic.

Arthur Fallowfield Another character that seemed to metamorphose into one of the favourites from *Round The Home*. Fallowfield was the wise Somerset farmer whose answer to everything was 'it lies in the soil'. This was a prototype version of the colossally popular Rambling Syd Rumpo.

The other most oft-recurring characters within the series, although they didn't appear in every episode, were Ambrose and Felicity (doddering idiots played by Williams and Marsden); Cecil Snaith (***Beyond Our Ken***'s roving reporter, played by Paddick); Arthur Figley (the pompous cockney, played by Williams); Seamus O'Toole (the public house poet, played by Pertwee); Stanley Birkinshaw (the sibilant splutterer whose speech is continually impaired by his ill-fitting dentures; one of his most notable performances was as part of the 400th anniversary of the birth of Shakespeare, when Birkinshaw delivers the 'To Be or Not To Be' soliloquy; played by Paddick).

The Arthur Askey Show

September–December 1958

Transmission Details

Askey Galore

(12 Weeks)

Written by
Dick Vosburgh and Brad Ashton (Weeks 1–4), Johhny Speight and Dick Barry (Weeks 5–9), David Climie and Pat Dunlop (Weeks 10–12)

The Cast
David Nixon, Anthea Askey, Sabrina and Vanessa Lee

Music by
Billy Ternent and his Orchestra

Produced by
Dennis Main Wilson

30 January 1957–17 April 1957
Broadcast Wednesdays 1900–1930
Broadcast on the Home Service

The Arthur Askey Show

Series 1 – (13 Weeks)

Written by
Bob Monkhouse and Denis Goodwin

'Arthur Askey – the Big Hearted Arthur of a thousand-and-one radio nights – was one of the first broadcasters to set his own highly individual fashions in fun' – *The Radio Times*

Arthur Askey made his name in the wartime comedy show *Band Waggon* where he forged one of radio's great double acts with Richard ('Stinker') Murdoch.

The Arthur Askey Show in 1958 saw the team of Askey and Murdoch together once more for this one-off series, which didn't resonate with quite the same gusto as *Band Waggon* in which these two fine performers shared a flat on top of Broadcasting House.

Joining these two in ***The Arthur Askey Show*** were the scriptwriting team of Bob Monkhouse and Denis Good-win, who had now established themselves as a rising double act. Their writing credentials were second to none: they'd penned such series as *Here's Howerd, Hip Hip Hoo Roy, It's A Great Life* and *Calling All Forces*. They also wrote the favourite characters of Mrs Purvis and Nola for Irene Handl and Pat Coombs,

who appeared in their series of *Leave It To The Boys* from 1960, which also boasted June Whitfield, Dick Bentley and Max Wall among its cast.

The thirteen-week run of ***The Arthur Askey Show*** from 30 September 1958 also included Diana Decker and Pat Coombs in the cast. It was produced by Leslie Bridgmont and music came from Bob Sharples with the BBC Variety Orchestra with Paul Fenhoulet.

The Cast
Arthur Askey, Richard Murdoch, Bob Monkhouse, Denis Goodwin, Pat Coombs and Diana Decker

Music by
Brian Sharples and the BBC Variety Orchestra with Paul Fenhoulet

Produced by
Leslie Bridgmont

Tuesday 30 September 1958–Tuesday 23 December 1958
Broadcast at 2000
Broadcast on the Light Programme

It's Great To Be Young

1958–1961

Ken Dodd is a household name owing to the power of television. He's a long-time variety performer who became a Radio 2 institution, particularly with *Ken Dodd's Palace of Laughter* and the phenomenally successful *Ken Dodd Show*. In 1958 he made his name with ***It's Great To Be Young***, an apt title, considering that Dodd was a mere 27 years old.

Comedy in the 1950s was immensely popular with listeners. The curious aspect was that so much was divided by accent. This was the era when the so-called 'northern' comics became increasingly popular. Ken Dodd was just one of a list of comics that included George Formby, Jimmy Clitheroe and Al Read.

James Casey was the series producer and co-writer, together with Frank Roscoe. Casey was himself from

Transmission Details

It's Great To Be Young

Series 1 – (11 Weeks)

Written by
James Casey and Frank Roscoe

The Cast
Ken Dodd, Peter Goodwright, Judith Chalmers and the Barry Sisters

Music by
The BBC Northern Dance Orchestra with Alyn Ainsworth and Jimmy Leach at the organ

Produced by
Frank Roscoe

Broadcast every Thursday at 2100
2 October 1958–10 December 1958
Repeated from Monday 9 March 1959 at 2100
Broadcast on the Light Programme

Series 2 – (8 Weeks)

Written by
James Casey, Frank Roscoe and Eddie Braben

The Cast
Ken Dodd, Peter Goodwright, Leonard Williams, Judith Chalmers, Karal Gardner and Jimmy Goldie

Music by
The BBC Northern Dance Orchestra with Bernard Herrmann and the Littlewood Songsters

Produced by
Frank Roscoe

Broadcast every Monday at 2000
14 November 1960–2 January 1961
Broadcast on the Light Programme

a first-rate comedy background, being the son of the popular comedian Jimmy James.

It's Great To Be Young was first broadcast on 2 October 1958. The cast was small: Dodd, Peter Goodwright, Judith Chalmers and the Barry Sisters; and the show's signature tune was 'Love Is Like a Violin'. Primarily, this was a sketch show with a strong northern edge, unlike the more gentle-paced situation comedies of the time like *Life With The Lyons*. The second series followed at the end of 1960 and the cast grew to incorporate Leonard Williams, Karal Gardner and Jimmy Goldie. An additional writer was recruited, a young Eddie Braben, who went on to massive success as writer for Morecambe and Wise.

Features of the show included 'A Journey to Doddyland', which has Uncle Ken reading imaginary tales from the equally imaginary Doddybook. There was a spot called 'Dodd's Mysteries of History', in which he solves those mysteries that have eluded the greatest minds of civilisation. The signature song from this series was 'Oh Boy, It's Great To Be Young'.

The Ken Dodd Show

1963–1967

The Ken Dodd Show followed the second series of *It's Great To Be Young* and was similar in formula. Characters and recurring sketches were the driving force of this show, all written to accommodate Ken Dodd's legendary breakneck speed of delivery. The cast was changed to include John Laurie (later of *Dad's Army* fame), as the crusty Scot from Invercockalekie, and Percy Edwards supplying a range of animal noises. Ray Fell, Judith Chalmers and Leonard Williams remained as stalwart support to Dodd.

The first series of ***The Ken Dodd Show*** was broadcast on 29 August 1963 and was written by Ken Dodd, writing for the first time, and Eddie Braben. With James Casey now engaged in writing *The Clitheroe Kid*, the new producer was Bill Worsley. Music was provided by the BBC Revue Orchestra with Malcolm Lockyer and Gerry and the Pacemakers.

Changes to the cast and production personnel were numerous and the second series, beginning on 24 May 1964, saw John Laurie replaced by another crusty Scot, Duncan Macrae. Patricia Hayes and Wallas Eaton joined the cast and Val Doonican provided the tunes. 'There is a touch of *The Sun*, of the Goons, and of *ITMA* in ***The Ken Dodd Show***,' said *The Radio Times* of this series.

By the third series, broadcast from 11 April 1965, Doddy's Diddy Orchestra was firmly established and recurring characters were creeping into the scripts. Among them were the Dowager Duchess, the Plummy Parson and the Cockeyed Cowboy called Clint.

Transmission Details

The Ken Dodd Show

Series 1

Written by
Ken Dodd and Eddie Braben

The Cast
Ken Dodd, John Laurie, Percy Edwards, Ray Fell, Judith Chalmers and Leonard Williams

Music by
The BBC Revue Orchestra with Malcolm Lockyer

Produced by
Bill Worsley

From 29 August 1963

Series 2

Written by
Ken Dodd and Eddie Braben

The Cast
Ken Dodd, Duncan Macrae, Patricia Hayes, Wallas Eaton, Percy Edwards and Judith Chalmers

Music by
The BBC Revue Orchestra with Malcolm Lockyer and Val Doonican

Produced by
Bill Worsley

From 24 May 1964
Repeated from 19 September 1964

The fourth series began in June 1966 with music by Dave Berry and the Cruisers. Graham Stark joined the cast of this show, which had now become a firm favourite, with characters that stayed with Ken Dodd for the rest of his career. The Diddymen were fictitious munchkin-like creatures from the town of Knotty Ash. The Knotty Ash Operatic Society were a recurring group, and another well-known character, Professor Chuckabutty, was introduced around this time.

Each show ended with the song that became Ken Dodd's theme tune – 'Happiness' – and rounded off with the catchphrase, 'Tattie-bye!' This was a show that, as the title suggests, was a vehicle for Ken Dodd. It was a mixture of straight gags learned from years of live theatre work and fantastic characters which reflect the sheer depth of imagination that this comic had when many of his contemporaries were merely telling gags or appearing in stifled situation comedies.

A further series of ***The Ken Dodd Show*** began on Radio 2 on 19 November 1967 at 1400. This was written once more by Ken Dodd and Eddie Braben and the cast were John Laurie (back again), Graham Stark and Patricia Burke with Bill Worsley producing.

Ken Dodd continued his work on the radio with further series in 1970, *Doddy's Daft Half Hour* in 1972, *Doddy's Comic Cuts* in 1973 and *Doddy's World of Whimsy* in 1975.

Series 3
Written by
Ken Dodd and Eddie Braben
The Cast
Ken Dodd, Duncan Macrae, Patricia Hayes, Wallas Eaton, Percy Edwards and Judith Chalmers
Music by
The BBC Revue Orchestra with Malcolm Lockyer
Produced by
Bill Worsley

From 11 April 1965

Series 4
Written by
Ken Dodd and Eddie Braben
The Cast
Ken Dodd, Duncan Macrae, Patricia Hayes, Wallas Eaton, Percy Edwards and Judith Chalmers
Music by
Dave Berry and the Cruisers
Produced by
Bill Worsley

From 15 June 1966

Series 5
Written by
Ken Dodd and Eddie Braben
The Cast
Ken Dodd, Duncan Macrae, Patricia Hayes, Graham Stark and Judith Chalmers
Music by
Dave Berry and the Cruisers
Produced by
Bill Worsley

From 18 December 1966

Series 6
Written by
Ken Dodd and Eddie Braben
The Cast
Ken Dodd, John Laurie, Patricia Burke and Graham Stark
Music by
Dave Berry and the Cruisers
Produced by
Bill Worsley

From 18 December 1966
Broadcast on Radio 2

Barker's Folly

March–May 1959

The Radio Times said in 1958, 'Eric Barker's reputation as an unconventional satirist of the human scene has grown with the years.'

First broadcast in 1959, ***Barker's Folly*** once again teamed Barker with Pearl Hackney. The husband-and-wife team played hosts to different guests each week, as they came to stay at their house in the imaginary village of Duxborough. *The Radio Times* previewed the show:

> As in any Barker household, there will be plenty of domestic troubles, and plenty of visitors. In the first week Eleanor Summerfield and Leonard Sachs are expected.

The most frequent guests were Deryck Guyler and Denise Bryer, as John and Mary Lawley, old friends of the Barkers. John was also Eric's bank manager.

Transmission Details

Barker's Folly

12 Weeks

Written by
Eric Barker

Featuring
Eric Barker, Pearl Hackney, Deryck Guyler and Denise Bryer

Produced by
Charles Maxwell

Broadcast 4 March 1959–20 May 1959
Broadcast Wednesdays 2130–2200 on the Light Programme

The Navy Lark

1959–1977

Most people will have heard of ***The Navy Lark***, but few below the age of 30 will have actually heard an episode from it. Compare the numbers that *did* hear it with those who heard *Hancock's Half Hour* or *The Goon Show*, and the listening figures will be very small. Yet, with a run of eighteen-and-a-half years, ***The Navy Lark*** was the BBC's longest-running comedy

Transmission Details

The Navy Lark

Series 1 – (16 Weeks)

Written by
Laurie Wyman

The Cast
Dennis Price, Jon Pertwee, Leslie Phillips, Richard Caldicott, Heather Chasen, Michael Bates, Ronnie Barker and Tenniel Evans
Music by
Tommy Reilly and James Moody
Produced by
Alastair Scott-Johnston

Sunday 27 March–12 July 1959
Weeks 1–16 transmitted at 1900; Weeks 4–16 repeated on the following Tuesday at 2000
Broadcast on the Light Programme

Series 2 – (26 Weeks)
Written by
Laurie Wyman
The Cast
Stephen Murray, Jon Pertwee, Leslie Phillips, Richard Caldicott, Heather Chasen, Michael Bates, Ronnie Barker, Tenniel Evans, June Tobin (for one episode only – 22 January 1960)
Music by
Tommy Reilly and James Moody
Produced by
Alastair Scott-Johnston

Friday 23 October 1959–Friday 8 April 1960
Weeks 1–10 transmitted at 1930; Week 11 (Christmas Day 1959) transmitted at 1935; Weeks 12–26

series (until *Week Ending* took over this mantle a few years ago). While it is true to say that this series didn't provide the kind of innovative scriptwriting exhibited in *The Goon Show* or *Round The Horne*, it did have some of the finest comic actors among its cast and the ensemble playing was of the highest quality.

In 1958 Laurie Wyman announced to the producer Alastair Scott-Johnston that he had an idea to build a series around the young and gifted comedy actor Jon Pertwee. Pertwee had previously finished a highly successful series called *Pertwee's Progress*, and Wyman rightly saw Pertwee not as a comedian 'but as an actor, a comic actor'. Pertwee had served in the navy for several years and it was decided that the Senior Service was to provide the backdrop to this new comedy.

With Pertwee as the anchor (for want of a better word) of this new series, Wyman had to flesh out the other main characters. He is quoted in an edition of *The Radio Times* as saying, 'I felt that we needed an idiot, and there was no one better at playing idiots than Leslie Phillips – so we got him.' The three leading characters of ***The Navy Lark*** each displayed different characteristics. Brashness, suaveness and naivety combined with idiocy were so brilliantly personified by Jon Pertwee, Dennis Price and Leslie Phillips respectively.

It took Laurie Wyman four months to get the first script to a finished state and when the programme was first listed in *The Radio Times* on 27 March 1959 it was described as, 'A Weekly and surely fictitious account of events in a naval detachment only loosely connected with the Senior Service.' The full cast list for this first series was:

Dennis Price	Lieut. Price the No. 1
Leslie Phillips	Sub-Lieut. Phillips
Jon Pertwee	Chief Petty Officer Pertwee
Richard Caldicott	Commander Povey
Heather Chasen	Joyce

With assistance from Michael Bates, Ronnie Barker and Tenniel Evans.

The action took place aboard *HMS Troutbridge* (see below for its full history), stationed in Portsmouth. The badge of the ship, which appeared in many photos and line drawings relating to the series, depicted a ship breaking through a bridge which is sinking into the sea (a testament to the incompetence, behind the wheel, of Sub-Lieutenant Phillips).

Such was the impact of this comedy that after only the third episode Herbert Wilcox sought to buy the film rights. *The Radio Times* wrote, 'Shooting will begin shortly in the Channel and the Admiralty have promised full cooperation and facilities.' The film was made with an entirely different cast, bar one actor, Leslie Phillips, who was at this time making a big name for himself in comedy films. As is the case with many radio comedy programmes of the time, no repeats were granted until a second or even a third series, but before the first series of ***The Navy Lark*** had come to an end the BBC decided to repeat the entire series on the Home Service on Saturdays at 1300.

However, all was not a smooth voyage for ***The Navy Lark***. After the success of the first series, Dennis Price left to pursue a once-in-a-lifetime opportunity to act on Broadway. (Unfortunately the play was a failure and Price was to regret this decision for the rest of his life.) Stephen Murray replaced Price

transmitted at 1930; Weeks 1–9 repeated on the following Tuesday at 2030; Weeks 13–26 repeated on the following Sunday at 1830
Broadcast on the Light Programme

Series 3 – (20 Weeks)

Written by
Laurie Wyman

The Cast
Stephen Murray, Jon Pertwee, Leslie Phillips, Richard Caldicott, Heather Chasen, Michael Bates, Ronnie Barker and Tenniel Evans

Music by
Tommy Reilly and James Moody

Produced by
Alastair Scott-Johnston

Wednesday 2 November 1960–Wednesday 15 March 1960
Weeks 1–20 transmitted at 1931; Weeks 1–20 repeated on the following Sunday at 1345
Broadcast on the Light Programme

Series 4 – (26 Weeks)

Written by
Laurie Wyman

The Cast
Stephen Murray, Jon Pertwee, Leslie Phillips, Richard Caldicott, Heather Chasen, Michael Bates, Ronnie Barker, Tenniel

Evans and Judy Cornwell
Music by
Tommy Reilly and James Moody
Produced by
Alastair Scott-Johnston

Friday 15 September 1960–Friday 9 March 1961
Weeks 1–26 transmitted at 1931; Weeks 1–26 repeated on the following Sunday at 1430
Broadcast on the Light Programme

Series 5 – (16 Weeks)
The TV Lark (10 Weeks)
The Navy Lark (6 Weeks)
Written by
Laurie Wyman
The Cast
Stephen Murray, Jon Pertwee, Leslie Phillips, Richard Caldicott, Heather Chasen, Michael Bates, Ronnie Barker, Tenniel Evans, Robin Boyle (Weeks 1–10) and Janet Brown (Weeks 1–10)
Music by
Tommy Reilly and James Moody
Produced by
Alastair Scott-Johnston

Friday 25 January 1963–Friday 10 May 1963
Weeks 1–16 transmitted at 2000; no repeats
Broadcast on the Light Programme

and stayed in the role of Captain until the very end of ***The Navy Lark*** in 1977.

The character of Chief Petty Officer Pertwee was central to ***The Navy Lark***'s success. Because he was the central character, it was Pertwee's plans and motives for personal gain that drove the plots forward. Vocally Jon Pertwee was highly dexterous and it is impossible to translate into words his nonsensical stutter (something that he resurrected for his role as the scarecrow Worzel Gummidge).

Although Wyman didn't significantly alter the character of Pertwee from the first series, he did expand upon Ronnie Barker's character of Able Seaman Johnson. Barker was gaining a large share of the audience's – and consequently the scriptwriter's – attention. Up to this point Barker was a largely unknown 30-year-old, having gained his radio experience in *The Floggits* with Elsie and Doris Waters and with Ted Ray in *Variety Playhouse.* His catchphrases, like 'You're rotten, you are', were becoming very quotable parts of the show.

It was Barker's exchanges with Pertwee that provided the biggest laughs of the show and set Pertwee and Johnson up as a kind of slapstick double act. Pertwee delighted in insulting Johnson whenever the mood took him, and this was more often than not. Most of these digs were weight-related: 'You barrel of lard' . . . 'my little rotund podge' . . . 'you great balloon-faced bumkin'.

This relationship of Pertwee and Johnson was the classic case of persecutor and victim. As with double acts before them, the downtrodden Johnson would always speak his mind, even if it meant a clip round the ear:

PERTWEE: **If you're gonna do a thing, do it right and proper. That's what I say.**

JOHNSON: **I know you do. I've been done right and proper ever since I knew you!**

Throughout the course of ***The Navy Lark*** this relationship stayed constant with Johnson playing the butt of Pertwee's insults. There was, however, a great feeling of 'us against them' in the way that they would team up to put one over superior officers like Commander Povey. Once again one has only to look at a double act like Laurel and Hardy to see that this device had been used long before ***The Navy Lark*** to great comedy effect.

Like Pertwee, Sub-Lieutenant Phillips (played by Leslie Phillips) was also trying to get the better of his superiors, but tended to fail because of an innate sense of incompetence and naivety. For eighteen years Laurie Wyman still managed to raise a laugh when it came to Phillips's complete inadequacy behind the wheel of *HMS Troutbridge.* Every time the order was given for 'full steam ahead' there was a sense of expectation with the audience as to what disaster Phillips would cause. In one early episode from 1960 the sounds of water followed by a deep creaking noise are remarked upon by Pertwee:

PERTWEE: **Blimey, we've taken the jetty with us sir!**

[Phillips retains his air of dignity and calmly gives the order:]

PHILLIPS: **Aaaah, stop engines.** [Pause] **Now how did I do that?**

Series 6 – (18 Weeks)
Written by
Laurie Wyman
The Cast
Stephen Murray, Jon Pertwee, Leslie Phillips, Richard Caldicott, Heather Chasen, Michael Bates, Ronnie Barker, Tenniel Evans and Judy Cornwell
Music by
Tommy Reilly and James Moody
Produced by
Alastair Scott-Johnston

Friday 27 September 1963–Friday 31 January 1964
Weeks 1–18
transmitted at 2000; no repeats
Broadcast on the Light Programme

Series 7 – (13 Weeks)
Written by
Laurie Wyman
The Cast
Stephen Murray, Jon Pertwee, Leslie Phillips, Richard Caldicott, Heather Chasen, Michael Bates, Ronnie Barker, Tenniel Evans and Jan Waters
Music by
Tommy Reilly and James Moody
Produced by
Alastair Scott-Johnston

Sunday 11 July 1965–Sunday 3 October 1965
Weeks 1–13
transmitted at 1400;

Weeks 1–13 repeated on the following Wednesday at 1931
Broadcast on the Light Programme

Series 8 – (13 Weeks)
Written by
Laurie Wyman
The Cast
Stephen Murray, Jon Pertwee, Leslie Phillips, Richard Caldicott, Heather Chasen, Michael Bates, Ronnie Barker and Tenniel Evans
Music by
Tommy Reilly and James Moody
Produced by
Alastair Scott-Johnston

Sunday 4 September 1966–Sunday 27 November 1966
Weeks 1–13 transmitted at 1330;
Weeks 1–13 repeated on the following Wednesday at 2000
Broadcast on the Light Programme

Series 9 – (10 Weeks)
Written by
Laurie Wyman
The Cast
Stephen Murray, Jon Pertwee, Leslie Phillips, Richard Caldicott, Heather Chasen, Michael Bates, Ronnie Barker, Tenniel Evans; Announcer: Michael de Morgan
Music by
Tommy Reilly and James Moody

COMMANDER: **Simple Mr Phillips. You omitted to cast off.**
PHILLIPS: [To himself] **Clumsy.**

Pertwee and Phillips were the scheming elements aboard the *Troutbridge*. Pertwee had the gift of the gab, which tended to get him off with no reproach, but Phillips had a habit of always saying the wrong thing at the worst possible time:

COMMANDER: **No Mr Phillips. I'm facing a most terrible domestic crisis.**
PHILLIPS: **We know. We've met her several times.**
COMMANDER: **You know I don't think it's going to be your day.**
PHILLIPS: **It never is actually sir.**

By the third series the show was so popular that the cast were chosen, by a poll of Women's Royal Naval Service personnel, to provide the entertainment for their 21st anniversary celebrations at the Royal Festival. *The Radio Times* claimed the show's popularity was so widespread that it was even liked by what CPO Pertwee calls the 'Hadmiralty'. During this second series a rehearsal was attended by the First Sea Lord Sir Charles Lambe, giving it a stamp of approval if ever there was one.

Unlike other comedy shows of this time ***The Navy Lark*** was synonymous with a real-life organisation who made the programme their own. To be more precise, the crew of the not too dissimilarly named *HMS Troubridge* were regular visitors to recordings at the invitation of the cast. A *Radio Times* article at the start of the third series said, 'The Navy and ***The Navy Lark*** have adopted each other.'

As any series grows it creates its own catchphrases and ethos. ***The Navy Lark*** was no exception. Two principles of the crew, which summarise very concisely their attitude, were: (1) 'If someone's got something on you, get something on him, quick'; (2) 'If you can't explain it, hide it and hop it.'

In an effort to avoid rehashing too similar plot lines, Wyman was beginning to work in newer situations. By the sixth series he had the *Troutbridge* going to sea in the Far East, the crew having a brush with an Iron Curtain shipping fleet and having to go in for limpet-mine disposal. Fresher backdrops were needed to give the same characters a new lease on life. This was a safer way of exploiting the characters than changing their profession outright (see *The TV Lark* below).

There is no doubt that ***The Navy Lark*** was a BBC institution by the time it last broadcast in 1977. It was listened to by millions of people, many of whom had absolutely no knowledge of navy life. However, the fact that it was adopted by navy personnel of all ranks made it that much more successful. It would be unfair to compare it to comedies like *Round The Horne* and *Hancock's Half Hour.* ***The Navy Lark*** was a safe sitcom, centred around the same few characters in largely the same few situations. It contained some first-rate ensemble playing and deserves to be remembered if only for the quite unique talent of Jon Pertwee.

History of HMS Troutbridge

In an article in *The Radio Times* on 16 November 1961 extracts of the 'official history' of *HMS Troutbridge*

Produced by
Alastair Scott-Johnston

Sunday 10 September 1967–Sunday 12 November 1967
Weeks 1–10 transmitted at 1330; Weeks 1–10 repeated on the following Wednesday at 1930
Broadcast on the Light Programme

Series 10 – (12 Weeks)

Written by
Laurie Wyman

The Cast
Stephen Murray, Jon Pertwee, Leslie Phillips, Richard Caldicott, Heather Chasen, Michael Bates, Ronnie Barker and Tenniel Evans

Music by
Tommy Reilly and James Moody

Produced by
Alastair Scott-Johnston

Sunday 16 May 1971–Sunday 29 July 1971
Weeks 1–12 transmitted at 1400; Weeks 1–12 repeated on the following Monday at 1815 on Radio 4
Broadcast on Radio 2

Series 11 – (13 Weeks)

Written by
Laurie Wyman and George Evans

The Cast
Stephen Murray, Jon Pertwee, Leslie Phillips, Richard Caldicott, Heather

Chasen, Michael Bates, Ronnie Barker and Tenniel Evans
Music by
Tommy Reilly and James Moody
Produced by
Alastair Scott-Johnston

Sunday 16 May 1971–Sunday 29 July 1971
Weeks 1–12 transmitted at 1400; Weeks 1–13 repeated the following Monday at 1815 on Radio 4
Broadcast on Radio 2

Series 12 – (13 Weeks)
Written by
Laurie Wyman and George Evans
The Cast
Stephen Murray, Jon Pertwee, Leslie Phillips, Richard Caldicott, Heather Chasen, Michael Bates, Ronnie Barker and Tenniel Evans
Music by
Tommy Reilly and James Moody
Produced by
Alastair Scott-Johnston

Sunday 29 July 1973–Sunday 21 October 1973
Weeks 1–13 transmitted at 1402; Weeks 1–13 repeated the following Monday at 1902 on Radio 4
Broadcast on Radio 2

were printed under the claim that they were 'taken from Admiralty files'.

Troutbridge keeps alive the memory of Admiral Sir Benjamin Troutbridge, who was born in 1741 and vanished in 1797. He is credited as the man who started the Battle of the Cape of St George with a howl of bad language which was misinterpreted as the ship's battle orders. Needless to say, Admiral Troutbridge sank with his ship shortly after this mishap occurred.

HMS Troutbridge was built as a general-purpose frigate and was completed in 1945 and served with 'average distinction' for thirteen years. Any naval undesirables were recruited to this one ship where they could all be watched over. Because CPO Pertwee has relatives in the Establishment and Lieutenant Murray's brother is an MP, questions have been asked in Parliament about a 'distressingly high mortality rate amongst admirals'.

Commander Povey is forever writing to the Admiralty to try to rid himself of his crew, who are more interested in personal comfort and commerce than the requirements of the navy. However the letter never reaches its destination. Suffice to say that *The Radio Times* obtained 'this top-secret information at enormous expense and that CPO Pertwee's ratings show no sign of pausing in their inflationary spiral'.

The TV Lark

At the end of the fourth series, ***The Navy Lark*** had gathered more listeners and was enjoying massive success. Laurie Wyman, with the producer Alastair Scott-Johnston, did, however, ensure that *HMS*

Troutbridge was written off so the cast could inhabit a new setting. In this case it was Troutbridge Commercial TV.

'The fact that our gallant crew know no more about TV than they did about the navy is no obstacle to their belief that the world owes them a living and can, somehow, be persuaded to cough up,' said *The Radio Times*.

The TV Lark was a risky experiment that lasted for ten episodes. The usual goings on were no different in practice, whether they were on a ship or in a TV studio. The crew, led by Director Leslie Phillips, included Jon Pertwee as the Floor Manager and 'Fatso' Barker on cameras. True to form, these characters constantly attempted to pull the wool over Producer Stephen Murray's eyes and, in so doing, succeeded in annoying the Deputy Controller of Troutbridge TV, Henry Povey (ex-Captain of the *Troutbridge*).

Added to the usual cast of ***The Navy Lark*** were Janet Brown as the Production Secretary and Robin Boyle as the Announcer. But the frolics at the television station were short-lived and on 5 April 1963 ***The Navy Lark*** was back in time for its 100th episode on 12 April. Although it was a risky experiment that perhaps didn't quite work it certainly succeeded in giving ***The Navy Lark*** a new lease of life.

Series 13 – (11 Weeks)

Written by
Laurie Wyman and George Evans

The Cast
Stephen Murray, Jon Pertwee, Leslie Phillips, Richard Caldicott, Heather Chasen, Michael Bates, Ronnie Barker and Tenniel Evans

Music by
Tommy Reilly and James Moody

Produced by
Alastair Scott-Johnston

Sunday 9 November 1975–Sunday 18 January 1976
Weeks 1–11 transmitted at 1402; Weeks 1–11 repeated the following Saturday at 1902
Broadcast on Radio 2

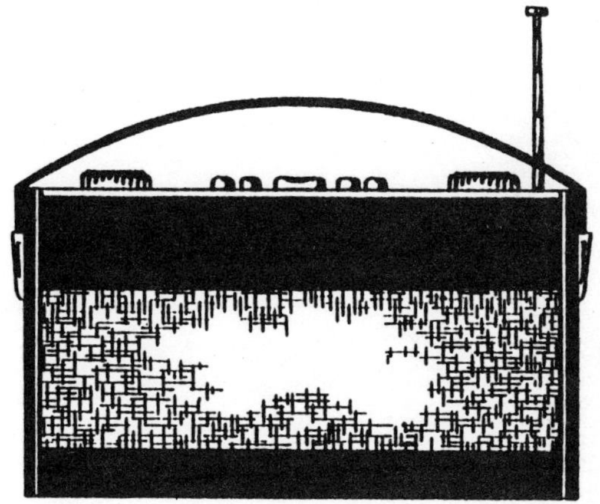

THE 1960s

The 1960s

Looking back at the output from the 1950s, you can see why it is cited as the 'golden era' of radio comedy. The BBC radio department managed to keep its audience, despite the ever-growing threat of television, which was reaching thousands of virgin viewers each day. It was inevitable that in the none-too-distant future radio would lose out in this battle for an audience. Sadly, the 1960s marked a definite decline in quality and quantity of the BBC's comedy output.

The Swinging Sixties have been more than adequately documented. It was a time when popular music had become the property of the young and with it the emergence of Radio 1 and numerous independent music channels, as well as the pirate stations like Radio Caroline. A vast split in the listenership that the BBC once had to itself had now been created. This was the decade when teenage tastes were well catered for by the emergence of mass media. No longer were there only children and adults – now there was the teenager, the adolescent. The teenagers didn't want to sit with the family around the radiogram on a Sunday lunchtime – technology provided them with cheap transistor radios on which to listen to their own shows.

So many of the radio stars of the 1950s were lured by television and film as the offers of more money and a far larger audience proved irresistible. Tony Hancock, Peter Sellers, Frankie Howerd, Kenneth Williams all appeared less and less on radio and unfortunately also seemed irreplaceable. But the 1960s did throw up stars who at times achieved phenomenal audience figures despite being very 'un-hip' in such an image-conscious time.

One example is Jimmy Clitheroe, whose radio show *The Clitheroe Kid* was heard by over ten million people at its height in the mid 1960s.

There were of course several radio series during the 1960s that could fall into the category of 'classics', notably *I'm Sorry, I'll Read That Again*, which saw the beginning of a new wave of comedians, spawned by the satire boom of the early 1960s. The establishment was no longer a taboo subject exempt from ridicule. Politicians, royalty and the aristocracy were all legitimate targets for lampooning.

This satire boom was spearheaded by the Oxbridge revue *Beyond The Fringe*, which starred Peter Cook and Jonathan Miller from Cambridge, and Dudley Moore and Alan Bennett from Oxford. *Beyond The Fringe* really opened the floodgates for a whole new coterie of performers who also wrote their own material, unlike so many of the established comedians who had gone before.

Hot on the heels of *Beyond The Fringe* followed *Cambridge Circus*, which included John Cleese, Tim Brooke-Taylor, Bill Oddie, Jo Kendall and David Hatch among the performers. This core of performer/writers was speedily snapped up by the BBC and it was only a matter of a couple of years before *Cambridge Circus* appeared as *I'm Sorry, I'll Read That Again*.

ISIRTA set the standard by which so many subsequent series were to be measured. It is important to stress, however, that the BBC didn't suddenly have a mass exodus of its previously established stars, replacing them only with young turks from Cambridge or Oxford University. Kenneth Horne, one of the Beeb's hardy perennials, was to become one of the best-known names in the history of the medium because of two seminal series from the 1960s: *Beyond Our Ken* and *Round The Horne*, which included Kenneth Williams, Bill Pertwee and Betty Marsden among its cast. Undoubtedly the influence of Oxbridge humour like *Beyond The Fringe* can be seen in shows like *Round The Horne*, which often ridiculed government goings-on and news items; but this was a show that came to be loved for its incessant innuendo and wordplay. In a decade when satire was all the rage, a show like *Round The Horne* succeeded as an antidote.

Round The Horne particularly has become one of the best-loved radio series of all time. However, it is a series that owes as much to the 1960s as to a variety tradition of the past. It was a show that targeted much of the popular culture of the time, which was so centred on London and Liverpool. The music, clothes, film and the whole ethos of the Swinging

Sixties were mirrored and sent up by the *Round The Horne* team. Both *I'm Sorry, I'll Read That Again* and *Round The Horne* had a very strong sense of controlled anarchy about them. This was the era of team comedy, when anything could happen – and often did.

Kenneth Horne's former partner from *Much-Binding-In-The-Marsh*, Richard Murdoch, teamed up with Wilfrid Hyde-White in a sitcom called *Men From The Ministry*. While the format of the situation comedy was certainly safer and kinder than other shows of the time, the target of government bureaucracy was very much in keeping with the satirical edge of so much comedy of this era. *Men From The Ministry* is a classic that deserves its place among the great shows of yesteryear. It is certainly influential and one only has to look at *Yes Minister* to see the similarities.

Perhaps the strongest indication of the decline in the standard of comedy output on the radio was the advent of series that had started life on television. The notable examples of this trend were the adaptations of *Steptoe and Son*, *Whack-O* and *The Likely Lads*. It wasn't that these were necessarily bad examples of radio comedy. *Steptoe and Son* was based on the original TV scripts, which were brilliantly funny, as was the *Likely Lads* radio series. It just showed a distinct lack of originality on the part of the heads of the light entertainment department.

It's A Deal

March–June 1961

Transmission Details

It's A Deal

13 Weeks

Written by
Ronald Chesney and Ronald Wolfe

The Cast
Sid James, Dennis Price, Wallas Eaton, June Whitfield and Robin Ray

Produced by
Tom Ronald

Thursday 9 March 1961–Thursday 1 June 1961
Broadcast at 2100
Broadcast on the Light Programme

The radio, TV and film star Sid James appeared in this 1961 series as a spiv-type property dealer with his eyes on anything he could get his claws into. 'In fact he was going to put in a bid for Buckingham Palace until he found out there was a sitting tenant.' Sid's character was not alarmingly dissimilar to the one he played opposite Hancock, always there to make a few quid even if he wasn't sure about the outcome. As a rising property tycoon he knew precious little about the business and 'fondly imagines that the Green Belt is a boxing trophy for novices'.

Joining him in his shady dealings was the smooth-voiced Dennis Price. Price was part of the company to add a veneer of old-school-tie respectability. Equally plummy-voiced was their secretary, Susan Corkindale, played by June Whitfield, 'who was born with a silver spoon in her mouth – and speaks as though it were still there'. Her father, Lord Corkindale, just happened to own those parts of London that Sid was dying to buy up. Benson, the general manager of the office, kept a watchful eye on the dealings and was played by Wallas Eaton with Robin Ray playing the last cog in the wheel – the office boy Steve.

The scripts for this thirteen-part series were written by Ronald Chesney and Ronald Wolfe, and Tom Ronald produced.

It's A Fair Cop

May–July 1961

Although this series was a one-off and ran for only eight episodes, it is of interest as it was the first radio series starring Eric Sykes. Sykes had made his name as a comedy writer of some repute, most notably as a co-writer of *The Goon Show* with Spike Milligan. He was already a household name and familiar face to many people, having starred in his own very successful TV series.

It's A Fair Cop was based around a country policeman at the Blossom Hill Station. He was a constable and answerable to his sergeant, Sgt Deryck Guyler. Ironically Guyler was to play a policeman, Corky, in the long-running BBC series *Sykes*. Above Guyler, at Blossom Hill, was Superintendent Leonard Williams.

Eric Sykes had a sister in this series played by Hattie Jacques, a partnership which was just beginning to be forged in his television series, which began in the previous year. The close partnership with Jacques lasted until her untimely death in 1980. Naturally, it could have been difficult to appreciate just how unlikely this brother/sister act was on the radio, but they were such well-known personalities that this wasn't an issue.

The permanent prisoner in cell No. 1 was Dick Emery. He has been in and out for a long time and so has learnt to make himself comfortable with the armchair and television set provided by his solicitous gaolers.

Writers of this one-off series in 1961 were John

Transmission Details

It's A Fair Cop

8 Weeks

Written by
John Junkin and Terry Nation

The Cast
Eric Sykes, Hattie Jacques, Deryck Guyler, Dick Emery and Leonard Williams

Music by
Ronnie Cass and Alan Roper

Produced by
Herbert Smith

Monday 22 May 1961–Monday 10 July 1961
Broadcast at 2000
Broadcast on the Light Programme

Junkin and Terry Nation, and Herbert Smith produced. Music was provided by Ronnie Cass and Alan Roper.

The Men From The Ministry

1962–1977

Transmission Details

The Men From The Ministry

Series 1 – (13 Weeks)

Written by
Edward Taylor

The Cast
Wilfrid Hyde-White, Richard Murdoch, Roy Dotrice, Diana Olsen, Edwin Apps, David Graham and Norma Ronald

Produced by
Edward Taylor

Tuesday 30 October 1962–Tuesday 22 January 1963
Weeks 1–13 transmitted at 2000;
Weeks 1–13 repeated from Saturday 9 February 1963 at 1310 on the Home Service
Broadcast on the Light Programme

Episode List
1. *The Great Footwear Scandal*; 2. *The Big Rocket*; 3. *Strictly For*

The influence of this light-hearted situation comedy about government life and bumbling bureaucrats is not as wide-reaching as *The Goon Show* or *Hancock's Half Hour* but it can be pinpointed as the forerunner to the phenomenally successful *Yes Minister*, which became one of the best-loved British comedy shows of all time. It was certainly one of the longest-running at fifteen years, starting life in 1962 and last heard in 1977.

The pace of this show is certainly slower than many of its counterparts. While *Round The Horne* and *I'm Sorry, I'll Read That Again* were firing gags at a breakneck speed, Wilfrid Hyde-White and Richard Murdoch, the stars of the show, were more reminiscent of a world that was being left behind. Times were indeed changing, but behind government doors the world of lunch at the club and stopping work to take tea in the afternoon was still alive and well and not concerned with life in the fast lane.

The announcement that introduced the show summarises it in a succinct way:

> A weekly tribute to that faithful army of public servants who direct our lives and whose function

is illustrated by their ancient crest, two crossed memos and bowler hat carrying a can.

Wilfrid Hyde-White, a very well-respected and well-loved film actor, was Mr Roland Hamilton-Jones, the head of the General Assistance Department. This was a department that, according to *The Radio Times*, 'exists to help any section that's over-loaded. One day aviation; the next, education: always, confusion'.

Playing opposite Hyde-White was one of the great names from radio, Richard Murdoch as Richard Lamb, the second-in-command and often referred to as 'Number Two'. Lamb keeps the office running, usually in the absence of Hamilton-Jones referred to as 'HJ' or as 'Number One'. The department is continually monitored by Sir Gregory Pitkin, usually very angry, and described in a later episode as being 'like Jekyll and Hyde. Half the time he's difficult and irritable and quite unpleasant, then something snaps and he really turns nasty.' Sir Gregory was played by the very popular actor Roy Dotrice.

Lamb and HJ have to keep a firm hand on their secretary, Mildred Murfin, played by Norma Ronald, who specialises in doing as little as possible in as short a time as possible. Mildred is the only representation of the real world and, as a nineteen-year-old, is a fish out of water in the department.

The other main character in the first series was Miss April Adams (Diana Olsen), who was the level-headed member of the team and on hand to help get the department out of the inevitable mess it finds itself in.

The first series of ***The Men From The Ministry*** was written and produced by Edward Taylor and

The Birds (with Percy Edwards); 4. *French Cricket* (with Betty Marsden); 5. *The War With The Isle of White*; 6. *Moderately Important Person*; 7. *The Rhubarb Pirates*; 8. *A Matter of Form*; 9. *The Magic Carpet*; 10. *The Spy in Black and White* (with June Whitfield); 11. *Island in the Sun*; 12. *Problem in the Park*; 13. *The End of the Road*

Christmas Special 1964

Broadcast on 24 December 1964 at 1930 with no repeat

Series 2 – (13 Weeks)

Written by
Johnny Mortimer, Brian Cooke and Edward Taylor

The Cast
Wilfrid Hyde-White, Richard Murdoch, Roy Dotrice, Norma Ronald, Joan Sanderson and David Graham

Produced by
Edward Taylor

Sunday 25 July 1965–Sunday 17 October 1965
Weeks 1–13 transmitted at 2100; Weeks 1–13 repeated on the following Tuesday at 2000 on the Home Service
Broadcast on the Light Programme

Episode List
1. *Pirates of Lakeview Reservoir*; 2. *Something*

About A Soldier; 3. *The Trouble With Cecil*; 4. *Mahboni Lies Over the Ocean*; 5. *The Man Who Made it Rain*; 6. *Train of Events*; 7. *A Degrading Business*; 8. *The Butcher of Glensporren*; 9. *Counter Spies*; 10. *A Question of Dundancy*; 11. *A Back-Dated Problem*; 12. *The Hole*; 13. *The Day The Martians Came*

Series 3 – (14 Weeks)

Written by
Johnny Mortimer, Brian Cooke and Edward Taylor

The Cast
Deryck Guyler, Richard Murdoch, Norma Ronald, Ronald Baddiley and John Graham

Produced by
Edward Taylor

Sunday 11 December 1966–Sunday 12 March 1967
Weeks 1–3 transmitted at 2130;
Weeks 4–14 transmitted at 2100;
Weeks 1–14 repeated from Monday 3 April at 1900 on the Home Service
Broadcast on the Light Programme

Episode List
1. *Rebel In Regents Park*; 2. *A Terrifying Weapon*; 3. *The Post Office Pantomime*; 4. *All At Sea*; 5. *Bowler Hats and Machine Guns*; 6. *On The Run*; 7. *A Gift For Sir Gregory*; 8. *The*

ran for thirteen episodes. Although not resolutely topical, this situation comedy did mirror issues that were in the news at the time. One example was the second episode to be aired, called *Big Rocket*, which was a comment on how little Britain was doing in the ever-expanding area of space travel.

The department find themselves transformed by direct order into the 'Space Information Bureau', responsible for a weekly bulletin to heighten Britain's profile in the space race. Mildred has stormed out of the office and Mr Lamb, wanting to go early to lunch, leaves a note for HJ next to the bulletin which explains Mildred's absence: 'Big rocket in the air, Mildred shot off early this morning. Mildred must be brought down to earth.'

Needless to say, when the teleprinter-operator comes to pick up the bulletin he picks up the note to HJ setting up the plot very nicely for total confusion. This kind of confusion was a regular occurrence in ***The Men From The Ministry***, which had its roots in British farce rather than in the new wave of satire.

The typical cross-purpose conversation takes place when Peterson, the editor of a paper, calls up for more information about a secret rocket called 'Mildred'.

PETERSON: **Can you give us some information about this big rocket?**

LAMB: **What big rocket?**

PETERSON: **This morning's big rocket. What was the name we were given? Ah yes, Mildred.**

LAMB: **Oh the Mildred business, good gracious you press boys get on to everything.**

PETERSON: **Mildred was fired this morning I understand?**
LAMB: **Not exactly fired, sort of shot off.**
PETERSON: **This was very sudden though, wasn't it?**
LAMB: **Not really, we have been building up to it for some time.**

When the papers and television are full of stories about Mildren Murfin, the first woman in space, HJ is keen to play along with it rather than admit that his department made a huge mistake sending the wrong piece of paper to the teleprinter. He bluffs to the Admiralty that she will be coming down in the North Sea. An American announcer on the spot remarks,

> Through a slight miscalculation Mildred came down, not in the North Sea, where so many sailors were waiting to pick her up, but in the deserted Thames Estuary. Here she was rescued by the foresight of Space Information Bureau's Roland Hamilton-Jones, who was patrolling this very area in a launch.

The show was an instant hit with audiences. It was a sitcom of the old school but had the added edge of gentle satire in that it ridiculed the government. Although another series was commissioned, audiences had to wait until 1965 for a second series, when another thirteen episodes were broadcast.

Diana Olsen was missing from the second series and was replaced by Joan Sanderson, one of the

Whitehall Circus; 9. *Customs of the Country*; 10. *Getting the Bird*; 11. *The Girl in the Case*; 12. *The Thing on the Beach*; 13. *A Slight Case of Demolition*; 14. *The Fastest Ship in the World*

Series 4 – (13 Weeks)

Written by
Johnny Mortimer, Brian Cooke and Edward Taylor

The Cast
Deryck Guyler, Richard Murdoch, Norma Ronald, Ronald Baddiley, John Graham and David Nettheim

Produced by
Edward Taylor

Sunday 18 February 1968–Sunday 12 May 1968
Weeks 1–13 transmitted at 1431; Week 1 repeated on Monday 19 February 1968 at 2045 on Radios 1 and 2; Weeks 2–13 repeated on the following Mondays at 1945 on Radios 1 and 2
Broadcast on Radio 2

Episode List
1. *Battle of the River Thames*; 2. *The Tubby Submarine*; 3. *A Matter of Breeding*; 4. *The Great Showbiz Fiasco*; 5. *Up The Poll*; 6. *Waterway To Go*; 7. *Dam Nuisance*; 8. *The Fastest Brolly in the West**; 9. *Lamb Takes a Gambol*; 10. *Four Men in a Wellington*; 11. *Out*

of This World; 12. *Muddlers in Law*; 13. *What Has Four Wheels and Flies?*

*This episode contained the song 'The Legend of the Men From the Ministry', which was sung by Graeme Garden

Series 5 – (14 Weeks)

Written by
John Graham and Edward Taylor

The Cast
Deryck Guyler, Richard Murdoch, Norma Ronald, Ronald Baddiley and John Graham

Produced by
Edward Taylor

Tuesday 30 June 1970–Tuesday 31 September 1970
Weeks 1–14 transmitted at 1930
Broadcast on Radio 4
Weeks 1–14 had previously been broadcast on the World Service from 15 March 1970

Episode List
1. *Bye Bye Mildred*; 2. *Bare Necessities*; 3. *Storm In A Teacup*; 4. *The Moving Target*; 5. *Oil Well That Ends Well*; 6. *The Bigger The Better*; 7. *Trouble In The Air*; 8. *Miss Chatterly's Lover*; 9. *The Pudding From Outer Space*; 10. *A Little Of What You Fancy*; 11. *A Bird In The Hand*; 12.

best-known faces in sitcoms on television throughout the 1970s and 1980s. Edward Taylor produced once more and co-wrote with Johnny Mortimer and Brian Cooke, who had also written for the first series of *I'm Sorry, I'll Read That Again*. Later on in its run, Taylor's co-writer was the actor John Graham who regularly appeared in the show playing a wide variety of smaller roles.

The second series of ***The Men From The Ministry*** was a huge hit with listeners. Another series was inevitable but series three saw the departure of Wilfrid Hyde-White, who moved out to Hollywood. It is a testament to the writing that even when one of the leading actors leaves, the show can continue to flourish with a replacement. In the story the reason that Hamilton-Jones left was his promotion to the Ministry of Expansion, where the attraction was a generous two biscuits with their tea.

Wilfrid Hyde-White was replaced in the cast by Deryck Guyler as Deryck Lennox-Brown. Guyler was another radio star who had appeared in *ITMA* as Frisby Dyke, Percy Palaver and Sir Short Supply. He was Eric Barker's partner in *Just Fancy* in the 1950s and was the crime-solving policeman Inspector Scott in the imaginatively titled *Inspector Scott Investigates*. Guyler went on to television playing opposite Eric Sykes as another policeman, Corky, in the hit show *Sykes*.

The series went on, with the department continually bungling every task put its way by the ever-angry Whitehall boss Sir Gregory. In *Sky High* from 1974 the department is meant to oversee the completion of a new skyscraper to house the Ministry of Social Security called 'Wilson Towers'. Lennox-Brown remarks drily, 'Don't tell me, it's leaning to the left?'

Lennox-Brown and Lamb are instructed to ban all tea breaks, which they do with a posted memo. Sir Gregory insists that they go up onto the top floor armed with binoculars and allay fears that people will be able to see in to the washroom of the Foreign Office. This was formula stuff. The department's role is set up within the first five minutes, which include gags about the subject, in this case about the slowness of builders. Sir Gregory calls in to give them their orders and the plot moves forward.

With Lennox-Brown, Lamb and Mildred on the top floor, the builders below have decided to strike on receipt of the memo from the department banning all tea breaks. The trio are stranded with the lift out of action and they think that the builders will return early in the morning. Lennox-Brown insists on survival measures with nothing to eat but a bag of potatoes that Lamb bought and a half chewed piece of chewing-gum in Mildred's bag. He starts to cook his briefcase by igniting it with the sun through his glasses:

LENNOX-BROWN:	**It will make a change from raw potato. I'm cooking this briefcase.**
MILDRED:	**Cooking the briefcase?**
LENNOX-BROWN:	**Well it's soft leather you see: it should taste just like a canteen steak.**

After a fortnight 'Creepy' Crawley from the next office has wormed his way into taking over the department with Sir Gregory's approval and Lamb is carving out his will in the concrete and is going mad:

Bringing The House Down; 13. *Fair Exchange*; 14. *Bill Stickers Is Innocent*

Series 6 – (7 Weeks)

Written by
John Graham and Edward Taylor

The Cast
Deryck Guyler, Richard Murdoch, Norma Ronald, Ronald Baddiley and John Graham

Produced by
Edward Taylor

Tuesday 11 July 1972–Tuesday 29 August 1972
Weeks 1–7 transmitted at 1225; Weeks 1–7 repeated on Thursdays at 1815
Broadcast on Radio 4

Episode List
1. *Conference Trick*; 2. *How Now Brown Cow?*; 3. *Sorry, Wrong Number*; 4. *The Desk Job*; 5. *Foul Play*; 6. *Something Of Value*; 7. *Taking Leave of Their Census*

Series 7 – (13 Weeks)

Written by
John Graham and Edward Taylor

The Cast
Deryck Guyler, Richard Murdoch, Norma Ronald, Ronald Baddiley and John Graham

Produced by
Edward Taylor

Tuesday 6 March 1973–Tuesday 29 May 1973
Weeks 1–13 transmitted at 1225;
Weeks 1–13 repeated on Thursdays at 1815
Broadcast on Radio 4

Episode List
1. *That's My Pigeon*; 2. *Don't Let Them Needle You*; 3. *Find The Lady*; 4. *Bridge Over Troubled Waters*; 5. *A Private Affair*; 6. *Food For Thought*; 7. *Getting It Taped*; 8. *Safe and Unsound*; 9. *The Expert Caper*; 10. *Flushed With Success*; 11. *Under The Weather*; 12. *Monkey Business*; 13. *Cheesed Off*

Series 8 – (13 Weeks)

Written by
John Graham and Edward Taylor

The Cast
Deryck Guyler, Richard Murdoch, Norma Ronald, Ronald Baddiley and John Graham

Produced by
Edward Taylor

Monday 17 June 1974–Monday 16 September 1974
Weeks 1–13 transmitted at 1815;
Weeks 1–13 repeated on Wednesdays at 1227
Broadcast on Radio 4

Episode List
1. *Plane Madness*; 2. *Vipers in the Bosom*; 3. *Great Guns*; 4. *I Want My Mummy*; 5. *One*

SIR GREGORY: **This is the end, the end! Do you hear? There's only one potato left and his eyes seem to follow me everywhere.**

They are eventually found, a month after first going onto the roof, and the news reports:

> Three civil servants were today brought down from a London skyscraper block after spending a month on the roof. It was thought at first they had been trapped there but a Ministry spokesman, Sir Gregory Pitkin, later denied this. He said, 'No civil servant could be that stupid. The three had in fact been researching the effects of exposure on the human frame. They had to assess the process of human deterioration and the two men had been chosen because they were half way there to start with.'

It is of little surprise that ***The Men From The Ministry*** was a firm favourite with listeners to the World Service. This was a slice of Old England and ex-pats abroad must have felt that this comedy was as English as listening to test match cricket. Such was the popularity of this show abroad that several episodes were produced exclusively for the World Service and were never heard on the home networks.

The show changed little in fifteen years and in this way has much in common with

The Navy Lark and *The Clitheroe Kid*. It was quality situation comedy that gently poked fun at the establishment without being smug or superior. The performances were first-rate, not altogether surprising with actors of the calibre of Richard Murdoch, Wilfrid Hyde-White and Deryck Guyler. It is worth listening to these genuinely funny episodes again as they are among the few examples of sitcom from this era to have aged very well.

Man's Meat; 6. *Ballet Nuisance*; 7. *Sky High*; 8. *A Break For Sir Gregory*; 9. *Health and Deficiency*; 10. *Big Deal*; 11. *They Fry By Night*; 12. *In The Picture*; 13. *She'll Have To Go*

Series 9 – (13 Weeks)

Written by
John Graham and Edward Taylor

The Cast
Deryck Guyler, Richard Murdoch, Norma Ronald, Ronald Baddiley and John Graham

Produced by
Edward Taylor

Monday 26 May 1975–Monday 18 August 1975
Weeks 1–13 transmitted at 1815; Weeks 1–13 repeated from Sunday 5 October 1975 at 1227
Broadcast on Radio 4

Episode List
1. *Nothing But The Vest*; 2. *That's My Boy*; 3. *All That Glitters*; 4. *Torn To Shreds*; 5. *Wool Over Their Eyes*; 6. *This, VAT and the Other*; 7. *The Great Trouser Troubles*; 8. *The Cabinet Crisis*; 9. *Chain Reaction*; 10. *All Change*; 11. *A Merry Dance*; 12. *A Sense of Power*; 13. *Postal Disorder*

Series 10 – (8 Weeks)

Written by
John Graham and Edward Taylor

The Cast
Deryck Guyler, Richard Murdoch, Norma Ronald, Ronald Baddiley and John Graham

Produced by
Edward Taylor

Tuesday 6 July 1976–Tuesday 24 August 1976
Weeks 1–13 transmitted at 1815; Weeks 1–13 repeated on Thursdays at 1227
Broadcast on Radio 4

Episode List
1. *All Cisterns Go*; 2. *A Problem Shared*; 3. *The Whitehall Castaways*; 4. *Off The Rails*; 5. *Penny Wise*; 6. *A Turn for the Nurse*; 7. *Seal of Office*; 8. *Birmingham is Revolting*

Series 11 – (8 Weeks)

Written by
John Graham and Edward Taylor

The Cast
Deryck Guyler, Richard Murdoch, Norma Ronald, Ronald Baddiley and John Graham

Produced by
Edward Taylor

Monday 4 July 1977–Monday 22 August 1977
Weeks 1–8 transmitted at 1830; Weeks 1–10 repeated on Wednesdays at 1227
Broadcast on Radio 4

Episode List
1. *Mission Inedible*; 2. *Horse Play*; 3. *Big Big Big Ben Bungle*; 4. *A Motley Crew*; 5. *Not On Your Telly*; 6. *One Way Only*; 7. *Take Your Pick*; 8. *Claws*

I'm Sorry, I'll Read That Again

1964–1968

Transmission Details

Cambridge Circus

The Cast
Humphrey Barclay, John Cleese, Graham Chapman, David Hatch, Jo Kendall, Tim Brooke-Taylor and Bill Oddie

Music by
Burt Rhodes and his Quintet

Produced by
Humphrey Barclay and Edward Taylor

Broadcast on Monday 30 December 1963

I'm Sorry, I'll Read That Again

Series 1 – (3 Weeks)

Written by
The Cast

The Cast
Tim Brooke-Taylor, Anthony Buffery, John Cleese, David Hatch, Jo Kendall and Bill Oddie

Music by
Burt Rhodes and his Quintet

Produced by
Humphrey Barclay and Edward Taylor

'A kaleidoscope of funny voices, catchphrase and innuendo revolving at breakneck speed and with complete disregard for logic' – Barry Took

Up to the 1950s, BBC comedy was the preserve of comics who had served their apprenticeship on the stage in music hall and variety theatres. The post-war wave of young comedians was the product of concert parties like Ralph Reader's RAF Gangshow. The likes of Hancock, Sellers and Milligan had little previous performance experience prior to joining the forces, but on leaving they sought work on the live circuit of variety theatres and training grounds like the Windmill Theatre. Live work was *de rigueur* for aspiring performers but in the 1950s there was an abundance of bookings in comparison with today. It was the 1960s that spawned a new generation of comedians unique to radio in that they had comparatively little live experience.

Those responsible for bringing about this new wave of young turks eager to prove themselves on the radio were the *Beyond The Fringe* group of Jonathan Miller, Peter Cook, Dudley Moore and Alan Bennett. Miller and Cook attended Cambridge University and Moore and Bennett were students at Oxford but were brought together for this Oxbridge revue which became legendary. Cambridge particularly had a tradition of university revue staged by the

Footlights group. From the early 1960s the list of Footlights members reads like an encyclopaedia of British comedy. Prior to this period members of the Footlights club saw revue merely as an amusing diversion from studies.

Beyond The Fringe was a reaction by Robert Ponsonby – the man in charge of running the Edinburgh Festival – to the unofficial Fringe productions put on by experimental theatre companies and university revue groups. He wanted an official late-night revue in a bid to cash in on the popularity of fringe revues. *Beyond The Fringe* was born in 1960 and, in the years following, virtually every committee of Footlights had what was to become a well-known name in comedy.

The Footlights revue from 1963, called *A Clump of Plinths*, was the next show to spawn a cast that was to follow the path recently trodden by the likes of Peter Cook into a new comedy establishment. The cast of this show was Chris Stuart-Clark, Jo Kendall, Tony Buffery, Bill Oddie, David Hatch, John Cleese and Tim Brooke-Taylor. The revue was staged in the West End by a very youthful producer called Michael White, who subsequently went on to stage *The Rocky Horror Show* in the 1970s and back *The Comic Strip* in the early 1980s.

The show's name was changed to *Cambridge Circus* and it was not directed by the original director, Hugh MacDonald, but by Humphrey Barclay, who had been involved with the past three years of Footlights revues. The only cast change was that of Tony Buffery, who left to pursue a more secure career, but his replacement was Graham Chapman, who had taken part in the 1962 revue *Double Take* with Barclay.

Friday 3 April 1964–Friday 17 April 1964
Weeks 1–3
transmitted at 2130
Broadcast on the Light Programme

Series 2 – (9 Weeks)

Written by
See below for writers' list

The Cast
Tim Brooke-Taylor, Graeme Garden, David Hatch, Jo Kendall and Bill Oddie

Music by
Bill Oddie supported by the Dave Lee Group

Produced by
Humphrey Barclay

Monday 4 October 1965–Monday 6 December 1965
Weeks 1–9
transmitted at 2200
Broadcast on the Light Programme

Writers' List
Week 1: Peter Vincent and David McKellar, and Graeme Garden
Week 2: Les Lilley and Chic Jacob, Humphrey Barclay, David Lund and Johnny Mortimer and Brian Cooke
Week 3: John Esmonde and Bob Larbey, Graeme Garden, David Lund, Peter Vincent and David McKellar, and Bill Oddie
Week 4: Graeme Garden, Johnny Mortimer and Brian Cooke, Bill Oddie and

Peter Vincent, and David McKellar
Week 5: Tim Brooke-Taylor, Graeme Garden, Johnny Mortimer and Brian Cooke, and Bill Oddie
Week 6: Graeme Garden, Les Lilley and Chic Jacob, Johnny Mortimer and Brian Cooke, and Bill Oddie
Week 7: John Esmonde and Bob Larbey, Clive James, Bill Oddie, and Peter Vincent and David McKellar
Week 8: John Esmonde and Bob Larbey, Graeme Garden, Eric Idle and Bill Oddie
Week 9: Tim Brooke-Taylor, Graeme Garden and Bill Oddie

Series 3 – (13 Weeks)

Written by
None listed

The Cast
Tim Brooke-Taylor, John Cleese, Graeme Garden, David Hatch, Jo Kendall and Bill Oddie

Music by
Bill Oddie supported by the Dave Lee Group

Produced by
Humphrey Barclay

Monday 14 March 1966–Monday 6 June 1966
Weeks 1–13 transmitted at 2200; Weeks 6–13 repeated from Saturday 23 April at 1200; Week 4

Barclay was keen to get a foothold within the BBC as a trainee producer. Having failed, his best option was to enlist the help of Peter Titheradge, who had been charged with the task of recruiting new talent from university revue to the Beeb. The BBC saw that this new wave was a fruitful resource to tap, and satire was becoming a more popular entertainment genre with shows like *That Was The Week That Was* gaining huge ratings for BBC television. Titheradge personally recruited Barclay as an assistant radio producer who was then to become instrumental in the *Cambridge Circus* revue, making the transition from stage into people's living-rooms.

An initial one-off show was recorded and edited for radio and broadcast on 30 December 1963. This retained the title of *Cambridge Circus* but the three subsequent shows broadcast on 3, 10 and 17 April 1964 were specifically recorded for the BBC in the studio under the new name of ***I'm Sorry, I'll Read That Again***. Roger Perry in his book *The Life Of Python* says of these early shows, 'The material was drawn from a mixture of old and new, and the format was themeless, permitting a broad latitude of attack.'

Little came of these shows in the way of commitment from the BBC and the cast departed for a six-week tour of New Zealand. Following this was a run of the show on Broadway. Owing to a less-than-enthusiastic review in the *New York Times*, the show closed within three weeks but very soon took up residence at a more suitable cabaret-style venue in Greenwich Village, where it played until the end of 1964.

The cast went their separate ways thinking that the project had run its natural course. Tim Brooke-

Taylor was the most active publicly, having landed a job on *The Braden Beat*, a popular comedy show for ATV. The person working on behalf of ***ISIRTA*** was the producer Humphrey Barclay, who was now established as a BBC Light Entertainment producer and was keen to capitalise on the three radio versions of *Cambridge Circus*/***ISIRTA*** that had already been broadcast.

The changes made on the personnel front concerned the omission of Tony Buffery, who was not available, and John Cleese, who was still in the States after a short run in the musical *Half a Sixpence* and a spell as a writer for *Newsweek*. Cleese's future writing partner, Graham Chapman, was replaced by another Cambridge University medical student, Graeme Garden.

Garden took over as President of Footlights the year after Tim Brooke-Taylor left in 1963, but ironically he had failed to be accepted as part of the revue that became *Cambridge Circus*. It was only after Garden had left Cambridge and had started on his three years at medical school that Humphrey Barclay asked him to become part of the ***ISIRTA*** team. The only other team changes brought John Cleese back for the second series in 1966 and omitted Graeme Garden for the third series later on in 1966.

As with many other

repeated on 13 June at 2200; Week 3 repeated on 20 June at 2200
Broadcast on the Light Programme

Series 4 – (14 Weeks)

Written by
None listed

The Cast
Angus Prune, Tim Brooke-Taylor, Graeme Garden, David Hatch, Jo Kendall and Bill Oddie

Music by
Bill Oddie supported by the Dave Lee Group

Produced by
Humphrey Barclay

Monday 3 October 1966–Monday 6 December 1966
Weeks 1–14 transmitted at 2200; Weeks 1–14 repeated on the following Saturday at 1400 (except Week 6 – broadcast at 1300)
Broadcast on the Light Programme

Series 5 – (14 Weeks)

Written by
None listed

The Cast
Angus Prune, T. Briddock, Tim Brooke-Taylor, Graeme Garden, David Hatch, Jo Kendall and Bill Oddie

Music by
Bill Oddie supported by the Dave Lee Group

Produced by
Humphrey Barclay

Sunday 23 April 1967–Sunday 23 July 1967
Weeks 1–14 transmitted at 1700; Weeks 1–14 repeated on the following Monday at 2200
Broadcast on the Light Programme

Series 6 – (14 Weeks)

Written by
None listed

The Cast
Angus Prune, T. Briddock, Tim Brooke-Taylor, Graeme Garden, David Hatch, Jo Kendall and Bill Oddie

Music by
Bill Oddie supported by the Dave Lee Group

Produced by
Humphrey Barclay and Peter Titheradge

Sunday 14 April 1968–Sunday 7 July 1968
Weeks 1–14 transmitted at 2130; Weeks 1–14 repeated on the following Friday at 1300
Broadcast on Radio 2

Series 7 – (13 Weeks)

Written by
Bill Oddie and Graeme Garden

The Cast
A. Gibbon OBE, Tim Brooke-Taylor, John Cleese, Graeme

innovative radio shows, it was often the later series that were the more memorable. One could perhaps account for the lack of real direction and inconsistency early on in the run of ***ISIRTA*** by the large amount of writers contributing material. The first series proper lists several individuals and writing partnerships including John Esmonde and Bob Larbey, Clive James, Peter Vincent and David McKellar and Eric Idle.

By the third series ***ISIRTA*** was being written by the cast and more regular characters were beginning to emerge. Some of these, like the frightfully uptight and emotionally repressed John and Mary, had first seen the light of day during *Cambridge Circus*. By the fifth series the two credited writers were Bill Oddie and Graeme Garden.

MARY: **John, why don't you admit it, you don't love me any more.**
[PAUSE]
JOHN: **All right, I admit it.**
MARY: **John, once we had something that was pure and wonderful and good. What's happened to it?**
JOHN: **You spent it all.**
MARY: **That's all that matters to you isn't it? Money. I despise you, I hate you. I don't know how I've been able to stand it. I suppose it's because I love you. I do love you John. I love you more than I can say. I need you John I . . . I . . . Please John don't look at pictures of nude women while I'm talking to you!**

By the third series there is a credit in *The Radio Times* for the music, which goes to Bill Oddie. During his Footlights days Oddie had concerned himself with the musical content of shows, a main ingredient of any revue-type entertainment. His most noticeable contributions to the writing of ***ISIRTA*** were parody songs, which he did to immense effect. It is often said of those composers who lampoon others' styles that they are lacking any real innovation of their own, but Oddie's songs were intrinsically funny *because* they were such accurate take-offs. Credit also goes to Dave Lee and to Leon Cohen, who orchestrated these songs with next to no rehearsal time.

By the sixth series in 1969 Humphrey Barclay had left to join Independent Television, where he remains today as a producer of note in the light entertainment field. David Hatch, who had been part of the cast, took over as producer and he still works at the BBC in a management position. Hatch played the butt of much of the humour because of his new role. He had taken a post as part of the authoritarian BBC and thus was ripe for insults.

ISIRTA were hardly the first to attack the authority of the BBC through comedy: *The Goon Show* had done it before and *Round The Horne* made it a speciality. But ***ISIRTA*** sounded their critical comments through the fictitious Radio Prune, which spawned *Prune Playhouse* and *Prune Forum*. Under the guise of Radio Prune, boundaries were forever being challenged and the material often bordered on smutty. This was very popular with the audience who seemed to rejoice in the risqué material or, as it was increasingly being called, irreverence:

MRS MW: **Dear Prune Forum, My husband and I have been experimenting in our**

Garden, David Hatch, Jo Kendall and Bill Oddie

Music by
Bill Oddie supported by the Dave Lee Group

Produced by
David Hatch and Peter Titheradge

Sunday 12 January 1969–Sunday 6 April 1969
Weeks 1–13 transmitted at 2130;
Weeks 1–13 repeated on the following Wednesday at 1945
Broadcast on Radios 1 and 2

The I'm Sorry Christmas Show

Broadcast on Thursday 25 December 1969 at 2045 on Radios 1 and 2

Series 8 – (13 Weeks)
'A New Improved Whiter-Than-Blue Radio Wash-Out.'

Written by
Bill Oddie and Graeme Garden

The Cast
A. Gibbon OBE, Tim Brooke-Taylor, John Cleese, Graeme Garden, David Hatch, Jo Kendall and Bill Oddie

Music by
Bill Oddie supported by the Dave Lee Group

Produced by
David Hatch and Peter Titheradge

lovemaking recently. We do it in unusual places at all times of the day and night. Just thought I'd tell you. PS, please excuse the shaky handwriting.

The studio audience revelled in the often painful and merciless play on words. The following example comes from 'Fish and Quips' – one of the many occasions when the cast would veer away from the direction of any plot and indulge in one-liners until they seemed to have exhausted every opportunity:

HATCH: **They're playing 'Salmon'.**
CLEESE: **'Salmon'?**
HATCH: **'Salmon-chanted Evening'.**
B-TAYLOR: **Or it could be 'I met her in Manta-Ray'.**
KENDALL: **And there's a little sole.**
GARDEN: **Oh yeah baby.**
CLEESE: **I didn't ketch that.**
GARDEN: **You must need a herring aid.**
CLEESE: **Don't shout – you'll give me a head-hake.**
KENDALL: **Don't carp.**

The puns continue for some time . . .

B-TAYLOR: **And another carrying today's newspaper.**
GARDEN: **Topical fish.**
B-TAYLOR: **That was a sharking one.**
KENDALL: **Don't be shellfish.**
CLEESE: **You're losing your sense of porpoise.**
B-TAYLOR: **I feel eel.**
HATCH: **Don't flounder.**

Sunday 15 February 1970–Sunday 8 May 1970
Weeks 1–13 transmitted at 2045
From 5 April 1970 Weeks 8–13 repeated on the following Wednesday at 1815 on Radio 4
Broadcast on Radios 1 and 2

Special Christmas Show

Thursday 31 December 1970 broadcast at 2000 on Radio 4

Series 8 – (12 Weeks)

Written by
Bill Oddie and Graeme Garden

The Cast
A. Gibbon OBE, Tim Brooke-Taylor, John Cleese, Graeme Garden, David Hatch, Jo Kendall and Bill Oddie

Music by
Bill Oddie supported by the Dave Lee Group

Produced by
David Hatch and Peter Titheradge

Thursday 6 July 1972–Thursday 28 September 1972
Weeks 1–12 transmitted at 1225; no Repeats
Broadcast on Radio 4

CLEESE: **Then whelk-ome to a sardine end.**
BAND: CHORD.

The revue style was certainly beginning to take shape by the sixth series with recurring characters like John and Mary, Lady Constance de Coverlet (the insatiable old lady played by an unrecognisable Tim Brooke-Taylor) and the inclusion of regular serials that parodied well-known series or books. In this respect ***ISIRTA*** was a cross between *Round The Horne*, with its catchphrase and regular characters, and *The Goons* with a reliance on sound effects and narratives.

In an episode broadcast in the ninth series in 1973 called *Jack The Ripper*, sound effects are used to maximum effect (and, true to form, often to *smutty* effect):

NARRATOR: **And that night Jack the Ripper struck again . . . and again**
F/X: *RIP*
BILL: **Ooooh!**
F/X: *RIP*
JO: **Oooooh!**
F/X: *RIP*
JOHN: (BUTCH) **Ere, wot's your game?!**
NARRATOR: **Next morning the news broke . . .**
F/X: *Breaking Glass*
NARRATOR: **On street corners, news vendors shouted the headlines . . .**
TIM: **THE HEADLINES!**
NARRATOR: **Queen Victoria was not amused . . .**

VICTORIA: **We are not amused.**
F/X: *RIP*
VICTORIA: **Oh, I don't know though . . .**

But like all great radio shows, which ***ISIRTA*** certainly was, it had its own style. Audience interaction was very evident with each pun greeted by resounding boos. Scripts were written with retorts to this kind of response included, and Cleese was often given the task of telling off the audience. This tended to fuel further the audience's desire to become part of the proceedings and this trend snowballed.

It was felt by the whole cast (and especially by Cleese) that this did at times get out of hand. The show wasn't made up purely of bad gags and ridiculous characters, like Tim Brooke-Taylor's portrayal of Spot the dog who did nothing more than bark. As a result, the more subtle material was beginning to get lost in the ensuing mayhem that seemed ever present in the studio. These fears never fully materialised and the audience always seemed to know when to stop.

Listening back to ***ISIRTA***, you can tell that the audience reaction is what adds to the show's quite anarchic feel. When the series started in the mid 1960s, the cast and production team were just out of university and had no experience of radio whatsoever; but their enthusiasm and raw talent carried the show through to ten series. The main criticism would be that it relied too much on clever wordplay and parody, avoiding any real innovation; but it was a very successful comedy show that aided its stars to move on to greater things and inspired many others to enter the medium of radio.

David Hatch wrote an article in *The Radio Times*

and broke it down to each cast member and what they did. It sums up the kind of style that the show put across:

Bill Oddie
is 2ft 6in small and big with it. He likes to think he can sing beautifully, but then pigs might fly. I am really quite fond of him, and he's nice as a pet.

John Otto (I'm the King Rat) Cleese
He plays all the cruel and viscous parts. He has a remarkably unpleasant manner but he juggles well. I suspect that he wears suspenders. A fool.

Tim Brooke-Taylor
Well, what a stupid name. I mean who does he think he is? His second name is Julian, which sums him up, I think. He does all the camp men's parts and a lot of the female voices. How contemptible!

Jo Kendall
She gets the female parts Tim can't handle. Rehearses men's voices in the bath. Please note that the first four letters of her name spell 'Joke'.

Graeme Garden
A bespectacled scruffy youth who does impressions and funny voices. He has recently qualified as a doctor so at least he's got something to fall back on to.

They are all doing awfully well on television and the critics keep saying how good they are. I'm just the feed man and occasionally I get feed up with the whole thing.

David Hatch

Benny Hill Time

1964–1966

Transmission Details

Benny Hill Time

Series 1

Written by
Benny Hill

The Cast
Benny Hill, Peter Vernon, Patricia Hayes, Frank Thornton and Jan Waters

Broadcast from Sunday 23 February 1964

Series 2

Written by
Benny Hill

The Cast
Benny Hill, Peter Vernon, Patricia Hayes; guests included Pearl Carr and Teddy Johnson

Broadcast from 21 February 1965

Series 3

Written by
Benny Hill

The Cast
Benny Hill, Peter Vernon, Patricia Hayes; guests included Elaine Taylor

Broadcast from 27 February 1966

Benny Hill never made a big name for himself on the radio but by the late 1950s he was regularly appearing on television. He did work on certain shows in the 1950s, among them a show called *Anything Goes*, which was broadcast from BBC West starting on 21 February 1952. The cast of this show, which was co-written by Hill, included Johnny Morris, who went on to fame as a children's TV presenter who talked to animals.

Hill also had three series of ***Benny Hill Time*** broadcast in the mid 1960s on the BBC Light Programme, which became Radio 2. He wrote much of his own material, as he did with his TV output, and the shows were coloured by his varied characters including the Teddy Boys, which he played with Peter Vernon, Peter Nobble, the film gossip, and Hans and Lotte Hill, the undersea explorers.

The first series was unimaginatively described by *The Radio Times* as 'a sort of revue', which also starred Peter Vernon, Jan Waters, Frank Thornton and Patricia Hayes. It began on Sunday 23 February 1964 and was repeated the following Wednesday.

The second series began on 21 February 1965 and included Pearl Carr and Teddy Johnson as guests. The third series started on 27 February 1966 and still included Patricia Hayes and Peter Vernon as cast members.

Round The Horne

1965–1968

During wartime service in the RAF Kenneth Horne made his first radio appearance in 1939 in the series *Ack-Ack Beer Beer*. In 1943, as an announcer on the Overseas Recorded Broadcasting Service (ORBS), he met Richard Murdoch. Together they wrote *Much-Binding-In-The-Marsh* as part of the services programme *Merry-Go-Round*. The BBC commissioned a first series of 37 programmes and *Much-Binding* continued from 1947 until 1953.

Throughout this period Horne continued to work within business and broadcasting. His business credentials included director of Triplex Safety Glass and chairman of Chad Valley Toys. In 1958 he suffered a stroke and lost the power of speech, forcing him to retire from his business and broadcasting duties. During his recovery he devised *Beyond Our Ken* and in May 1958 he returned exclusively to the entertainment field and by the end of that year *Beyond Our Ken* was attracting over ten million listeners. Throughout the 1950s and 1960s he appeared in over 50 different radio and television programmes, including his own TV series *Horne A Plenty* for Thames TV. But it was as the establishment anchor-man in ***Round The Horne*** that he will be most remembered.

Round The Horne's ground-breaking mix of wordplay, innuendo and camp caricature proved to be an irresistible combination, pulling a regular audience of fifteen million listeners and making it one of the best-loved programmes in radio history. It was a direct successor to *Beyond Our Ken*, during which time

Transmission Details

Round The Horne

Series 1 – (16 Weeks)
('Five characters in search of the authors' – *The Radio Times*)

Written by
Barry Took and Marty Feldman

The Cast
Kenneth Horne, with Kenneth Williams, Hugh Paddick, Betty Marsden and Bill Pertwee; Announcer: Douglas Smith

Music by
The Fraser Hayes Four and Paul Fenoulhet and the Hornblowers

Produced by
John Simmonds

Sunday 7 March 1965–Sunday 20 June 1965
Weeks 1–11 transmitted at 1430; Weeks 12–16 transmitted at 1330
Broadcast on the Light Programme

(Personnel change – Paul Fenoulhet replaced by Edwin Braden after episode six)

Series 2 – (13 Weeks)

Written by
Barry Took, Marty Feldman
The Cast
Kenneth Horne, with Kenneth Williams, Hugh Paddick, Betty Marsden and Bill Pertwee; Announcer: Douglas Smith
Music by
The Fraser Hayes Four and Edwin Braden and the Hornblowers
Produced by
John Simmonds

Sunday 13 March 1966–Sunday 5 June 1966
Weeks 1–13
transmitted at 1330
Broadcast on the Light Programme

Series 3 – (21 Weeks)
(Personnel credits as Series 2)

Sunday 5 February 1967–Sunday 25 June 1967
Weeks 1–21
transmitted at 1330
Broadcast on the Light Programme

Series 4 – (16 Weeks)
Written by
Barry Took, Johnny Mortimer and Brian Cooke, and Donald Webster (credited for the first six weeks only)
The Cast
Kenneth Horne, with Kenneth Williams, Hugh Paddick and Betty Marsden;

Kenneth Horne and his colleagues (Kenneth Williams, Hugh Paddick, Betty Marsden and Bill Pertwee) had already established themselves as one of the strongest ensembles in radio.

The new series was written largely by Barry Took and Marty Feldman (50 out of the total 66 episodes), who injected wit and satire into their scripts, which were consistently of the highest standard. Each show seemed to have a cast of thousands played by the same four highly accomplished actors from *Beyond Our Ken*, Kenneth Horne, the anchor-man, once again stopping the entire proceedings from spinning out of control.

Musical relief for the series was provided by the Fraser Hayes Four: 'They may play a little flat but where they come from they aren't allowed anything sharp,' said Horne. Innuendo continued to be rife within the scripts and ***Round The Horne*** still makes the listener raise an eyebrow after nearly 30 years: 'I'm not being *serviced* on this show. No, I need the *servicing* duckie. I can cope with more than this. This doesn't stretch me. I'm used to enormous parts.' (Kenneth Williams).

This was a series that achieved huge ratings and occupied the coveted Sunday lunchtime slot. *The Radio Times*, in an article prior to the fourth series maintains that: 'Many a Sunday lunch will be hurried, delayed, or just plain interrupted to catch every word.'

Barry Took and Marty Feldman were the writers of three series with the fourth written by Barry Took, Johnny Mortimer and Brian Cooke. Took had been part of the team way back in 1958 when he and Eric Merriman wrote the first two series of *Beyond Our Ken*. Took left in 1959 to write *Take It*

From Here and it wasn't until 1965 that he made a return to the Horne stable to write ***Round The Horne*** with his partner Marty Feldman. They added a speed to the show which was lacking at the end of the run of *Beyond Our Ken* and there were far more topical references to films, fashion and even politics. They even invented what can only be described as a new language for some of their regular characters. In 1968 *The Radio Times* commented on the show:

> 'This is satire, also in the best sense: intelligent and amusing comment on the time; creative comment too, to the extent that it can invent its own language and still be intelligible.' (See under Rambling Syd Rumpo and Julian and Sandy.)

Kenneth Horne died in February 1969.

Announcer: Douglas Smith
Music by
The Max Harris Group
Produced by
John Simmonds

Sunday 25 February 1968–Sunday 9 June 1968
Weeks 1–16
transmitted at 1400
Broadcast on Radio 2

Regular Characters

KENNETH WILLIAMS
J. Peasmould Gruntfuttock, bumbling old fart and self-styled sage. *Chou-en Ginsberg M.A. (Failed)*, the crazed Japanese would-be master criminal. *Rambling Syd Rumpo* 'Picturesque, homespun, folksy twit.' Syd would regularly greet his audience with 'Hello my deary-os' before dipping into his 'gander bag' to perform obscure folk songs. The combination of Williams's extraordinary vocal dexterity and Took's and Feldman's inimitable rustic gibberish made these pastiches sound far more risqué than they actually were.

NURK YOUR THROBBERS
AND AWAY WE GO!

Ye Nergs and Bogels of bonnie Glen Postule,
Oft have I greebled amongst your trees,
And whirdled my lassie among your nettles,
Sworn my devotion, and stung both my knees
from Posselswaite Lament

Hit him in the nadgers with the bosun's
plunger,
Slap him on the grummet with a wrought iron
lunger,
Cuff him in the moulies with the Captain's
glunger,
Till his bogles dangle
from Sea Shanty Medley

BETTY MARSDEN
Daphne Whitethigh, loosely based on the television cook Fanny Craddock; changed her name from Fanny Haddock, which she had for *Beyond Our Ken*. *Lady Beatrice Counterblast (née Clissold)*, 'The pure brass of the Music Hall'.

BILL PERTWEE
Seamus Android, Irish chat-show host of limited vocabulary cruelly lampooning Eamonn Andrews.

HUGH PADDICK and KENNETH WILLIAMS
Julian and Sandy, gloriously over-the-top celebration of camp with this duo named after Julian Slade, the composer of *Salad Days*, and Sandy Wilson, the composer of *The Boyfriend*. Their scripts were liberally sprinkled with 'Polari', a gay slang of the period, e.g. 'bona' (good), 'fantabulosa' (extremely good), 'riah'

(hair), 'varda' (look), 'ecaf' (face), 'lattie' (house), 'lallies' (legs), 'omipalone' (homosexual).

Their outrageous badinage contrasted sharply with the polite respectability of Kenneth Horne (although he did occasionally lapse into 'Polari' himself).

'I'm Julian and this is my friend Sandy' – used every episode.

'Hello, Mr Horne, how bona to varda your eek again' – used virtually every episode.

'I could do something wild, with a couple of creepers up his trellis' – from *Bona Homes and Landscape Gardens.*

'You have a rummage Mr Horne. Jules will follow you round and make suggestions' – from *Bona Gift Boutique.*

'He's a miracle of dexterity at the cottage upright' – from *Bona Song Publisherettes.*

BETTY MARSDEN and HUGH PADDICK

Dame Celia Molestrangler and 'Ageing Juvenile' Binkie Huckaback, invariably playing the terribly terribly intense Fiona and Charles:

'I know you know.'
'I know you know I know.'
'I know you know I know you know' and so on.

After the 1960s

As this book has shown, the impact and influence of shows as far back as the 1930s have been colossal. There have, of course, been series that started after 1969 that certainly owe much to series like *ISIRTA* or *ITMA*. Consciously or not, writing style is adapted and changed slightly to suit certain performers, but keeping an eye on the past often improves shows of the future.

The Navy Lark was, until a few years ago, the longest-running series on BBC radio. This is no mean feat considering shows like *Rays A Laugh, Educating Archie* and *Take It From Here* all clock in around a highly commendable ten years. *Week Ending* took over the mantle of longest-running show and owed much of its early success to the satire boom of the 1960s. The wave of comics like Cleese, Cook, et al. created a newer wave. With Oxbridge-educated producers now firmly ensconced at Broadcasting House, it was natural for them to look to the same system that shaped them for new talent.

After the *ISIRTA* generation in the 1960s came producers like John Lloyd and Griff Rhys Jones in the 1970s. Also fresh out of Footlights, they were eager to repeat the same kind of success as their predecessors and did so with absolute assurance. The Hancock and Goons generation of writers and producers – the last remains of the music hall/variety tradition – had now forged careers in the lucrative television market. The late 1960s saw the end of many long-running shows, the most marked decline being the adaptation of television series like *Steptoe and Son, The Likely Lads, Dad's Army, Whack-O* and many others. Production values decreased significantly during this period with resident bands being trimmed down or phased out and BBC venues being shut down. A major factor was the start of independent television in the mid 1950s, which by the late 1960s could afford to pay for big stars. For so long radio had spawned television series but by 1970 it seemed decidedly second-class by comparison.

The 1970s were a rather barren time for radio comedy. Shows like *The Clitheroe Kid* and *The Navy Lark* were in their last throes, as was *ISIRTA*. Two shows emerged in the 1970s that drew upon the week's news for comic inspiration: *Week Ending* and *The News Huddlines*.

Week Ending was, and still is, a training ground for new writers, and is one of the few platforms offering the inexperienced worksmith a professional outlet. It existed before the arrival of John Lloyd but he was one in a long line of producers to cut his producing teeth on this low-budget show. The style, taking the week's news and writing topical sketches and monologues with a few non-topical but just very amusing sketches, was one that he expanded on when he moved to television. *Not The Nine O'Clock News* was one of the biggest hits of the early 1980s that launched the careers of its stars. Like *Week Ending*, it used a plethora of writers all contributing small segments on a weekly basis. This is still the way *Week Ending* works now.

In 1975 John Lloyd was also responsible for the production of *The News Huddlines*, now the longest-running radio show with a live audience. Revolving around the talents of Roy Hudd, June Whitfield and Chris Emmett, this show was an instant hit. *The News Huddlines* seems a far less tired show than *Week Ending* – due to the live audience reaction and the speed, sheer talent and interplay of the three main cast members.

The biggest shake-up of comedy since the satire boom of the 1960s emerged also at this time. What was to become known as 'alternative' comedy created a very loud bang on the cultural scene. The Comedy Store, based on American clubs where stand-up comics would each perform for around twenty minutes, was hardly new. The Establishment Club in the 1960s did much the same thing but it was the ferocity with which many of the acts performed that created attention. Alexei Sayle, Rik Mayall and Keith Allen all paved the way for other comedians like Jenny Eclair, Mark Steel, Mark Thomas and a whole new movement of comics. Many say that this was comedy born out of a political discontentment but it is likely that this new movement was a product of a shake-up in music during the punk era, where the 'have a go if you want' mentality created a new wave of creativity. It was also easier for an aspiring comic to get gigs. Whereas the only path was to enter clubland with its relics from a bygone era, clubs like The Comedy Store had an open mike policy where the only thing that wasn't tolerated was racist and sexist material. In retrospect, the first few years of this movement contained their fair share of dross, with a high turnover of participants, but by the mid to late 1980s there was a far more established and more professionally run 'comedy circuit' with a large number of quality acts. Radio took its time to really wake up to this new movement.

Television was quick to make stars out of *The Comic Strip*; Sayle, French and Saunders, Mayall and Edmonson, etc. These new performers didn't make numerous radio series as so many before them did because Channel Four took the risk of commissioning often terrible series from many unseasoned turns. Some worked and some didn't. But while this new channel was risk taking, BBC radio seemed to be lagging way behind. Apart from *Week Ending* and *The News Huddlines*, its big comedy success story was the long-running *Radio Active*. Once again, the team responsible for this radio spoof series was ex-Oxbridge. This is still a funny series but did nothing to tap into the new comedy resource. *Fundation* came closer with a show that was broadcast from The Woolwich Tramshed, launching the careers of two young teachers called Hale and Pace, but it wasn't until the end of the 1980s that radio producers turned to the comedy circuit for fresh impetus.

All the success stories from the circuit have made radio shows – John Hegley, Jeremy Hardy, Harry Hill and Mark Steel to name but a few. The *Mark Steel Solution* was one of the most original and well put together radio formats for years. *Harry Hill's Fruit Corner* is a throwback to the days before satire – he is a comedian who owes far more to Tommy Handley, Harry Worth and Eric Morecambe than to Peter Cook.

The recent shake-up of Radio 1 has been a boon to radio comedy, because the monopoly that Radio 2 and 4 seemed to have was effectively removed. Radio 1 expanded its remit to include comedy shows; only in the evening and only for an hour. Their direction was somewhat more upbeat and the first big Radio 1 comedy success story to emerge was *The Mary Whitehouse Experience*. This was a fast-paced show that once again mixed up various elements – stand-up, topicality, sketch humour – and put them together in a more up-to-date package that appealed to a younger audience. Most Radio 1 listeners would probably never have thought of listening to any radio comedy if it weren't for this.

It is only recently that the BBC seems to have woken up to the importance of its radio comedy output, both past and present. It is wonderful that cassettes of all the big shows of the past and even some of the less well-known ones are now on sale, and that many are selling in large quantities. But over the past ten years many shows that emerged on radio – like *Whose Line Is It Anyway?*, which popularised improvisational comedy in this country – were lost to independent television. This isn't the fault of radio as it lies firmly at the foot of BBC TV bosses, too slow to see the potential of these shows.

The 1990s have seen a resurgence in radio comedy. With *The Mary Whitehouse Experience* making the leap to television (BBC2!), yet another generation of comedians is emerging. Not surprisingly, many of these are products of the Oxbridge system but their humour seems less political and more parody based. The big shows to have emerged in the past few years have been *On The Hour*, a spoof radio news show that became *The Day Today* on BBC2; *Knowing Me Knowing You*, a spoof chat show and creation of Steve Coogan that made the transition to BBC2 in 1994; and *Fist Of Fun*, which was a Radio 1 show that has now become a BBC2 series. It is encouraging to see the BBC holding on to its more popular shows and radio comedy in a stronger position than it has been for 25 years.

Bibliography

Radio Luxembourg – The Station of the Stars, Richard Nichols (Comet, 1983)
Joyce Grenfell Requests the Pleasure (Futura, 1976)
It's All in the Book, Al Read (W H Allen, 1985)
Radio – The Great Years, Derek Parker (David and Charles, 1977)
The Wireless Stars, George Nobbs (Wensum, 1972)
Good Morning Boys, Ray Seaton and Roy Martin (Barrie and Jenkins, 1978)
Crying With Laughter, Bob Monkhouse (Century, 1993)
The Goon Show Scripts, Spike Milligan (Sphere, 1972)
More Goon Show Scripts, Spike Milligan (Woburn, 1973)
Before Your Very Eyes, Arthur Askey (Woburn, 1975)
The ITMA Years, Ted Kavanagh etc. (Woburn, 1974)
On the Way I Lost It, Frankie Howerd (W H Allen, 1976)
Tommy Handley, Ted Kavanagh (Hodder and Stoughton, 1949)
Solo For Horne, Norman Hackforth (Angus and Robertson, 1976)
Take It From Me, Jimmy Edwards (Werner Laurie, 1953)
Life With the Lyons, Bebe Daniels and Ben Lyon (Odhams, 1953)
Steady Barker, Eric Barker (Secker and Warburg, 1956)
I Wanna Tell You a Story, Max Bygraves (Star, 1976)
The Glums, Frank Muir and Dennis Norden (Penguin, 1979)
Mr Showbusiness, Vic Oliver (Harrap, 1954)
Raising the Laughs, Ted Ray (Werner Laurie, 1952)
The World is Full of Charlies, Charlie Chester (NEL, 1974)
The Fool on the Hill, Max Wall (Quartet, 1975)
ITMA, Francis Worsley (Vox Mundi, 1948)
Three Times Lucky, Jimmy Jewel (Enigma, 1982)
The Golden Age of Radio, Dennis Gifford (Batsford, 1985)
Still On My Way to Hollywood, Ernie Wise (Arthur Barker, 1990)

Laughter in the Air, Barry Took
Kindly Leave the Stage, Roger Wilmut (Methuen, 1985)
Radio Variety, John Watt (Dent, 1939)
Make 'em Laugh, Eric Midwinter (George Allen and Unwin, 1979)
They Made Us Laugh, Geoff Mellor (Kelsall, 1982)
The Guinness Book of Sitcoms, Rod Taylor (Guinness, 1994)
Jack of All Trades, Jack Warner (1975)